THE SOCIETY OF THE ENLIGHTENMENT

THE SOCIETY OF THE ENLIGHTENMENT

The Rise of the Middle Class and Enlightenment Culture in Germany

RICHARD VAN DÜLMEN

Translated by
Anthony Williams

Polity Press

This English translation copyright © Polity Press 1992

First published in 1992 by Polity Press in association with Blackwell Publishers

First published as *Die Gesellschaft der Aufklärer: Zur bürgerlichen Emanzipation und aufklärerischen Kultur in Deutschland*
© Fischer Taschenbuch Verlag GmbH, Frankfurt am Main 1986

Editorial office:
Polity Press
65 Bridge Street
Cambridge CB2 1UR, UK

Marketing and production:
Blackwell Publishers
108 Cowley Road
Oxford OX4 1JF, UK

ISBN 0 7456 0815 9

British Library Cataloguing in Publication Data

A CIP catalogue record for this book is available from the British Library.

Typeset in 11 on 13 pt Baskerville by Best-set Typesetter Ltd., Hong Kong
Printed in Great Britain by Billing & Sons Ltd, Worcester

This book is printed on acid-free paper.

CONTENTS

Introduction

The development of the Enlightenment and the emancipation of the middle class were interdependent processes. Under the prevailing conditions – the growing concentration of power in the hands of the state and the dissolution of feudal society – these processes created important pre-conditions for the emergence of middle-class society and culture. The appearance of numerous organizations, circles and societies from the early eighteenth century onwards provided an important focal point of, and forum for, progressive and reformist discourse and activity and the emergence of the middle class. They attracted an ever increasing number of scholars, progressive state officials and the educated middle class. Ultimately, they contributed to the emergence of a 'new' middle class, though they never severed links with traditional society or challenged the authority of the state. Obviously, there were more efficient media of the Enlightenment, and disciples of the Enlightenment operated at several levels; but the societies of the Enlightenment provided such disciples with the best outlets for their extensive interests; the societies were the most tangible form of the socio-cultural process of Enlightenment.

A multitude of societies emerged under similar circumstances, but with various names: first on the scene were the language societies and the learned academies, then Freemasonry and the public-spirited societies and, lastly, secret societies, reading circles, literary clubs and so many kinds of political organizations that it is now no longer possible to estimate their number. The societies were the focus of articulation for a great variety of interests, depending on the respective phase of the Enlightenment and the social status of its champions: learned and academic and practical and reformist interests, intellectual education and middle-class and reformist social intercourse, free self-determination and class-less exclusivity. However, the Enlightenment's claim to universality, and the achievement of social reform through the dissemination of knowledge and self-education were common to them all. This is what distinguishes the societies of the Enlightenment from the traditional feudal communities and middle-class organizations of the nineteenth century.

The societies of the Enlightenment are no longer an unknown quantity for historical research. There are numerous accounts of learned academies, public-spirited societies and especially Freemasonry, particularly since many of the organizations have continued from the eighteenth century until the present day.[1] However, both the older and the more recent monographs are mainly concerned with a positivist reconstruction of the historical development of the respective institutions. It long went unrecognized that the wide range of societies, clubs and organizations in the eighteenth century constituted a unified movement sustained by the spirit of Enlightenment and emancipation, making a significant contribution to middle-class society and culture. And, furthermore, sociologists, not historians, were the first to undertake systematic analyses of the special contribution that the societies made to the emergence of the middle-class public at large.[2] The study by Jürgen Habermas, which received a favourable reception from historians and initiated a fresh study of the societies of the Enlightenment, occupies pride of place. However, to date, it has not resulted in any important synthesis. The fundamental studies undertaken by Thomas Nipperdey (1972)[3] and Otto Dann (1976)[4] represented initial progressive inroads of a specifically historical character. However, their preoccupation with the history of the clubs, organizations and societies of the nineteenth century leads them to overlook the importance of the societies of the Enlightenment. Certainly, the former have many similarities with their successors, but their importance lies essentially in the fact that they created a new elite culture that challenged the ideas of a class-based social order without representing specifically middle-class interests.

In the meantime, so much material has become available – detailed studies[5] and essay collections[6] – that a structured outline of the problem is now possible.[7] It does not, however, fall within the scope of this study to embrace each and every society and convey a complete picture – certain non-Enlightenment societies, such as the Rosicrucians and the Christian societies, have been ignored. Nor is it claimed that, in concentrating on the clubs, organizations and societies, the study adequately considers every aspect of the communication process of the Enlightenment or the history of the socialization of those who championed its cause. There were many possible ways for the committed champion to engage in agitational activity and satisfy his needs for social inter-course, but the fact that the societies became so widespread is evidence that they provided him with the best arena for his activity. Thus, the societies focus the history of the problems of the Enlightenment and the emerging middle class.[8]

First, there is an outline of the socio-political context of the Enlightenment, its scope for development within the framework of absolutism and traditional feudal society. This is followed by a systematic attempt to chronicle the genesis and flux of the societies of the Enlightenment using a typology of the principal mani-festations to distinguish between the various phases. This is in-tended to reveal the extent to which the societies depended on the situation in society at large. It is also intended to reveal the correlation that exists in the social process of middle-class emerg-ence between the problems of the Enlightenment and the cultural self-image of its proponents.

1

ENLIGHTENMENT AND TRADITIONAL SOCIETY IN THE EIGHTEENTH CENTURY

In Germany, the Enlightenment developed under the conditions of a society with a predominantly feudal structure.[1] Although absolutism gave rise to many egalitarian tendencies, hardly any of the eighteenth-century systems of government were interested in radical social reform and, as yet, there had been no socio-economic threat to the social order.

The aristocracy remained the most privileged estate with a monopoly on the exercise of power and government. The middle class monopolized the trades and commerce, and the peasantry continued to produce sufficient food for the population in a state of political nonage. Given this framework, social erosion, the emergence of a new social class which breached feudal barriers, was due more to the increasing requirements of absolutism for skilled administrators than to any expansion of a commercial middle class. They were to improve 'economic' efficiency and intellectual capabilities, but they became the driving force behind a process of state and social reform. The new functional elite of other sectors of society did not appear until later. Governmental administration and the endeavours of the administrators to impose a new, rational basis upon the state resulted in the emergence of a new social class. This subsequently evolved into a 'new' middle class, the educated middle class. Despite the fact that they were long to remain socially entrenched in feudal society, their desire for reform spawned a new consciousness based on the concepts of purposefulness, morality and reason in place of feudal honour and tradition. It became increasingly necessary for members of this elite to prove their academic credentials, which only served to reinforce this trend.

These circles spawned a learned and progressive culture characterized by high moral standards. At first, it remained a private affair, but it then made a rapid entrance onto the public stage, forcing society for the first time to question the political and social basis of the traditional social order.

The process of Enlightenment was on a relentless march from the early eighteenth century onwards – now stagnating, now accelerating. During the initial stages, this process was sustained by a small class of scholars, then by circles of men in the public eye, until, towards the end, it embraced nearly all educated men. In the final analysis, however, from the point of view of eighteenth-century society as a whole – the aristocracy, the urban population and the peasantry – the process was shaped by only a minority of the population. Only a minority yearned for a new identity beyond the realms of traditional society, though, initially, without drawing the obvious social conclusions either for themselves or for others. Ultimately, 'revolutionary' groups were of minor importance.

The true focal points and power factors of society rested in the princely court, the Church, the estates, and the household until well into the eighteenth century. These represented the social milieu of the majority of the population, upon whom they exerted an almost exclusive formative influence. This also applied to most disciples of the Enlightenment.

Although the eighteenth-century process of separating government from the court resulted increasingly in an administration which was institutionally and socially independent of court circles and a bastion of the middle class, the court remained the central seat of power until the end of the eighteenth century, and was restricted mainly to the aristocracy. It was a closed and exclusive world with its own customs, and, for the most part, it remained hidden from public view within numerous palaces whose splendour was evidence to all the uninitiated, including government administrators, of their exclusion from high society. At court, the aristocracy indulged in social intercourse characterized by refined manners and customs. It was a milieu whose distinguishing features were permissiveness and secularity. Displays of ostentatious splendour were the status symbol of the aristocracy. They remained aloof from the middle class and focused their attentions on the ruling princes. The court aristocracy enjoyed great privileges, living off their estates or holding lucrative positions of state. At the end of the century, court life no longer enjoyed the social dominance that it did at the beginning, but it was still the central point of social focus. Thus, many enlightened men of letters endeavoured not only to attain positions of state based at court, but also to satisfy their ambitions for a financially secure existence and social recognition, aristocratic rank. A third factor was that they would then be in a position to pursue their reformist ambitions more effectively. Benign absolutism had attracted many middle-class academics and intellectuals, thus opening up aristocratic society. However, it also spawned social tensions. These tensions persisted regardless of the aristocracy's adoption of the new literature and philosophy, abandonment of their traditional contempt for public office and willingness to cooperate in reforming society. The decisive influence in the emergence of many of the proponents of the Enlightenment was their governmental background at court. The life-long endeavours of Adolph von Knigge, a leading propagator of the societies, clubs and organizations, give a clear indication of the problems resulting from this marriage between the court and the reformist middle class.

The Church was a world of its own. Its social and cultural eminence went unchallenged until well into the eighteenth century, despite the loss of some of its power and autonomy which it had suffered as a result of its clash with the state. This is true for all religious denominations. Ecclesiastical affairs were dominated by clerics trained in theology. Lay influence was negligible. Faith, with the state's blessing, was a monopoly of the Church, and no alternative interpretations were permitted. The authorities showed little interest in wielding secular powers against heretics, but, nevertheless, criticism of the Church long continued to have serious consequences, especially professional consequences. However, the Church not only manipulated the population's social views and perceptions of faith through the exercise of this monopoly, it also had a decisive influence on public morality and education. There were endless opportunities for the exercise of ecclesiastical influence at primary and grammar school level as well as in the universities. The Church did not possess any autonomous rights of disposal; it was simply fulfilling 'state' responsibilities. These monopolies remained until the last third of the century. However, not all the advocates of the Enlightenment challenged them as a matter of principle. There were no objections to an enlightened Church. Although most leading ecclesiastical positions were the preserve of the aristocracy and the respectable middle class, less senior positions were accessible to the lower classes. Thus, in the eighteenth century, significant numbers of the lower middle class were, for the first time, able to occupy positions other than the most lowly. In addition to providing permanent financial security, for many of those championing the Enlightenment, the Church, like public administration, also opened up vistas for effective agitation. Many disciples of the Enlightenment were clerics: alongside government administration, ecclesiastical posts provided the most complete intellectual fulfilment and thus, despite strict regimentation, they were much in demand. However, it soon became clear that here, too, there was a limit, as exemplified by the commitment to the Enlightenment of Karl Friedrich Bahrdt.

The estates were another example of a self-contained world in which the population of the eighteenth century was still very much entrenched and which exerted a formative influence upon many champions of the Enlightenment. The estates had also forfeited some of their political power, but they were still a powerful social force. Nobody was able to choose their estate; they were born into it. This fact controlled both private and professional lives. Individual needs were subordinated to collective norms. The estates were not professional organizations: they were lifelong communities controlling every aspect of religious, family and economic life. They permitted neither economic expansion nor communication between the estates. The feudal world was a closed world, characterized by marked social distinctions and controlled in the main by the 'respectable' classes. This particularly applies to the feudal corporation, but also to the merchant class. However, the system of estates was by no means inflexible: their numbers increased with their spheres of activity. Even university scholars regarded themselves as an estate with their own tradition and code of honour, permitting only limited 'extravagances'. The eighteenth-century feudal structure was no longer hermetic; increasingly, the new classes of government administrators and clerics refused to conform to the prescribed model. However, despite their self-image as enlightened individuals transcending the barriers between the estates, in many respects, many of those who championed the cause of the Enlightenment remained, as far as their family and professional lives were concerned, rooted in feudalism. Personal problems did not arise as long as professional interests and private commitment to the Enlightenment did not clash. However, the moment that this commitment spawned self-awareness, feudal barriers were breached.

The fourth element exercising a decisive social influence during the eighteenth century was the household, the traditional whole 'household' as a component part of feudalism. Within the household, the life of each and every individual was subordinated to the whole, and everyone was designated a role which was defined down to the last detail: the master of the house, the lady of the house, the children and the labourers and servants. This was the case in merchant, academic and peasant households alike. Like the individual estate, the household was both a production and a social community subject to a traditional set of rules. A patriarchal structure and community bonds, material and economic interests and security and domestic happiness were all bonded together to form an integrated whole, permitting few opportunities for individualism. The household also underwent a social transformation in the eighteenth century, but, nevertheless, it was still a fundamental component of the experiential horizon of those who were the advocates of the Enlightenment. Complete breaks seldom occurred: compromises were made much as they were in court circles, in the Church and in the estates. While publicly conforming to the traditional order, the proponent of the Enlightenment privately preached the cause and pursued interests transcending feudal divisions. 'Escape' from the traditional order had many different starting points, but in every case scholastic training, familiarity with the new literature, mainly acquired through periodicals, and contact with like-minded individuals exercised the major influence. Courtly society and feudal customs began to lose some of their appeal as self-confidence increased, and groups which did not conform to the traditional order and drew their sense of identity from communication spanning feudal divides were able to establish themselves on a firm footing.

It is essential to grasp fully the individual social consequences of these four domains, including their influence upon the social and professional lives of the advocates of the Enlightenment and the scholars. Only then will it be possible to understand, firstly, how slowly the process of Enlightenment progressed during the course of the eighteenth century, not becoming a social force until the end of the century, and, secondly, how strongly the Enlightenment and its call for morality and reason, or rather the subordination of the whole of society to the laws of morality and reason, represented a new phenomenon which in the long term challenged the legitimacy of the old world.

Providing that these calls did not extend beyond the private domain, thus remaining a matter for the individual, the advocate of the Enlightenment and his milieu seldom experienced any problems – he pursued his new activities alongside his old. The dynamism which, in the long term, was to transform society did not develop until the process of self-education generated criticism of state and society and groups of champions of the Enlightenment drew, at least for themselves, the obvious social conclusions from the new moral and rational postulations and broke with traditional society. This process was part of a general political and economic transformation, but it also possessed a dimension of its own. In the eighteenth century, it was not the lower classes who voiced deep-seated dissatisfaction but rather an educated middle class who had reached maturity in the service of the state, the Church and the economy. Literary and philosophical activity and debate played a uniquely forceful emancipatory role in the eighteenth century: they were the media of middle-class self-realization. However, the middle-class social concepts based on the tenets of reason had originally been the objectives of scholars, intellectuals and educated members of society long before they were adopted as standard by society as a whole. These objectives not only influenced the perceptions of those who remained aloof from the world at large; they were soon exercising a social influence upon those sections of the middle class engaged in intellectual self-articulation, thus, for the first time, breaching the dam of the traditional social framework. To a certain extent, a new force emerged to challenge the traditional institutions of the court, the Church, the estates and the household. Initially, it was solely a private affair of the middle class, but it then became the model for social behaviour in general.

The fact that the process of emancipation in Germany was achieved through the medium of education was by no means an indication that there had been a retreat on the political front. The acquisition of knowledge and the process of self-realization were social processes. The challenge to traditional society, the cultivation of common reformist interests, the process of self-organization and public political agitation were fundamentally new factors in the history of European civilization.

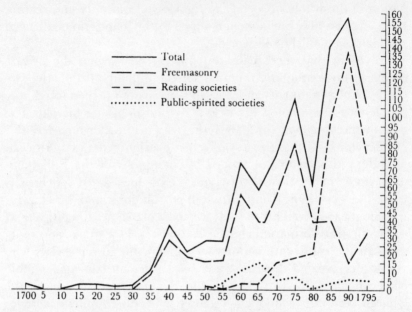

Figure 1.1   The development of societies, clubs and organizations in
the eighteenth century in order of dates

The objective of this study is to portray this process of the
cultivation of new media of communication in a feudal society.
This process is interwoven with the history of middle-class self-
discovery and the perception and articulation of middle-class interests. Although the impact of this process of emancipation was
not felt until the beginning of the eighteenth century, its origins
lie much further back in time. This fact was exploited by the
champions of the Enlightenment themselves in order to bestow
upon their cause a long and illustrious history. Indeed, important
characteristics first appeared in the various societies of the six-
teenth and seventeenth centuries.

2

LEARNED AND LITERARY SOCIETIES IN THE SEVENTEENTH CENTURY

THE HUMANIST SODALITIES

The appearance of the first free associations was linked to the development of the secular culture of humanism.[1] A new class of scholars came into existence outside the Church and the universities and created a new and free medium of communication, the so-called sodalities, which was independent of all guild, monastic and corporative ties. This medium of communication satisfied the new needs both for social intercourse transcending the estates and for learned discourse. In addition, it also generated the conditions for the emergence of secular, non-theological knowledge. The sodalities were only the beginnings of free association, and, due to the limited sources available, only a general reconstruction of their organizational structure is possible.

Even before 1500, loose circles of scholars had come into existence in university, and other towns and cities throughout Germany. As a new medium of communication, the opportunities for personal contact and private discussion offered by these circles complemented those supra-regional contacts and connections which already existed as a result of the expansion of publishing and the emergence of 'Commercium litteratum'. However, the German arch-humanist, Conrad Celtis (1459–1508), was the first to organize these circles into leagues of friendship and learned societies, and his secular habits and self-image were adopted as the programme of German humanism.[2] The Emperor also gave him his full support. In imitation of Italian humanism and humanist societies, of which the platonic academy in Florence and the literary society in Rome are outstanding examples, Celtis organized many urban-based sodalities into centres of humanist thought. The Heidelberg circle spawned a 'Sodalitas litteraria Rhenana' and in Vienna, the humanists founded the 'Sodalitas litteraria Danubiana'. These became the best known of the sodalities, and most humanists soon regarded themselves as members of one or the other. However, this did not satisfy Celtis. His ambition was the foundation of a national literary sodality. In 1501, the Nuremberg parliament bestowed royal privilege upon him. However, Celtis did not achieve his ambition. The 'Collegium poetarum et mathematicorum' of Vienna University, comprising the leading members of the Danube Sodality and founded with the full support of the Emperor, achieved greater success. Its aim was to offer a humanist alternative to the traditionalism of Vienna University Faculty of Arts, and it specialized in the cultivation of the modern arts and sciences, such as poetry and mathematics, as well as history, philosophy, cosmography and the classics. However, neither the German literary sodalities nor the Collegium survived the passing of Celtis: the social conditions essential for the flourishing of creativity were absent, and there was no theoretical programme which would have united all the humanists.

The sodalities and, to a lesser extent, the Vienna Collegium, pursued three objectives: firstly, they regarded themselves as an association of learned friends with the same humanist interests. They met in private, assisted each other with their literary endeavours, recited didactic pieces as a testimony to their eloquence, performed plays and enjoyed many a social occasion dining with their hosts. The aim of all this was to engender a new spirit of learning which would reject the grand theatrical disputations of the scholastics, who were mainly concerned with the application of formal logical acumen and the use of complex technical language during the debate of a dialectical problem. Instead, in the tradition of the ancient world, this new learned spirit would gravitate towards the conviviality offered by the small circle of learned friends. The sodalities were also learned societies where the future of the arts and sciences was debated. Celtis expected the sodalities to propose source material and make common publishing suggestions. Nothing was to be published without proof-reading and prior sodalist consent. Thus, the individual writer exposed himself to the criticism of his peers whenever he risked such an undertaking. Lastly, the sodality cherished an image of itself as the humanist shield against the all-powerful scholasticism of the universities. It spawned cells as a basis for the reform of private and public education: the famous obscurantist letters originated from the Erfurt sodality, and the founding objective of the Vienna Collegium was the provision of an institutionalized safeguard for the new humanist programme.

LANGUAGE SOCIETIES

Independent societies emerged a century later in the form of the so-called language societies, which were also the first lasting free associations with a definite organizational shape.[3] They were very different from the 'Christian Societies' of Johann Andreae and their aims were more akin to those of the humanist sodalities. They also survived to a certain extent in the so-called 'German' societies of the eighteenth century, or at least the 'German' societies claimed them as their antecedents. The term 'language society' is somewhat ambivalent: in the first place, it embraces both highly organized societies and casual groupings of literati. Secondly, for these societies, German language and literature was only one, albeit important, element in the enhancement of virtuous and patriotic behaviour. The same societies might also reasonably be called societies of virtue, and, indeed, some of them were. The 'Fruchtbringende Gesellschaft' ('Fruitful Society') founded by Prince Ludwig von Anhalt in 1617 was the largest and best known of the language societies, but there were numerous others, some of which were of notable importance. Some examples are: the 'Deutschgesinnte Genossenschaft' of Philipp von Zesen founded in Hamburg in 1643,[4] the 'Pegnesischer Blumenorden' ('Pegnesian Floral Order') of Georg Philipp Harsdörfer founded in Nuremberg in 1664, and the 'Elbschwanenorden' founded by Johann Rist in Wedel between 1656–60.[5] In addition, there were some smaller societies: the 'Aufrichtige Tannengesellschaft' founded by Jesaias Rompler von Löwenhalt in Strasbourg in 1633, the 'Neunständige Hänseschaft' founded in 1643–4, also by Philipp von Zesen, the 'Poetisches Kleeblatt' of Johann Christoph Becher, founded in Strasbourg in 1671, and the 'Belorbeerte Tauben Orden' of 1693, of which neither the founder nor the place of origin are known;[6] and there were also the 'Istergesellschaft' in Lower Austria[7] and the 'Tugendliche Gesellschaft' in Saxony, which were both informal associations of aristocratic women.[8] The most influential and best known of the societies were the 'Fruitful Society' and the 'Pegnesian Floral Order'.

The Fruitful Society

The 'Fruitful Society' originated in princely and aristocratic circles and in imitation of the Italian model.[9] It was founded as a means of satisfying the ambitions of some members of the literary and aristocratic elite to strengthen and refine the German language as a counter to the growing cultural influence of French, and to improve and defend moral standards and virtue against the threat posed by the turmoil of the Thirty Years' War. This was one of the first Protestant national and patriotic movements.

The cultivation of High German was a central issue: it was to be preserved 'as far as possible, free from alien vocabulary both in essence and in form'. However, this was a secondary objective. More important were public displays of 'sensibility and wisdom, virtue and courteousness, usefulness and delightfulness, and the geniality of moderation'. It was especially important that the members should behave in a 'kind, genial, and friendly manner' towards one another, and 'improper address and crude raillery' were forbidden.[10]

Positive achievements, such as, for example, literary publications, were not required of the members. Generally speaking, they were expected to display a moral and ethical posture at all times and show commitment to the societal aims. Under its first head, Prince Ludwig von Anhalt, the society made extraordinary progress. During the period 1617–50, 527 members were admitted, and by 1680, the 'Order of the Palms', as it was also known, had a total of 890 members. In keeping with the aristocratic and political interests of the prince, the majority of members were aristocrats, even though it was expressly intended that neither class nor religious denomination should be a membership factor. The membership did include numerous commoners, among them most of the famous German baroque poets, but, despite the number of literati among their ranks, almost no Protestant clergymen. They were excluded on the grounds of their tendentious reputation. However, most conspicuous of all by their absence were Catholics and women whose exclusion was a silent rule. This resulted in the emergence of organizations of aristocratic women.

A potential member could only be admitted upon proposal by an existing member. Personal applications for membership were not admissible. Upon admission, each member received a societal name, a motto and an emblem: Prince Ludwig von Anhalt, the society's first president, was known as the 'Provider', his emblem was a well-baked loaf of wheat bread and his motto 'Nothing Better'. Martin Opitz, the famous baroque poet, went under the name 'Crowned Head', his emblem depicted a laurel tree under a panoply of leaves and his motto was 'With These'. The societal name was not a secret name; its purpose was to emphasize the existence of 'equality and a society among unequals'.

Furthermore, the literary publications were to serve 'the common good', not to promote the reputation of the individual.[11] Most of the members abided by this rule, and even Harsdörfer, who founded his own society and was a respected man of letters himself, published his works under the name of the 'Fruitful Society'.

Typically, the membership was divided into two groups: those living outside the society's catchment area around Köthen-Weimar and who were scattered throughout Germany received a 'letter of acceptance' upon admission. In such cases, correspondence was the only means of contact with the society. This could lead to an exchange of intellectual ideas, but in the main it was confined to the admission formalities. Publishing under the societal name was the only other connection that such members had with the society. In the case of those members admitted in person, the procedure was altogether different: there was a formal admission ritual. The members were seated around a table with the president of the society in attendance. The newcomer took an oath to the statutes, whereupon he received his name, motto and emblem. A ritual of conviviality terminated this ceremonial part of the proceedings: the new member was presented with a glass and the other members drank a toast to his health. This 'practical joke' was borrowed from the traditional admission rituals of the guilds.

The Fruitful Society had a simple organizational structure: there was a president, and a treasurer responsible for matters of correspondence and maintaining the membership list. Generally speaking, the president's main function was the admission of new members. However, this did not preclude the possibility that general meetings might be held in Köthen or Weimar on the occasion of the admission rituals, but, however desirable they might have been, such meetings seldom materialized.

In the main, the prince was preoccupied with improving his standing, especially among men of letters, by the bestowal of favours, and he was very successful in this quest. For their part, poets and writers sought membership as a token of recognition of their intellectual achievements by the court upon which they were dependent. Although the society itself seldom made any efforts to achieve its goals, such as engaging in project collaboration on the Italian model, no writer, no matter how famous, scorned membership. Its ranks included Andreas Gryphius and Georg Philipp Harsdörfer, Friedrich von Logau and Johann Michael Moscherosch, Martin Opitz and Caspar Stieler, and Johann Rist and Philipp von Zesen. A considerable number of them were also members of other societies.

It has continually been emphasized that the language societies of the seventeenth century made scarcely a single contribution towards the improvement of German literature. On the contrary, it is maintained that they never progressed beyond indulging in a vain, courtly game. Although the society itself might not have exerted any directly creative influence upon literature, and although its association with the court might have been so intimate as to be injurious to its well-being, this is just one side of the coin. What was a fundamentally new phenomenon was the fact that, for reasons of the promotion of patriotism, the upholding of morality and the improvement of literature, men of letters from all over Germany joined forces. In addition, despite its shortcomings, the society was the first to dispense with aristocratic and middle-class distinctions and to silence the confessional differences between members of the Reformed and the Lutheran churches. This was all the more remarkable at a time when confessional arguments had reached their peak and the aristocracy was increasingly making a conscious effort to keep aloof from commoners. While, as has already been pointed out, collaboration, whether in the drafting of the statute or in the common authorship of literary works, was rare, and large-scale projects non-existent, the literati did nevertheless agree on a joint programme which contributed to the development of a patriotic consciousness based on German baroque poetry. Only the individual achieved fame, but, nevertheless, the society did contribute to the standing of a national Protestant culture.

The Pegnesian Floral Order

In contrast with the 'Fruitful Society', the 'Pegnesian Floral Order' emerged from a tightly knit association of poets.[12] In 1644, on the occasion of a double wedding, Georg Philipp Harsdörfer and Johann Klai, two well-known pastoral poets, composed a 'Pegnesian pastoral poem set among the meadows of Berinorgia and led in song by Strephon and Clajus'. In a way, it was composed as a festive social cameo commissioned for private performance, and out of it grew the idea of a floral order. This society also introduced societal names. The order's emblem were the panpipes, which was meant to suggest that, in the same way as these individual tubes are united into a single pipe and play in harmony, so, too, these shepherds of Pegnitz are to direct all their efforts and all their poems towards a single aim, that of the celebration and aggrandizement of the Glory of God, and the practice and propagation of the teachings of virtue and of German language and poetry. In terms of its organizational structure, this society is difficult to describe. The society only assumed the form of a language society proper, with a clear membership policy restricted exclusively to the Nuremberg area, upon Sigmund von Birken's assumption of the presidency. There was a set of statutes from the outset, but it did not appear in print until 1716.[13]

This association of poets was primarily concerned with the furtherance of the German language, but, as moral objectives, virtue and the glory of God were equally as important. It was intended that the 'Crowned Heads of the Pegnesian Floral Order' should give 'their countrymen' cause

> to cultivate the purity of the German language in its spoken and its written forms. If, as is to be expected, this objective cannot be attained among all the people, then let at least those whose profound knowledge of the arts and sciences distinguishes them from the masses exploit this opportunity to improve their command of their mother tongue, and thus clear the way for their early admission to the most praiseworthy Order of Palms.[14]

In the early years, under Harsdörfer, the Floral Order experienced a literary high-water mark on the occasion of the Nuremberg peace celebrations of 1649–50. Harsdörfer, Birken and Klai exploited the occasion for their own celebration of the peace. The peace of Westphalia was celebrated among the Nuremberg shepherds as a national festival, and their subsequent literary works published in honour of the celebrations revealed an intellectual national consciousness in which the traditional concept of the Reich was combined with a new linguistic and cultural concept of the nation.[15]

The 'Floral Order' was much less widely known than the 'Fruitful Society', and membership increased only slowly. By 1658, Harsdörfer had recruited only 16 members. The order made its most significant strides under Birken who, by 1681, had recruited a further 58 members, mainly from the ranks of Nuremberg's upper middle class: they were either natives of Nuremberg or had grown up in the city, and most of them had studied in Altdorf. Besides academics, priests, jurists and preceptors, the membership list also contained the names of several merchants. The aristocracy was not well represented. A further marked contrast between the membership composition of the 'Floral Order' and that of the 'Fruitful Society' is that the former admitted both Catholics and women; indeed, by 1681, thirteen women had been accepted for membership. Birken was convinced 'that the nature of this sex did not preclude them from possessing the qualities of virtue and wisdom'.[16] And rightly so: the most famous female novelist of the seventeenth century, Maria Catharina Stockfleth, was one of those female members.

The order was based exclusively in and around Nuremberg, and even the president was supposed to be a resident of the city. Initially, the poets met on the banks of the River Pegnitz, then on the property of Andreas Ingolstätter, a merchant, and subsequently in the 'Irrhain' Inn, near Krafthof, which was especially fitted out for the purpose. The society had many prominent members, but there was a dearth of famous writers and poets, particularly the likes of the preacher, Johann Dilherr, who exercised such a powerful influence over Harsdörfer,[17] and Catharina Regina von Greiffenberg, who was both a resident of Nuremberg and a friend of Birken.[18] Birken evidently kept his literary and personal friendships separate from his commitment to the order.

Under Birken's influence, in particular, the original small society of poets blossomed into a language society proper. It could stand comparison with the 'Fruitful Society', but it had a completely different character. At first, the society was called simply the 'Pegnitz Floral Order', then, as Birken bestowed upon it a religious and devotional veneer, the 'Crowned Heads of Pegnitz Shepherds' and the 'Pegnitz Society of Shepherds'. Birken and his colleagues lauded the carefree way of life of the shepherd as an 'ancient, necessary, innocent estate pleasing to the Lord Almighty'. The poetical world of the shepherd was cultivated as a social cameo, not as a serious attempt to change the real world but rather as a light-hearted representation of an idealized, fictional way of life for entertainment and edification. At first, the idyllic world of the shepherd was depicted purely in accordance with secular and pagan conceptions, but it subsequently became endowed with a religious and mythical meaning: the shepherd ceased to be the symbol of innocent and ordinary man and became the symbol of the Saviour. The pursuit of 'vanity' was prohibited. Instead, the 'main objective' was 'the furtherance of the Glory of God', and all the members were urged to 'make every effort to praise their Shepherd of Souls, Jesus Christ, in spiritual song'.[19]

Grand projects were of no interest to the Pegnesian Shepherds, and neither did they indulge in public displays of ostentation. The prestige of membership was small in comparison with that of the 'Fruitful Society'. The *raison d'être* of the order was social intercourse and a common love of pastoral poetry. There was little room for individualism within the Floral Order, but, nevertheless, it was characterized by a private atmosphere. The society was idealist: there was no discrimination on the grounds of estate, religious denomination or sex. Instead, educated members of the middle class were united in a national and patriotic consciousness transcending any denominational barriers. This was the new, idyllic world of the shepherds extending beyond the household, the estates and the Church.

LEARNED SOCIETIES

Literary circles of friends were the first free associations, but they were soon joined by learned societies whose interests lay in the

fields of natural philosophy and the natural sciences. The emergence of these societies was a riposte to the official study of science
within the universities, which remained rooted in Aristotelianism
and closed its eyes and ears to the modern methods and instruments of the new experimental sciences. It was also a riposte to
the social isolation of scholars in quasi-feudal corporations where
innovation was anathema and where there was no place for anyone lacking formal academic training, or for independent scholars,
despite the fact that, since Bacon and Descartes, such men had
been the foremost pioneers of natural science. These new demands
and interests called for new forms of organization. Learned academies did not emerge until the eighteenth century. However, several
smaller societies were established during the course of the seventeenth century. Their histories give some indication of how arduous a task it was to establish associations of mutual interest.

An early attempt at founding a society of philosphy and natural
science was undertaken by the mathematician and philosopher,
Joachim Jungius (1587–1657): he founded the 'Societas ereu-
netica' in Rostock in 1622.[20] Not much is actually known about
this society, but, according to surviving statutes, what is known is
that a group of scholars, under the leadership of a president,
intended to conduct research into the 'truth of reason and experience'. The procurement of instruments and equipment was to be a
joint effort. Each member was to specialize in a single field. The
remarkable concept was the scholar's right to his own intellectual
property. Important decisions were to be taken collectively, including the expulsion of members, for which the agreement of the
whole membership was required. In order to protect both the
research work and the researchers, the statutes were not to be
made public knowledge. In his conviction that 'though the flesh is
mortal, the thoughts are eternal', Jungius was the first to propagate the doctrine of cooperation between scientists through the
free exchange of views. Subordination to the president was total,
but the individual member still had some rights. Among Jungius's
close associates there was much interest in these bold ideas, but,
probably as a result of the incipient turmoil of the Thirty Years'
War, the founding of the society came to nothing.

Much more widely known is the 'Academia Naturae curiosorum', the so-called Leopoldina, which was founded in Schweinfurt in 1652 by the doctor and urban physician, Johann Lorenz
Bauch, together with three friends.[21] This is the only one of the

earliest societies to have survived to the present day. Its history is a documentation of the long, hard road that the institutions of natural science have trodden. Although the society was based on the Italian model, the oft-repeated claims of a connection with Francis Bacon's 'Nova Atlantis' are completely without foundation. Initially, it was exclusively an association of doctors 'for the development of medical science, the benefit of our fellow-men, and the exploration of truth'.[22] It was not intended to be a public academy, but rather a private association of scientists who 'are Naturae Curiosi, thirsty for knowledge in matters of natural science'. At that time, natural science was regarded as more the collection and observation of natural curiosities than an experimental science aimed at making new discoveries.

At the head of the society was a president whose home town was the society's base. Not until the nineteenth century did the society find a permanent home in Halle. Each member had to choose a research topic from the realm of botany, zoology or mineralogy. In addition to the powers of the whole and its constituent parts, and the effects of the medicines obtained, the names, synonyms, genesis, natural habitats, differentia and types also had to be detailed. In order to achieve these aims, the members were expected to conduct their own research as well as rely upon third party sources. Everyone was expected to conduct their research independently and joint research was rare. General meetings were also a rarity; in fact, due to the great distances separating the members' places of residence, they were practically out of the question. Only those who lived in and around Schweinfurt met together occasionally.

This society also bestowed societal names. It seems to have been of some importance to the society to make the fact of its existence widely known. To this end, each member received a signet ring bearing a coat of arms depicting an open book. On one page of the book, there is an engraving of a plant, and on the other, of an eye illuminated by rays of light breaking through a group of clouds. Two serpents, one on each side, their bodies and tails coiled around the ring, hold the book in the grip of their jaws. 'Nunquam otiosus' was chosen as the societal motto.

Although, from the outset, there was no lack of earnest intent, the learned society still experienced serious problems in recruiting members, raising funds and achieving public recognition. The famous philosopher and mathematician, Gottfried Wilhelm

Leibniz, clearly recognized the problems faced by a society of natural scientists in the seventeenth century. He regarded the 'Collegium Naturae Curiosorum' more as 'a sign of our willingness that we (Germans) have made a start, just like young birds starting to fly, as it were. But it is also a sign of our shortcomings that those who show willingness have not been given a helping hand'.[23] Here, Leibniz was alluding to the lack of court support. In both England and France, in contrast, considerable interest was forthcoming from this quarter. But Leibniz also points to the other difficulty of the society: that of actively proving its worth. It only collected material and showed no desire to make any new discoveries on the basis of 'its own experience'. It was thus no wonder, he thought, that the society was failing to excite any attention.

The situation did not change until, thanks to the committed intervention of the Silesian doctor, Philipp Jacob Sachs von Lewenhaimb, contacts were established at the Court of Vienna, and Emperor Leopold I bestowed recognition upon the society in 1672. A few years later, in 1687, the society was elevated to the status of Imperial Academy with the title 'Sacri Romani Imperii Academia Caesareo-Leopoldina-Naturae Curiosorum' and granted extensive privileges. Chief among these were the right to award academic degrees and complete freedom from censorship, which safeguarded the free exchange of scientific views against interference on the part of the state and the Church. This was a privilege which became a matter of central importance to scholars during the course of the eighteenth century. However, none of this meant that the society had secured any direct financial support. This was not forthcoming until 1712, by which time the society was able to call itself 'Academia Caesarea Leopoldina-Carolina Naturae Curiosorum'. But public recognition alone did not secure the society's existence: of equal importance was the society's publication, the 'Miscellanae curiosae medico-physicae Academiae Naturae Curiosorum sive Ephemeriden', which first appeared in 1670, again at the initiative of Sachs. Later, the title was changed at regular intervals. This meant that it was now possible to keep a broad international readership abreast of scientific results. This was the first specialist publication in the fields of medicine and natural science. However, since it was published in Latin and, true to the society's statutes, contained more in the way of curiosities than actual research in the modern sense of the term, unlike contemporary English-language scientific publications, it long remained largely ineffective.

In comparison with the eighteenth-century academies, the Leopoldina never became particularly well known and its membership consisted chiefly of learned doctors, including some foreigners. All they had in common was a perception of medicine as a polyhistorical science. Thus, what was fundamentally new was not the perception of science but the emergence of a community spirit under the protection of the Emperor.

3

The Republic of Scholars

There had already been a series of attempts to establish societal organizations during the seventeenth century. Generally speaking, despite the fact that the motivating forces behind all these efforts were morality and patriotism, there were three main basic standard models: a linguistic and literary model, such as the literary societies; a society of natural philosophy, such as the Leopoldina, which was an association of medical science; and, finally, one of Christian learning, but this never progressed beyond the stage of utopian projection. These associations, foundings of associations and attempts to found associations were all, to a greater or lesser extent, the result of private initiatives by private individuals wishing to form associations outside the existing forces of authority, such as the court, the Church and the estates. These individuals were not fully integrated into these institutions, but nevertheless, they still retained some feudal and authoritarian characteristics. The reformist impulse is unmistakable: their aspirations were either the creation of a new form of literature, a purified language, which would make a contribution towards the stimulation of patriotic consciousness, or the liberation of science from scholastic disputation in order that it might serve the well-being of mankind. All such associations were founded by representatives of the elite. They came mostly from the middle class (but also from the aristocracy) and had made a name for themselves as scholars independent of existing academic institutions. All these associations cherished both Christian and patriotic ambitions and a pragmatic objective. However, only those which adapted themselves most enthusiastically to the existing order, while at the same time manifesting a definite and clearly perceptible mission with which to gain the recognition of both the forces of authority and the general public, had any hope of success. Not counting the Nuremberg Order (the Floral Order), the only society to survive beyond the seventeenth century in Germany was the Leopoldina.

The history proper of the societies of the Enlightenment as media of middle-class self-determination and culture did not, however, begin with the societies of the seventeenth century, even though these did provide important foundations. Two great societal movements mark the beginning of the process of middle-class self-organization. These are the learned society, a creation of Gottfried Wilhelm Leibniz, and the literary society, which was founded by Johann Christoph Gottsched and his German Society in Leipzig (see map 1). Although both could point to their predecessors and both learned from the diverse experiences of societies abroad (in Italy and England), they also represented something fundamentally new, and as such they created the foundations for the development of the Enlightenment in Germany.[1]

THE LEARNED SOCIETY

Leibniz and the learned society

The figure at the centre of the societal movement in Germany at the end of the seventeenth and the beginning of the eighteenth centuries was Gottfried Wilhelm Leibniz (1646–1716). It was his lifetime ambition to found a learned society which satisfied both the demands of the new sciences that research should be conducted jointly on the basis of practicality and relevancy, and the expectations of the state that practical science should advance the common good. This combines theoretical and political interests as well as those of philosophy and the individual sciences. Leibniz is the source of the most far-reaching eighteenth-century concepts. He was familiar with the development of the organization of scientific interests both in Germany and elsewhere and he adopted their traditions. Furthermore, as a court-based rather than an active university scholar, he knew how best to adapt to the contemporary political structure. He thought that a court-based science organization, rather than the traditional institutions of learning, would be more likely to lead the new sciences to victory and free 'societal' life from the spirit of rational science.[2]

Leibniz first developed the idea of a learned society during his years in Mainz; although his 'Societas philadaelphica' of 1669, in which he called for a union of scholars along the lines of the religious orders, still bore utopian characteristics, in 1671, in his 'Outline of an Idea for the Establishment of a Society in Germany to Embrace the Arts and Sciences', he produced a detailed plan for the furtherance of theoretical knowledge and its practical application through the foundation of a learned society. This was, according to Leibniz, the only way of ensuring the contentment of the human race. This aroused little interest at the Court of Mainz and thus, after his return from Paris, in 1672/3, he again called upon scholars to found a society, this time an Imperial society. Nature itself and the treasure chest of the intellect were to be the fount of knowledge, not writings. By this time, he had probably already approached somewhere in the region of fifty scholars. During his time at Hanover, he did not at first pursue any ambitions other than supporting the efforts of a historic Imperial college in Vienna to found a society. Leibniz's first major success was in Berlin. Here, in collaboration with the court chaplain, Jablonski, he succeeded in persuading the electoral prince to set up first an observatory and then a society. After the electoral prince had issued an order at the beginning of 1700 'to establish an Academy of Science and an Observatory in Berlin',[3] Leibniz drew up the foundation charter and became academy life-president. According to the foundation charter, the society was to

> strive towards the development, improvement, complete understanding and correct application of beneficial studies, the sciences and the arts, useful information and anything else that is relevant. This can be achieved by observing the works and wonders of God in nature, and also by commenting upon, describing, and applying the inventions, artistic creations, processes and teachings of nature. As a result of this, the scattered treasure of human knowledge might be gathered more closely together within a framework, supplemented and exploited to the full.[4]

However, it was to be a further ten years before the formal inauguration. Leibniz did not remain idle during this time: on the contrary, he attempted to build up a whole network of scientific societies in various countries. His discussions and negotiations in

Dresden, St. Petersburg and Vienna progressed well, but these projects did not develop beyond the planning stage, despite the support of Peter the Great in Russia and Prince Eugene in Vienna. They do, however, reveal how far-reaching were Leibniz's concepts. Leibniz was the instigator of very many initiatives, but it was only in Berlin that he achieved any real success. Even here there were interminable problems and his concept fell victim to repeated truncation.

What preoccupied Leibniz was not some small, loose association of scholars; his ultimate goal was an academy of science which was recognized and supported by the state, such as those with which he was familiar in England and France. Not until there was such an academy did he expect science to make any systematic progress or exert any influence upon government or social policy to improve the status of the scholar. The academy was conceived as an all-embracing scientific, economic and cultural authority of the state, and he hoped that it would enable him to combine theory with practice. Thus, he stated that:

> The purpose [would be] to combine theory with practice and to improve not only the arts and sciences but also the country and the people, agriculture, manufacturing and commerce and, in a word, food. Also, to make discoveries which redound profusely to the Glory of God and assist in the perception of His miracles, and thus in the implantation and dissemination of the Christian religion, strong government, stability and morality among peoples partly heathen, partly still ignorant, even barbaric.[5]

Above all else, his primary concerns were the furtherance and the practical implications of scientific knowledge. At the same time, Leibniz hoped that this would also assist in shaping state, economic and cultural life in the spirit of mercantilism. Furthermore, it was intended that the academy should also promote education, publishing and the study of language and history. Leibniz even placed the Far East Mission at the service of science.

> Meanwhile, it has been most humbly suggested to us that it would be of service to an objective of such stature that is so well-pleasing to God to found a certain scientific society which would have its main headquarters at our place of residence in Kölln on the River Spree. Through foreign members and epistolary and verbal com-

munication with individuals and other societies, it is intended
that the society should conduct all kinds of useful investigations
and produce all kinds of reports, extracts, writings, instruments,
discoveries, demonstrations, experiments, observations, tests, ma-
chines, models, exotica, and other natural specimens, summaries,
descriptions, proposals and ideas for collection and study. In addition, where necessary, it should, of its own accord, out of dutiful-
ness most befitting and upon request most gracious, most humbly
furnish its report, thereby restricting itself to studies and the sciences. In a word, the supervision and aggrandizement of science.
We have not simply adopted this proposal, but also, of our own
accord, most humbly improved upon it so that it should be at one
and the same time a society that is German in spirit and one which
is chiefly concerned with the glory, well-being and acceptance of
the German nation, and with learning and language. We were
induced to this undertaking all the more because the Good Lord
blessed our Germany in a multitude of ways, in the course of which
He also ignited such a flame of teaching that the darkness which
blighted the Christian peoples was banished, and the truth, particularly in the Church and its institutions of learning, was led
back into the light of day. Nobody can deny that in all the fields of
study, in the sciences and in the arts, many important truths, yes,
even the art of printing, which is the best means of conveying noble
thoughts to posterity, emanate from Germany. For this and many
other reasons it is incumbent upon us as upstanding patriots not
only to concern ourselves to the best of our ability with cultivating
the common interests of our fellow Protestant estates, but also with
the preservation and aggrandizement of the dignity of the Fatherland. (General Instructions for the Society of Science of 11 July
1700 (Berlin)).[6]

Prior to the foundation of the Berlin Academy, Leibniz's main
concern had been to establish a scientific programme. Although
his concepts were diverse, they all conformed to a similar pattern:
a practical and realistic leaning, a summary of all the practical
implications and an emphasis on usefulness, particularly for the
state. The Berlin Academy's General Instructions of 1700 provide
an insight into Leibniz's ideas for the consolidation of a learned
academy.[7] The academy's patron was the electoral prince. It was
headed by a president. Membership was open to anyone of academic distinction, irrespective of social origin or religious denomination. However, a distinction was made between active members
from Berlin, correspondence members from outside Berlin and

honorary members. The latter were granted membership in return for services rendered, usually of a financial nature, or the prestige which their membership bestowed upon the academy. This policy had the advantage of ensuring that research remained the responsibility of the full members while at the same time providing a court presence. The president was assisted by a consilium comprising the departmental directors and the secretary. This 'intima societas' was responsible for all important decisions and all the society's financial affairs: the proposal of members, editing scientific publications and the responsibility for instruments and equipment. Each department was supposed to hold monthly meetings, including an open lecture. The academy consisted of four departments: 'res physicae' (medicine, physics and chemistry), 'res mathematicae' (mathematics, astronomy and mechanics), German language, including general and ecclesiastical history, and literature, including oriental literature and any literature which, as was expressly stated, 'might help to spread the gospel among non-believers'.[8]

The society was a state institution *par excellence*, and regarded itself as such. However, Leibniz's structural organization guaranteed a high degree of independence: it was the exclusive remit of the Republic of Scholars to determine both what should be done and how it should be done.

The learned society as envisaged by Leibniz flourished during the course of the eighteenth century, and even Leibniz himself noted that 'judging by the popularity of societies, this would appear to be a secular age'.[9] There were many attempts to establish learned societies throughout Germany, mainly in court centres. This was due to a desire both to be close to the seat of power and to keep the universities at bay, from whose cultivation of science the societies were at pains to disassociate themselves. The Berlin, Göttingen,[10] Munich and Mannheim[11] societies became the most widely known. The societies seldom achieved the ambitious objectives enshrined in their statutes, and they only became true cultural and scientific centres to a limited extent. Nevertheless, membership was a great honour: it frequently represented the ultimate recognition of scientific and academic achievement, and most advocates of the Enlightenment were anxious to attain it. Most members were government officials, physicians and professors, in other words, members of the educated elite who were openly loyal to the new sciences. The aristocracy received favourable treatment, though they did not attain any positions of prominence. Apart from theology, politics, speculative philosophy and law, most academies were subdivided into three departments: mathematics and natural philosophy, history and philology. Priority was devoted to those subjects which promised results, although specialist knowledge was increasingly regarded as general knowledge, with the result that the societies often became associations of specialists. However, there was no shortage of scientists who were able to overcome this limitation and exploit the opportunity for research offered by the societies. Joint research and general debates of scientific problems were mainly the concern of private circles. The focus of societal attention was private research, albeit of an empirical kind fostering community spirit. Annual publications of collections of essays were the most common method of communicating new discoveries. At the same time, these publications were a record of societal achievement. The societies' main priority was to offer public support to research activity, for which funds had always been scarce. In addition, in order to create the basis for historical research, the societies undertook publishing projects on a large scale.

The academy lectures were also of central importance. Lectures were held both in public and in private. They reflect the individual member's perception of science and serve as a history of the problems faced by the sciences and of the changing face of scientific objectives during the course of the eighteenth century. Finally, the academy sponsored an annual open competition which anyone was free to enter, regardless of academic membership or formal education. The best entries were awarded prizes in public ceremonies. This was a powerful instrument: on the one hand, it could be used to stimulate broad public involvement with the academy, and on the other, to promote the reputation of previously unknown scholars among the educated public at large.[12]

Academy-sponsored research regarded itself as 'independent' research, in other words, it was not usually subject to either government or ecclesiastical censorship. The scientists themselves supervised the work of their colleagues and they only lent their support to projects which they regarded as beneficial to both state and society. There were no problems as long as this selectivity only affected the field of individual empirical research. However, especially during the second half of the eighteenth century, fundamental issues increasingly became topics of debate. Thus, the socio-political activity of the academies assumed a controversial quality. After all, the source of these new points of view was hardly irrelevant: these were academies with full state support and protection whose value judgement might exercise political influence. However, towards the end of the century, the activity of these academies went into decline.

The sole purpose of the academies was to serve the progress of science. Ultimately, they had no master: they were answerable only to truth and reason. However, the regional academies included a high proportion of senior state officials who regarded them as their personal mouthpiece: they were exploited both as an instrument of theoretical sabotage *vis-à-vis* state plans for reform and as an offensive weapon in the struggle against opponents of government policy. The learned debate practised by the academies played an important role in the conflicts between the state and the estates and the state and the Church, and it contributed towards the triumph of absolutist and mercantile interests.

The academies were institutions of learning in which the virtue of critical reason sponsored empirical and practical research, thus contributing towards finding solutions to practical social problems. This emphasis on social reform received the blessing of the state. Central to the self-image of each and every member of an academy was learned Enlightenment. Central to learned Enlightenment was the exposition of mundane relationships for the purpose of improved exploitation and state planning. In contrast, humanitarian and middle-class interests had yet to play a role. Generally speaking, there was no sudden movement towards the debate of political and social principles. In this sense, the academies were not really progressive, critical institutions with which enlightened members of the middle class could stake their political claims, achieve their dream of self-determination and shape their lives as they saw fit: they were, and remained, scholarly institutions for safeguarding the march of progress. The history of the electoral Bavarian Academy of Science is an example of the advantages and the limitations of an academy.

The Bavarian Academy of Science

On 2 July 1759, the founder of the Bavarian Academy of Science, Georg Lori, wrote jubilantly to Gottsched in Leipzig:

> Your honour will have expected a few dozen new comets to appear
> in the sky sooner than an Academy of Science in Bavaria. Never-
> theless, this miracle has come to pass, and sooner than even we
> expected. On 12th October last year, four brave souls took the
> decision to follow in the footsteps of the Swiss pioneers and dedicate
> themselves to the freedom of science. Thus, plans were laid for the
> foundation of an academy. No sooner had the group been rein-
> forced by the recruitment of some rural prelates and scholars to the
> cause, and the government informed of our intentions, than the
> electoral prince took the opportunity of the occasion of his birthday
> to bestow his official sanction. After the Jesuits had realized that
> the academy could no longer be split, they tried desperately to gain
> control. There are some young Turks among the membership
> whom the university censors (in other words, the Jesuits) were
> anxious to bridle. Only our resolution secured our victory over
> these hypocrites. The academy has been freed from all forms of
> control and external censorship.[13]

Of all the German states, Bavaria was regarded as the least
progressive and the most susceptible to the dark forces of superstition, and thus, the founding of the Bavarian Academy of Science was an event of some significance.[14] However, there had
been consistent and serious attempts to establish a learned society
in Bavaria ever since the beginning of the eighteenth century. The
'Nutz- und Lusterweckende Gesellschaft der vertrauten Nachbarn
am Isar-Strom' in Munich, which resembled a court association of
government officials and priests, is well documented. There was
also a learned circle based around the German-language scientific
periodical 'Parnassus Boicus', which was sponsored mostly by
monks. Both these associations remained ineffective. However, in
1758, the young government official and jurist, Georg Lori (1723–
86), succeeded in uniting the two sets of protagonists of Catholic
scientific Enlightenment, the monks and the secular government
officials, in a private association, the 'Bavarian Learned Society'.
It was this society from which, twelve months later, in 1759,
following the bestowal of the sanction of the electoral prince, the
Academy of Science of the Electorate of Bavaria emerged.

In Bavaria, three factors characterized the societal movement,
and thus also the academy:[15] firstly, Bavarian patriots were
anxious to match the achievements of the other states in the field
of secular knowledge and to exploit the practical implications for
the benefit of the Bavarian state and of Bavarian society. De-

spite all international leanings, the decisive factor for Bavarian advocates of the Enlightenment remained patriotism. Secondly, the learned culture of the monasteries was the main standard bearer of learning which, under the influence of French culture (Maurists), was enjoying something of an academic heyday during this period. As a result, the monasteries were increasingly opening their doors to the literary and philosophical culture of Protestantism.[16] Thirdly, learning was imbued with a pronounced anti-Jesuit streak from the very outset.[17] The Jesuits dominated the entire Bavarian education system, and opposition to them was almost the academy's *raison d'être*: as an alternative to the Jesuits, the academy propagated positive historical research, an open mind towards the new sciences and rejection of ecclesiastical scholasticism. In line with their philosophical convictions, the academy's first members were adherents of the philosophy of Christoph Wolff. The patronage of the electoral prince provided the Bavarian advocates of the Enlightenment with a focal point for their political interests under the protection of the state. It possessed its own funds and enjoyed freedom from censorship. The aim of the academy was to conduct research of every conceivable kind, 'to disseminate all the practical sciences and liberal arts throughout Bavaria', excluding, however, 'religious (and) legal matters'.[18] The guiding principles of the academy were truth and practicality. The statutes state: 'Consideration will only be given to the truth, and the truth must rest on firm foundations. Sectarian and ill-founded prejudices will be ignored.' Similarly: 'All things German, and particularly Bavarian, are of legitimate interest to the academy.'[19] Thus, the academy, as a centre of learning, declared itself out of bounds for both the corporative education system (the University of Ingolstadt) and political and religious debate. In Lori's view, this was the only guarantee of academic independence.

In general, the academy's organizational structure was in line with this insistence on independence. Like the Berlin Academy, the Bavarian Academy clearly became a court institution. Nevertheless, within these limitations, the academy regarded itself as a free association of scholars. At the head of the academy was the president, appointed by the electoral prince from among his ministers. The president's responsibility was to ensure adherence to the rules of the academy. He was unable to make any changes without the consent of the senate. In addition to the president, the senate comprised the vice-president, a director and the secretary.

The president was assisted by the vice-president who was elected each year by those members in attendance at the general meeting. As a rule, a senior member of the aristocracy was elected for the sake of propriety. The vice-president deputized for the president, attended all meetings, bore the responsibility for 'order and prosperity' and was bound 'to prevent outbursts of bad temper or insulting language'.[20] Like the president, the vice-president was also unable to make any unilateral decisions. The upholding of research and academic standards was the responsibility of the two directors, the director of the department of philosophy and mathematics and the director of the department of history. The directors were elected by the full members on an annual basis, and they submitted academic progress reports to the academy's meetings. The most important position of all was perhaps that of secretary, who was elected by the full members in attendance at the general meeting. He shared responsibility for the 'well-being' of the academy with the president, the vice-president and one of the directors. In addition, he was responsible for the minutes of the meetings, all the academy's correspondence and the completion of the academy's projects.

There were three types of members of the Bavarian Academy: honorary members, full members and foreign members. Honorary members and full members had to be residents of Bavaria. The sole arbiter of membership was the meeting. Social rank or status were sufficient for honorary and foreign members. However, a candidate for full membership was required to submit a sample treatise. The applicant was only admitted to membership on condition that his treatise met with the approval of the members. Where this was the case, the application for membership was granted and the new member received a certificate. All members were bound to further the reputation of the academy, and all members were free to propose new members. Honorary members were not required to conduct any research activity, and foreign members were only required to submit a single essay. In contrast, full members were required to submit a treatise each year, participate in the academy's meetings and always be willing 'to assist' their fellows. All research work was subjected to the critical scrutiny of the general meeting. However, the researcher was permitted to adhere to his original opinion. Membership of the academy offered the individual the opportunity of publishing his work and participating in the process of objective criticism of research methodology. It also afforded him complete protection: all members were obliged to defend any of their fellows who suffered unjust criticism.

There were two formal meetings per year, and the president sent invitations to attend to all local members. The first of these meetings was held on the occasion of the electoral prince's birthday. At the same time, it was also a founder's day celebration. The second meeting was reserved for prize-giving, commissioning new research topics, elections, the admittance of new members and progress reports on the state of the academy's health. On the whole, the academy used these meetings as a public relations exercise. However, the academy also held the more important general meetings from which the general public was excluded. The purpose of these meetings was to debate the academy's progress. The general meeting was attended by the president, the vice-president, the directors, the secretary and any full member able to attend. The debate was rigidly controlled and it was expressly stated that the sole basis for every vote was to be 'love of the truth'; no vote was to be cast 'in the heat of the moment'. The academy adopted a democratic structure: in practice as well as in theory, actual decision-making authority and research was the responsibility of the full members. In other words, this responsibility rested with a relatively small circle of Munich-based middle-class government officials and clerics who made their mark in the world in the service of the academy.

There was great interest among the wider enlightened public in the academy, and, despite continuous difficulties at every turn and internal strife among the members which paralysed activity, the scientific work of the academy progressed well. The publication of the *Monumenta Boica*, a large collection of source material, and of the academy's treatises in German, hitherto an exception to the rule for scientific publications, rated as particular achievements. The academy's public lectures and the creation of chairs of natural science and philosophy also contributed towards the goal of reaching broad sections of the public. The gradual development of the academy's activity was reflected in a rapid rise in membership. In 1769, after ten years, the academy had a membership of 181, of which there were 68 full, 73 foreign and 40 honorary members. 124 of the members were Catholics, a disproportionately high number, but there were also 57 Protestant members. The classification of the membership into professions is a revealing exercise. During the first years, the academy was not dominated by professional academics or professors: 57 members came from the ranks of the clergy, 56 from among the ranks of government officials, and a further 24 were physicians or scientists (see table 3.1). The academy regarded itself as an institution which

Table 3.1 Membership structure of the Bavarian Academy of Science, 1759–85

Year	(1)	(2)	(3)	(4)	(5)	(6) (a)	(6) (b)	(7)	(8)	Total
1759	17	14	8	8	8	27	6	–	–	88
New members:										
1760	2	1	1	2	2	–	–	–	–	8
1761	4	5	1	–	4	3	–	1	–	18
1762	–	2	–	2	4	5	–	1	–	14
1763	2	1	–	–	3	11	1	2	–	20
1764	1	–	2	1	–	4	–	1	–	9
1765	1	–	2	–	2	2	–	1	–	8
1766	2	1	–	–	1	3	–	–	–	7
1767	–	1	–	–	–	–	–	–	–	1
1768	1	1	2	1	–	–	–	–	–	5
1769	–	–	1	–	–	2	–	–	–	3
1770	–	–	–	3	–	–	–	1	–	4
1771	1	–	–	1	2	1	–	1	–	6
1772	2	–	–	1	–	–	–	–	–	3
1773	1	–	1	–	4	1	–	2	1	10
1774	1	–	–	–	2	1	–	1	1	6
1775	3	5	3	3	1	–	–	–	–	15
1776	–	4	3	1	1	1	1	3	–	14
1777	1	2	2	4	1	–	–	2	–	12
1778	–	–	5	–	2	–	–	–	1	8
1779	–	3	1	1	–	–	–	1	–	6
1780	–	1	1	3	1	–	–	1	–	7
1781	–	3	3	2	–	–	–	1	1	10
1782	1	1	2	–	–	2	–	–	–	6
1783	–	1	1	1	–	2	–	–	–	5
1784	1	2	–	2	2	1	–	1	–	9
1785	–	–	–	2	2	–	–	1	–	5
1759 to 1785	41	48	39	38	42	66	8	22	4	307

(1) = Court officials; (2) = Govt. officials (mainly jurists); (3) = University professors (secular); (4) = Historians, archivists; (5) = Physicians and natural scientists; (6) = Theologians, (a) = Catholic, (b) = Protestant; (7) = Miscellaneous professions; (8) = Details not known.

Source: L. Hammermayer (1983) vol. 1, pp. 368 and 380 ff.

transcended the divisions between the estates and religious denominations, and in principle this was true: the only reason that Catholic members were in the majority was the fact that there was a large number of monks among the active membership at the academy's base in Munich. The receptivity of Catholic Enlightenment is reflected in the academy's open-door policy *vis-à-vis* Protestants. The presidency, the vice-presidency and honorary membership of the academy remained the preserve of the aristocracy. This was not in keeping with the goals of a society which wished to overcome the divisions between the estates and in which achievement, not social class, was meant to be the determining factor. However, the aristocracy had little influence on the conduct of research: their function was to serve as a shield against the considerable number of anti-Enlightenment forces in Bavaria. In addition, the aristocracy also provided the academy with a direct line of communication with the electoral prince. Not every full member of the academy satisfied the conditions for membership, which were enshrined in the statutes, and hence, the academy was not wholly an association of outstanding talent. Nevertheless, proof of achievement was still one of the main conditions of membership.

In general, the academy conducted its scientific activity in an unspectacular manner, and some of its historical and philosophical treatises were of negligible importance. The academy specialized in local and regional studies, among which was the *Monumenta Boica*. The academy performed a major role in the service of the Enlightenment in Munich, and, to some extent, set the standards for public debate. The reason for this was the commitment displayed by the members of the academy towards the Enlightenment, though they only strove to achieve their goals either within or through the academy. There were three complex themes which captivated the attention of the Bavarian public at large during the period 1765 to 1775. The origin of their dramatic impact was a central political action of Bavarian government officials who belonged to the academy.

In 1766, the director of the department of philosophy, Peter von Osterwald, anonymously published 'Vermund von Lochstein's Reasons For and Reasons Against Clerical Immunity in Secular Matters', which galvanized the Bavarian clergy and the Church into action.[21] Von Osterwald propagated the subordination of the Church to the state, thus laying the foundations for the creation of the Bavarian National Church. Von Osterwald refrained from commenting upon this issue before the academy, but, nevertheless, the accusation that the academy was behind this attack on the Church by the state was not wholly without foundation. A clearer demonstration of the relationship that existed between activity on behalf of the Enlightenment under the protection of the state and academic self-representation is provided by the commitment to the Enlightenment of the academician Ferdinand Sterzinger, the 'Bavarian Thomasius': in 1766, he made a public speech entitled 'The Common Prejudice of Active Witchcraft', which unleashed the so-called 'Bavarian War of the Witches'. Sterzinger not only fulminated against the existence of a widespread and Church-sponsored belief in witches, but also against belief in superstition and the forces of magic which enjoyed some measure of support from Bavarian Catholic monasteries.

For the enemies of the academy, this address provided confirmation of their belief that the academy was a bastion of anticlerical Enlightenment. Indeed, during this period, the academy had developed into a platform of enlightened debate enjoying both the protection of the state and the active support of the electoral prince. The third subject of controversy was educational reform. The complex debate on the German educational and secondary school systems had been initiated by two speeches: 'The Importance of an Efficient Institution to the German Education System' by Heinrich Braun in 1768, and 'The Effect of the Gradual Creation of Primary and Secondary Schools on the Electorate of Bavaria' by the renowned Ingolstadt expert on constitutional law, Johann Adam Ickstatt, in 1744. For the first time, the state began to expand its educational efforts beyond the universities to include the education of the lower social classes. Braun and Ickstatt were later actively involved in the reform of the education system.[22]

Revealingly, it now became a matter of principle that reform plans were debated among the wider educated public and no longer solely by government committees behind closed doors. Ultimately, this public involvement was of great service to the cause of reform. Originally, the academy had constituted nothing more than an association of academics who concerned themselves exclusively with problems of a historical and physical, and hence, technical, nature, and only attracted 'esoteric' interest. It had transformed itself into a forum for public debate which pursued a policy of Enlightenment with such vigour that it was able to initiate public debate of plans for reform prior to their implementation. The result of this transformation was a dramatic increase in the spheres of responsibility of the academy's members in the cause of the Enlightenment: in addition to matters of learning and science, they now included political and public problems, the relationship between the state and the Church, superstition and primary education. The service which the academy performed in the cause of the Enlightenment contributed to the successes achieved by the advocates of the policy of enlightened reform.

In 1789, following the accession of Karl Theodor to government office, the academy created a third department, the department of literature, and thus, temporarily, the academy also promoted contemporary literary and aesthetic issues, in addition to those of politics and the Enlightenment. This department was created as a result of the efforts of the Bavarian proponents of German language, literature and theatre rather than those of the academics. These efforts coincided with those of the 'German Society' in Mannheim, which now belonged to Bavaria. In Mannheim, the most prominent activists were the two journalists, Lorenz von Westenrieder and Karl von Eckartshausen. The activities of the literary department produced few results, but its literary competitions were very popular among the public at large: Johann Gottfried Herder, who had been appointed General Superintendent of Weimar in 1766, won first prize for his entry in a competition entitled 'How did literature affect the customs of the early peoples?'

The academy had originally been founded solely as an institution of learning with no interest in ecclesiastical or political issues. However, in the face of the polarization of the intellectual public and the Enlightenment, this goal proved illusory. Once the academy embraced issues of concern both to the public at large and to the Enlightenment and turned its attentions to literature and language, it increasingly came under the influence of the League of Illuminati, which had been founded in 1776. Many Munich members of the academy had joined the League, including almost all the members of the department of literature. In consequence, the prohibition of the League in 1785 also resulted in the disbandment of this department. Ideologically, the academy had nothing in common with the League of Illuminati: right up to the end of the century, the academy propagated a very moderate form of Catholic Enlightenment, whereas, in contrast, the League of Illuminati belonged to the radical wing of the Enlightenment. After 1785/6, the academy led a quiet existence until it was reorganized at the beginning of the nineteenth century.

In a short space of time, representatives of Bavarian academic and empirical interests had managed to establish the Bavarian Academy of Science under state protection. Although the academy had had no political or ecclesiastical aspirations, it nevertheless quickly became an established forum of the Enlightenment with a political programme. As long as the academy continued to support the reform programme of Bavarian benevolent absolutism, it continued to enjoy the support of the electoral prince. However, as soon as the academy posed a threat to the interests of the state as a result of Illuminati infiltration, it was brought to heel.

THE LITERARY SOCIETY

The literary societies were both a complement and an addition to the learned societies and the academies of science.[23] The original intention of the learned societies had been to include the cultivation and promotion of language and literature, particularly German language and literature, among their fields of activity. However, they then abandoned this idea for reasons of expediency. Thus, a new type of society was founded, the literary society, the society of *belles-lettres*. The literary societies continued in the tradition of the language societies, though they pursued much more far-reaching ambitions.

The primary goal of the literary societies of the early eighteenth century was the cultivation of High German, not simply as the language of academia, but as an everyday language in which it would be possible to discuss all important issues. This goal was a declaration of war on the use of dialects and Latin in academic debate. The literary societies were not concerned with the dissemination of arcane and learned knowledge affecting only tiny groups of scholars: they intended to promote the use of correct speech and well-founded argumentation as replacements for blind faith and mere opinion. Most of all, they intended to promote the moral standards of the middle class. It was intended that people should liberate themselves from the bonds of tradition and authority by the exercise of their own faculty of reason in the thought process. Lastly, the literary societies openly professed their belief in the existence of a single German nation: they practised the purification and use of German as a means of awakening a national consciousness, which would transcend local interests and call for the creation of a single nation state. In order to achieve this end, the literary societies channelled their efforts in two different directions. Firstly, they were directed at themselves with the objective of achieving the goal of mutual education, assistance and criticism among the membership: every member enjoyed equal rights, and every member was free to voice his opinions. Secondly, the societies produced joint literary efforts as a means of exerting 'external' influence. These literary endeavours were not intended to be entertaining: they were intended to influence and educate contemporary society, not by any bland and learned means, but by means of stimulating reflection upon moral and mundane issues unconnected with politics and theology. Thus, for the first time, all aspects of professional and domestic life became public issues. The literary societies focused on emancipatory concerns and the concerns of the early period of the Enlightenment much more clearly than the learned societies.

At the beginning of the eighteenth century, there were many attempts to found literary societies under many different designations. The two most important were the 'German Societies' of Johann Christoph Gottsched, which were modelled on the learned societies and were intended as the mouthpiece of the Enlightenment for the educated classes, and the so-called moral and patriotic societies, the fruit of friendship circles whose objective was to influence public opinion, primarily through the publication of 'Moral Weeklies'.

The Hamburg Moral and Patriotic Society

The 'Moral Weeklies' were the first German-language publications to attempt to reach a wider public readership beyond the world of the scholars, and, motivated by secular ambitions, to set moral standards.[24] No longer were secular and ecclesiastical authorities to be the sole arbiters of daily life. Instead, education and experience were to enable the individual citizen, of his own accord and independent of any form of secular or ecclesiastical authority, 'more accurately to perceive' all issues, ranging from child-rearing to housekeeping and including God, the world and mankind. The moral weeklies propagated education until the age of maturity, including, for the first time, for women. Thus, the moral weeklies were the first middle-class journals of the Enlightenment. Previously, there had been little open discussion of morality, and this makes the rapid dissemination of the moral weeklies all the more surprising. However, ultimately, the readership remained restricted to the wealthy and those receptive to learning. In Hamburg, 'The Patriot' had soon attracted a potential readership of between 12,000 and 15,000. The actual circulation of 'The Patriot' lay between 4,000 and 6,000, a considerable number indeed at that time.

The strongholds of the weeklies were the cities of Leipzig, Zurich and Hamburg, in other words, commercial centres beyond court influence. In Leipzig, where there was a short-lived Contributors' Association, which had no direct connections with the 'German Society', Gottsched wrote almost all the contributions for his weekly himself. In contrast, the 'Millers' Discourses' of 1720 was published by a society which had been founded for that very purpose: the Society of Millers. This society had been established by the two most eminent Swiss writers and teachers at the Zurich gymnasium, Johann Jakob Bodmer (1698–1783) and Johann Jakob Breitinger (1701–76), together with some clerics, jurists and physicians. The members of the society held regular meetings and produced weeklies of joint authorship whose objective was the improvement of virtue and good taste. However, compared to Gottsched and the Hamburg circle, they were of negligible influence. They helped to strengthen middle-class self-consciousness, but they too often strayed towards religious and moral and theological subject matter.[25]

The two Hamburg societies, the 'German-Speaking Society' and the 'Patriotic Society', were closely interlinked, and both had grown out of friendship circles with strong connections among the municipal authorities.[26] However, the 'German-Speaking Society' survived for only two years, between 1715 and 1717, and had only six members, including the eminent writer and municipal councillor, Barthold Heinrich Brockes (1680–1747).[27] The society held regular meetings each Saturday at the home of one of the members in order to debate German-language issues and to exchange and discuss publications. Unfortunately, there are no records available which might offer an insight into the society's style of debate. However, it is revealing that the meetings were strictly divided into two halves, official and unofficial. This was probably an attempt to prevent the meetings from becoming purely social gatherings, a problem with which many societies, both contemporary and those of later date, were familiar. Prior to disbandment following the departure of some of its members, the society had held 41 meetings in 1715 and 43 in 1716.

The 'Patriotic Society', which should not be confused with the later 'Patriotic and Public-Spirited Society', was of greater significance than the 'German-Speaking Society'. It was founded in 1723 with a total of eleven members: the remnants of the 'German-Speaking Society', and some new adherents, scholars and jurists.[28]

> They set aside one evening a week for the purpose of refreshing their spirits in intelligent and convivial conversation after work, which for most of them consisted of important public office. By popular consent, the society's statutes prohibited ostentation and vanity, gloom and time-wasting: the focus of all their attention and deliberations was the common good. As if around a pivot, all debate revolved around the benefit, the honour and the approval of the common good. Hence, they could think of no better designation for their society than one which indicated concern for the Fatherland. To this end, each meeting was devoted to selected observations on, and the perfection of, natural justice, ethics, statesmanship and good housekeeping. They committed their efforts to paper, now in fun, now in earnest, depending upon circumstance. Lastly, in imitation of their resourceful colleagues abroad, they decided that in order to reach a wider audience, it would be a useful exercise to publish some of their deliberations. In a word, they produced 'The Patriot'. (A report by M. Richey, 1728/9.)[29]

The Patriotic Society developed out of a loose, free association of friends who met together regularly, gave themselves a set of statutes and debated cultural and social issues. Within twelve months, an editorial committee had been established for the purpose of producing a moral weekly entitled – in keeping with the society's aims – 'The Patriot'. Little is known about the way the editorial committee operated. However, the committee did have more and better qualified staff than that of the 'German-Speaking Society': they were all experienced operators with excellent contacts among the municipal senate, which helped them to keep the hostile Church and municipal parliament at bay. Publication of

'The Patriot' was discontinued in 1726, but during its lifetime, it had exercised considerable influence and had covered all aspects of society and social life.

The term 'patriot' was defined by one of the society's members:

> A patriot has the best interests of the Fatherland at heart. He accepts the Lord God, respects the clergy, cherishes truth and order and respects authority. He honestly endeavours to contribute towards the common good, not simply because he wishes to be a patriot himself, but also, as far as he is able, to convert others into patriots, in other words, to demonstrate to them the obligations they owe to the Lord and the Fatherland.[30]

Discontinuation of 'The Patriot' did not signal the end of the Patriotic Society. Indeed, the society continued to recruit new members, including Prince Karl I of Brunswick and Wolfenbüttel, whose election as patron ended the society's independence of the aristocracy. The society continued to hold weekly meetings, though the circle was continually declining in number due to the death and departure of many of its members. Until his death in 1747, Barthold Heinrich Brockes remained the society's key figure.

The Patriotic Society had been a political association from the outset, and this trait became markedly more apparent following the discontinuation of 'The Patriot'. The moral and fraternal society, whose meetings had been subject to strict rules and regulations, was transformed once more into a loose debating circle comprising a few select scholars of the political ruling class: where the concept of the common good had previously been only the subject of abstract debate, the goal was now the realization of the ideal. Subsequently, the members of the Patriotic Society engaged in varied forms of activity, but they all drew inspiration from the programme of 'The Patriot' between the years 1724–6, for which they had been jointly responsible. The Patriotic Society was an academic and learned debating society devoted to the common good. The close ties between the society and the Hamburg political elite facilitated the political realization of the society's intellectual ideas, a scenario which was probably unique to the city of Hamburg and one which later redounded to the benefit of the 'Public-Spirited Society'.

Gottsched and the German societies

One of the leading figures in the literary societal movement at the beginning of the eighteenth century was Johann Christoph Gottsched (1700–66), a writer of the early Enlightenment. Prior to his appointment to the chair of Logic and Metaphysics at the University of Leipzig in 1734, he had been a freelance journalist who had made his mark as the founder of various successful journals, or 'Moral Weeklies'. His 'Vernünfftige Tadlerinnen' and 'Biedermann', propagated middle-class virtues: 'My main objective was the eradication of irrationality and vice among my compatriots and the furtherance of reason and virtue.'[31] He not only pursued this objective through his writings, but also through the founding of literary societies in imitation of the 'Académie française'. However, he failed to obtain the necessary state support, and was thus unable to establish a permanent institution.[32]

Gottsched attempted to achieve his societal objectives at three levels:

1   In 1724, he had become a member of a long-established student society in Leipzig. In 1731, he began to transform this society into a completely non-provincial German Society for the cultivation of language, poetry and speech. It was planned as a forum for sweeping linguistic reforms. The first head of the society was Gottsched himself. He made strenuous efforts to achieve wide acclaim for the society, including the publication of 'Contributions to the Critical History of German Language, Poetry and Speech' in eight volumes between 1732 and 1734. However, in 1738, internal difficulties resulted in his estrangement from the society, and he resigned all his offices and terminated his membership altogether.

2   Following his transformation of one student society in Leipzig, Gottsched attempted to initiate and participate in the founding of a whole network of subsidiary societies, particularly in university towns and cities, using Leipzig as his base. Societies were established in Jena in 1730, Göttingen in 1738, Greifswald in 1740, Königsberg in 1741, Helmstedt in 1742, Bremen in 1762 and Altdorf and Erlangen in 1756.[33] The organization of all these societies conformed more or less to the Leipzig model; in other

words, they were living proof of Gottsched's ubiquitous influence. However, the German Societies still possessed a large measure of independence and pursued differing interests. Gottsched's additional links with the learned societies in Olmütz, Munich and Erfurt are further evidence of the grand design of his concept.

3 Finally, taking his concept a step further, he also made strenuous efforts to establish German Academies at the Imperial Court in Vienna and at the centre of power in Saxony, the city of Dresden, in order to accomplish his plans for the creation of a single cultural nation through linguistic reform with the full support of the state. However, neither the Emperor nor the electoral prince of Saxony were willing to cooperate. Thus, in 1754, Gottsched made a fresh attempt to establish a 'Society of *Belles-Lettres* and the Liberal Arts', whose members, according to Gottsched, were not to rest 'until their diligent efforts and zeal had convinced all foreigners that the Germans are one of the most intelligent and educated of nations and that German literature and the German language are as indispensable, didactic and aesthetic as their own'.[34]

The society did become a reality, and it attracted many collaborators. However, like all Gottsched's grand and ambitious projects, it failed to attract the patronage of the electoral prince.

All German societies were, according to their statutes, open to 'all aficionados of the German language', irrespective of estate and religious denomination. Nevertheless, it was considered essential that membership should not be open to all: Gottsched preferred 'gifted people', 'aristocrats and university graduates, professionals and other particularly talented people'. In other words, Gottsched envisaged elitist societies which would enjoy social prestige.

Most of the members of the German societies were either representatives of the urban middle class (priests, teachers and professors) or students. Some, a very few, were aristocrats. Thus, they had a university, even an academic, background, and were motivated by ambitions transcending secular and ecclesiastical divisions. The societies deliberately remained aloof from the common people.

The membership of the Göttingen German Society[35] (1738 to 1755). President: Professor Johann Matthias Gesner:

Honorary members		**Full members**	
(282 in total, all resident outside Göttingen)		(206 in total, all students)	
Priests, theologians	76	Law students	65
Professors	51	Theology students	56
Government officials (senior)	38	Medical students	7
Headmasters, teachers	28	Profession	
Physicians	19	unknown	78
Women	12		
Aristocrats (no details of profession available)	28		
Officers	3		
Merchants	2		
Profession unknown	25		

There was one objective which was shared by all the German societies: by means of close contact with each other in tightly knit groups, each member was to recognize the errors of his 'provincial language' and avoid it in both its spoken and its written forms 'in order that he might avoid sounding unintelligible, or even ridiculous'.[36] For this purpose, all local members were required to attend weekly meetings – those members who did not live locally were specifically requested to attend whenever they were in the vicinity. In Leipzig, for example, such meetings were held every Wednesday afternoon between 3:00 and 5:00 for the purpose of preparing and reading brief speeches, letters, short translations, grammatical observations, critical examinations of ideas and language and literary extracts and criticisms 'comprising both forms of eloquence'. The members of the Leipzig society were meant to abandon the traditional regional spoken and written models. Instead, they were to use their own common sense, maintain the purity of the German language and speak and write 'High German' 'in a form which is intelligible throughout Germany'.[37]

Critical examination of the contributions was equally as important as this 'stylistic freedom'. The meetings were a forum for open debate as well as a platform for readings and lectures. However, it should be noted that the statutes attempted to determine the conduct of such debates. Half-baked and uncoordinated responses were not permitted: each problem, ranging from 'the style of the contribution as a whole' to individual expressions, was subjected to the critical reasoning of the participants in strict order. Interruptions and deviations from the subject were prohibited. All those present could have their say in good time, but criticisms had to be modest, brief and devoid of any suggestiveness and satire. Hence, 'civilized' debate was one of the hallmarks of the society. Those contributions which survived the criticism of the members unscathed and those issues which had been settled during the course of the debate were recorded and archived at general expense. They were not intended for actual publication. However, any member who did intend to publish some of his writings was obliged to submit them to another member for assessment. A reference copy of all such publications had to be deposited with the society library, which was open to members only.

A characteristic feature of the early advocates of the Enlightenment was reciprocal criticism. It was both a replacement for secular and ecclesiastical censorship, to which the society refused to submit, and a guarantee of adherence to the policy agreed in open debate.

The German societies were not only platforms for readings and open debate in private meetings. They also held extraordinary meetings every three months for the purpose of determining publishing plans and the admittance of new members. All members were invited to attend. Selected members held public speeches on the occasion of the electoral prince's birthday. Prizes were awarded on the basis of a majority vote for the best literary efforts, and the names of the prize-winners were subsequently published in a reputable newspaper. In Leipzig, during the book fair, special public meetings were held which were open to any non-member accompanied by a member.[38] However, as in the case of the learned societies, such public displays, though important as exercises in public relations, were merely sideshows: reading sessions and open, didactic debates among groups of German-language enthusiasts imbued with the ideals of the early Enlightenment retained pride of place. Nevertheless, Gottsched was not remiss in bringing the activities of the Leipzig Society to the attention of the educated public, and thus subjecting them to rational public scrutiny.

Although the emancipatory and critical ambitions of Gottsched's German society revealed traces of utopianism, it was, nevertheless, the first society with clearly defined objectives. The relevance of Gottsched's concept for large numbers of educated men of letters, particularly in university cities, is reflected in the sheer number of German societies which were established in rapid succession. In comparison, nationally, the learned societies were much less in evidence, despite their more pronounced orientation towards the court. Of course, all the credit for the breakthrough which the Enlightenment achieved is not due to the German societies, and much of the literature they produced was second-rate and bombastic. However, for the members of the German societies, the meetings which they attended marked important new milestones and experiences which became crucial factors in their subsequent careers.

In the first place, professional men and students from all walks of life held regular debates in defiance of all feudal, secular and ecclesiastical divisions in order to improve their command of German, write texts and discuss new works of literature. These meetings can be regarded as early forms of philosophical seminars. In the second place, the individual regarded himself as an equal among equals among whom force of argument alone was decisive, not the views of traditional authoritarianism. Despite the formality, the quality of the debate was determined by the reasoning power of the individual and by the judgement of one and all. Everyone was open to criticism. The didactic process proceeded along democratic lines, and everyone was at liberty to express his opinion. The only forms of control were the strict societal rules and the critical scrutiny of the membership, exercised free from feudal and ecclesiastical interference. The safeguarding of freedom of opinion was an important issue for the societies, one they would have preferred to have had settled by virtue of electoral privilege. However, the German societies were not comprised of groups of men who questioned the legitimacy of the authoritarian and feudal structure of society at large, demanded the right to apply reasoned criticism to all spheres of life and publicly propagated freedom of expression, including the abolition of public censorship. On the contrary, Gottsched and his followers were firm supporters of absolutism: they, too, excluded the common people from the didactic process. The 'German literati' restricted their demands to the intellectual independence of the 'scholars'; they did not broach the issue of political subservience.

As a scholar rather than as a citizen or an inhabitant of a particular country, the scholar is as free as the most powerful monarch on earth. As a monarch recognizes only God and the sword as his master, so, too, the scholar recognizes only reason and the might of the pen. Thus, providing that he is able to defend his actions before that great Throne of Judgement, Reason, and providing that he is not forced to surrender by a mightier pen and made to bow to the logic of its conclusions, a scholar can think, conclude, teach and write anything he wants.

However, it should be recognized that this freedom is subject to the restriction that the scholar may not publicly teach or write anything which redounds to the disadvantage of his country of residence. However, this constraint is not imposed upon him in his capacity as a scholar but in his capacity as a citizen duty-bound to consider the reputation of his country. If he were not resident in that country, it would not be in a position to restrict his freedom. A common interest in learning brings these scholars into daily contact with each other and unites them into a Republic of Scholars which recognizes no lord and master. (The Composition and Constitution of the Republic of Scholars, in 'Delights of the Soul of Reason', I 1745).[39]

For Gottsched, too, the scholar as a scholar is answerable only to reason, in whose realm he recognizes no lord or master, neither Church nor prince. As a scholar, the scholar is a free man. However, Gottsched also lent equal emphasis to the fact that, as a citizen, the scholar may not say anything he pleases in public. As a subject, he remains wedded to the feudal, political and ecclesiastical world.

Provided that a clear distinction was made between the learned and the feudal worlds, Gottsched could not perceive any contradiction between the scholar's independence in the one and his position of subservience as an ordinary subject in the other. However, it was only a question of time and mentality before this became problematic. As long as the free Republic of Scholars debated only learned issues, personal conflicts were few and far between. However, the moment that the Enlightenment discarded the cloak of learning and began debating social issues, even feudalism itself, this distinction engendered serious problems, which had still not been resolved by the end of the eighteenth century.

The societies of the early Enlightenment, such as the learned academies and the literary and moral societies, were gatherings of intellectuals who regarded themselves as scholars: these intellectuals represented all walks of professional life, though most of them came from the higher reaches of feudal society. The societies were independent of traditional corporations, havens in which the members were able to devote themselves to their learned, scientific and literary interests in the exclusive pursuit of truth, free from interference, particularly on the part of the Church. The societies represented the first stage in the process of Enlightenment, a first phase of middle-class self-determination in which scholars first publicly aspired to 'middle-class' ambitions. The member of a society ceased to be accountable to traditional models and rules: he was accountable to reason alone. However, research was not conducted into every field of learning. The subjects of research and debate were the new experimental sciences and the German language, which promised to yield some practical benefits. This excluded topics connected with the state, the Church, politics and religion, though not in order to avoid possible conflict. The reason for this was to focus on common areas of interest and to safeguard debate which was free from interference on the part of the authorities. Thus, the society was a haven of self-determination, a Republic of Scholars in which the members were free to exchange views across feudal, authoritarian and secular divides.[40] In the best interests of mankind, the society set standards of objectivity. However, these applied only to the field of learning, not to the sphere of personal life. They had no emancipatory aspirations. The societies were keen to obtain state recognition, though only in order to obtain the protection of the state for independent research and reasoned debate.

Learned academies and learned and literary societies were the product of the intellect and the interests of the early Enlightenment. Although they were of crucial importance to eighteenth century learning, they were of minor importance to the process of middle-class emancipation. In addition, they had an insufficient number of members to unleash any large-scale movement.

ASSOCIATIONS OF 'CIVILIZED' MEN

The rapidly expanding societies of the second phase of the Enlightenment, around the middle of the eighteenth century, heralded the appearance of completely new organizational forms.
These organizations enjoyed support which, for the first time,
extended far beyond the intellectual class. However varied and
diverse the objectives of these organizations might have been, it
was now no longer possible to categorize them simply in learned
and academic terms; they also contained some elements of 'middle-
class' reformism. Two groups achieved prominence: the secret
society of Freemasons and the so-called patriotic and public-
spirited societies (see map 2). These societies represented the two
main strands of the Enlightenment: behind a cloak of secrecy,
Freemasonry aimed to create a 'private' moral world independent
of the state and the Church in which to further the development of
men who, in accordance with the laws of enlightened reason,
chose to deport themselves in a moral and reasonable manner; the
patriotic societies aimed to function 'openly' on behalf of the state
and society in the interests of the common good, that is, to
strengthen patriotic consciousness and achieve the goals of the
Enlightenment by means of practical proposals and reformist
endeavours.

THE ORDER OF FREEMASONS

The Order of Freemasons was one of the most widespread and
important forms of eighteenth-century associations.[1] It exerted an

unusually strong attraction upon broad sections of an aristocratic and middle-class elite, both in free cities and absolutist states. As one of the 'most powerful social institutions in the moral world', it accorded completely with the emancipatory aspirations of the educated middle class.[2] Furthermore, its esoteric cult of secrecy, the origins of which were transplanted far back into the mists of time, aroused great interest. In a strange way, it combined rational and 'irrational' and progressive and mystic elements which exerted both an attractive and a disorientating influence. From the very beginning, the secrecy of the Freemasons resulted in endless literary speculation. The immediate causes of this were Freemasonry's mysterious origins and the complex manner in which it spread during the course of the eighteenth century. However, the wealth of eighteenth-century writings on the order by Freemasons and non-Freemasons alike was also a contributory factor.

Although the Order of Freemasons was a secret society, much information still permeated the outside world. Both their literature and the identity of their members were well known. Freemasonry was not only debated by Freemasons. Generally speaking, no society was the subject of so much heated literary debate as Freemasonry, even among circles which had little or no connections with the order.[3] The morals and rituals of Freemasonry played an important role in literature:[4] mention need only be made of Karl Philip Moritz,[5] Christoph Martin Wieland,[6] Johann Wolfgang von Goethe[7] and particularly of Wolfgang Amadeus Mozart and his 'Magic Flute', in which masonic moral teachings are proclaimed on stage for public consumption. The following is a popular masonic ditty dating from 1791:

> Brothers, your hands in unity!
> This hour of grand festivity
> shall lead us on to heights sublime!
> Mundane flee, depart this scene!
> Our unity, our harmony
> Shall e'er endure, to the end of time.

> We praise and thank our earthly master
> of hearts and minds,
> Eterne creator!
> The noble goal of our sacred quest
> light, virtue and justice blessed
> through the might of the hallowed sabre.

Those on this star among the best,
Humankind in East and West,
In North and South, your spirits high,
From truth and virtue ne'er depart,
Love God and Man with all thy heart,
This shall be our battle-cry![8]

The high expectations of well-known writers reveal the extent
to which late eighteenth-century intellectuals were affected by
Freemasonry. No lesser figures than Gotthold Ephraim Lessing[9]
and Johann Gottlieb Fichte[10] perceived the roots of middle-class
society in the secret Order of Freemasons, regardless of the fact
that contemporary Freemasonry in no way conformed to this
ideal. In 'Ernst and Falk', Lessing writes: 'Essentially, Freemasonry and middle-class society are of the same age. Both originated side by side, always presuming, that is, that middle-class
society is not just an offspring of Freemasonry.'[11]

Like the academic movement, Freemasonry was an international movement, and it has retained its international character to
the present day. At the beginning of the eighteenth century, the
Order of Freemasons, as a loose association of different secret
societies, very quickly branched out from its starting-point in
England and spread throughout Europe. It began to gain a foothold in Germany as early as the 1830s. On one side, it was
fostered by national centres of trade, and this led to the founding
of lodges in almost all large commercial and trade fair centres. At
the initiative of circles in England, the first lodge ('Absalom') was,
not surprisingly, founded in Hamburg.[12] In 1758, Crown Prince
Friedrich became a mason. This played a major role in the spread
of Freemasonry and had a formative influence on the specific
character which this process assumed in Germany. The Crown
Prince bestowed court respectability upon Freemasonry, encourag-
ing the aristocracy, the middle class and the military to follow his
lead. Lastly, French aristocrats and officers also introduced Freemasonry into the German courts, resulting in close links between
German Freemasons and French culture. This was particularly
the case in Western Germany.[13]

Freemasonry spread throughout the whole of Western Germany, and then in Saxony-Thuringia, the Rhineland and all the
large residential and university towns and cities. By the end of the
century, a lodge was established in almost every provincial city in

Germany as far down as the extreme south. Although the Catholic Church had forbidden its followers to join the ranks of the Freemasons, the lodges contained as many Catholics as Protestants. Those centres sympathetic towards the Enlightenment quickly became masonic strongholds. Frequently, Freemasonry proliferated in existing societal centres. There were probably some 250 to 300 lodges in Germany. It is not possible to ascertain their exact number because many lodges were short-lived, changed name or split into two or more different lodges. Furthermore, there were some so-called blind lodges, that is, lodges not officially recognized by either masonic system. It is equally difficult to calculate the total number of Freemasons. There was a multi-membership system, lodges with only 10–20 members and lodges with several hundred members. Including those of only short duration, the total number of German Freemasons is estimated at between 15,000 and 20,000.[14] This in itself can lead to an underestimation of Freemasonry's importance in the rise of an elitist culture:

> It was the first widespread, independent organization of the nascent German middle classes, the first form of voluntary association of private individuals no longer conforming to the traditional models of corporative association and – in contrast to, for example, the conventicular system of the Pietists – no longer pursuing exclusively religious objectives.[15]

Freemasonry appealed to the entire aristocratic and middle-class upper strata.[16] As was the case with other societies, it held less appeal further down the social ladder. The odd innkeeper among their ranks was usually the owner of the inn where the Freemasons held their meetings. The lodges were open to all members of the upper social strata without exception. Indeed, as far as can be ascertained from the available material, there were almost as many aristocratic members, especially those from the higher aristocracy, as middle-class members. It must be said, however, that even where there was a much larger proportion of middle-class members, the leadership still remained in aristocratic hands. There were also exclusive middle-class and aristocratic lodges, but they were usually merged. This is a generally accepted fact. However, a more detailed examination of the social structure of the individual lodges reveals a picture that differs considerably from region to region. This is because there were considerable differences between, for example, the trading centre of Hamburg[17] and the residential city of Weimar, or the administrative city of Wetzlar and the Imperial capital of Vienna.[18] To a large extent, this reflects the different social structure of the individual cities. Most lodges included a 'class of notables' who had close links with a particular court or with some administrative body. This includes both middle-class and aristocratic state officials. In contrast, there were as few scholastic members (except in the university cities) as clergymen and theologians. However, there was an obvious increase in the numbers of merchants, especially in cities such as Aachen and Leipzig (see below).

Munich 1781[19]

Lodge: St Theodor vom guten Rat

Members: 91 (including 39 aristocrats)

Court and administrative officials	38
Officers	16
Clergy/theologians	15
Jurists	9
Painters	2
Monastic officials	2
Musicians	2
Professors	1
Merchants	1
Physicians	1
Profession unknown	4

Bayreuth 1781[20]

Lodge: Alexander zu den drei Sternen

Members: 69 (including 38 aristocrats)

Court and administrative officials	33
Officers	22
Jurists	5
Landlords	2
Merchants	2
Chemists	2
Physicians	1
Profession unknown	2

Of these, number from Bayreuth 15

Leipzig 1787[21]

Lodge: Minerva zu den drei Palmen

Members: 137 (including 26 aristocrats)

Court and administrative officials	27
Merchants	25
Hereditary gentlemen	12
Professors	10
Jurists	9

Wetzlar 1784[22]

Lodge: Joseph zu den drei Helmen

Members: 90 (including 43 aristocrats)

Court and administrative officials	30
Members of Imperial supreme court	17
Jurists	10
Officers	9

Physicians	7	Clergy/theologians	2
Architects	3	Lay assessors	2
Wine merchants	3	Physicians	2
Clergy/theologians	2	Government presidents	2
Painters	2	Councillors (Nuremberg)	2
Watchmakers	1	Professors	1
Bankers	1	Justice ministers	1
Booksellers	1	Profession unknown	12
Profession unknown	34		
		Of these, number from	
Of these, number from		Wetzlar	30
Leipzig	59		

Weimar 1781[23]

Lodge: Amalia
Members: 55 (including 30
   aristocrats)

Aachen 1778/94[24]

Lodge: Zur Beständigkeit
Members: 176 (including 22
   aristocrats)

State officials	23	Merchants	121
Physicians	6	Physicians	9
Officers	4	Officers	9
Professors	2	Clergy/theologians	6
Merchants	2	State officials	5
Students	2	Jurists	3
Musicians	2	Artists	3
Bankers	1	Musicians	2
Court printers	1	Industrialists	2
Profession unknown	12	Captains	1
		Profession unknown	15
Of these, number from			
Weimar 30		Of these, number from	
		Aachen	76

Relatively large numbers of intellectuals, temporarily fascinated by Freemasonry, became lodge members, at least for a short time: Goethe and Wieland, Lessing and Moritz, Georg Forster and Friedrich Heinrich Jacobi. However, the uniquely social element is the fact that during the last third of the century, large numbers of the new administrative elite, that is, highly placed state officials, frequented masonic lodges and discovered this new form of enlightened social intercourse. There were virtually no artisan or female members. Artisans were only present in the brotherhoods of lowly social origin, and women only made an appearance on the occasion of grand masonic festivities which were not part of lodge activity proper. There were no barriers for the upper social classes. It redounded very much to the prestige of Freemasonry that it included among its ranks King Friedrich II of Prussia and Emperor Franz Josef I, the spouse of Maria Theresa. This was not, however, always of benefit to the order's original progressive aspirations. Denominational barriers were almost unknown, and the lodges were frequented by Catholics, Reformists and Lutherans alike. The spread of Freemasonry to the provincial cities apparently met increasing aristocratic and middle-class demands for new forms of social intercourse, demands which neither conventional modes of communication nor court life were able to satisfy.

The lodges were frequently havens for officers and bucolic aristocratic and middle-class state officials seeking to alleviate their social and cultural isolation. It was often in masonic lodges that they made each other's acquaintance. Thus, many of the contacts between members of the new administrative elite were forged by Freemasonry. Freemasonry spread and increased in importance at a remarkable rate during the latter half of the century, despite the innumerable internal amd external difficulties which beset the Order. On the one hand, the Catholic Church attempted to forbid Catholics from joining the secret Order of Freemasons (1738/51).[25] However, the prohibition bulls were as ineffectual as the attempts of the secular ruling princes to ban Freemasonry, particularly during the later persecution of the Illuminati.[26] Freemasonry survived all assaults from the outside, though in the process it changed character considerably. More serious, however, were the internal difficulties concerning the spread of Freemasonry. These were caused by competition between several different systems of Freemasonry, all of which claimed from the outset to be the true form of Freemasonry. There was soon such a confusion of systems and dependencies, best symbolized by the multitude of different rituals, that even the Freemasons were confused. This is definitely one of the reasons for the demise of the literary prominence of Freemasonry after only a short period of time. There were disputes, separations and new associations. There were repeated, and mostly fruitless, attempts to re-establish unity at conventions of all strands of Freemasonry. The internal divisions were exacerbated by the secret societies which were established on the fringe of Freemasonry. There had always been one rational and progressive wing and one that was more irrational and mystical, but the growth of the League of

Illuminati and the Order of the Golden and Rose Crosses at the end of the eighteenth century, both of which permeated the existing systems of masonic lodges,[27] caused such a chasm between the two wings that there was a danger that the rational core would be smothered and that Freemasonry would lose its separate identity altogether. There was no longer any link between a lodge infiltrated by Illuminati and one which professed a belief in Rosicrucianism. The former was a progressive lodge making emancipatory demands and the latter resembled an Order of Knights pursuing objectives bordering on the anti-progressive. This was one of the main reasons for the existence of several lodges in the same city or at the same court at one and the same time.

Classical Freemasonry, the original so-called Johannes Freemasonry of Hamburg, is characterized by a simple trigradal system, the apprentice, the fellow of the craft and the master mason, and a rational and progressive programme. Alongside this system, there soon appeared so-called Scottish Freemasonry, imported by way of France, a system of *hautes grades* which proclaimed its origins to be the Order of the Knights Templar. This system had an additional four grades.[28] More widespread than Scottish Freemasonry was the Strict Observance developed by Freiherr K. G. von Hund. The Knights of the *hautes grades* saw themselves as the successors of the Knights Templar. They bestowed Latin names, mottoes and coats of arms upon their orders, and believed in an unknown Grand Master. While this involves some element of Catholic religious mysticism, the system of the theologian J. A. Starck, whose teachings were not without influence, bears even more similarity to forms of Catholic ritualism: he established a cleric at the head of each grade.[29] The masonic lodges were apparently transforming themselves into quasi-secularized orders of knights in which hierarchical models were displacing the basic 'egalitarian' structure. Finally, the military physician von Zinnendorf began propagating the Swedish system based on gnostic and Christosophic teachings, recruiting mainly aristocratic lodges. There was now such a degree of confusion that masonic conventions became necessary as a means of finding fresh areas of unity. The collapse of Strict Observance, that is, of the breakaway *hautes grades* system, and the revival of the 'rational' wing under the Weimar court counsellor, Johannes Bode, and the Wetzlar supreme court official, Franz von Ditfurth, at the famous Wilhelmsbad Convention in 1782, marked the end of the strife between the different doctrines.[30] This resulted in the founding of the 'Eclectic League' in 1783, which returned to the trigradal system of Johannes Freemasonry and put an end to knightly tomfoolery. 'We do not have the slightest intention of forging any new systems or creating any sects. Our desire, our purpose, our endeavours have the objective of promoting tolerance, Enlightenment, freedom of thought, philanthropy and well-being.'[31]

Originally, the individual lodges were autonomous. However, at the regional level, they soon entered into association with each other, though, as mentioned above, the various groups were integrated into different systems as a result of the different interpretations of Freemasonry and its ritualistic customs. There was soon communication between these groupings at the official level: intensive contacts were developed and discussions were held, culminating in the staging of conventions. This was a unique development in the history of societies, and it resulted in the constant expansion of a nationwide communication network outside the traditional forms of communication. One important effect of this was that this network soon began to foster official inter-masonic communication and to create a public arena in which masons were able to fraternize and establish their own progressive environment and permanent social community. Insofar as the individual member wished to broaden his horizons, the opportunity of making 'the acquaintance of many upstanding people' was of great importance.[32] This opportunity offered the mason the chance to escape the confines of his own narrow milieu, a milieu defined by his religion, class and linguistic and national background, and to regard himself as a member of an international fraternity. Reciprocal visits, frequent travel and recommendations, etc. transformed the lodges into centres of international public communication and individual contacts. The lodges welcomed German and non-German guests alike and fêted them in style. This involved a considerable broadening of horizons, particularly for middle-class masons.

The lodge, the 'moral' nucleus of Freemasonry, was the social focal point. The purpose of the meetings was not to impart wisdom or mutual instruction in practical and theoretical problems but rather to enjoy a cultist experience of fraternal association: initially, this entailed a strict renunciation of the mundane external world of politics and the estates. 'It is not permitted to discuss matters of state, or religious, family or any other matters of minor interest or controversial content in the lodges.'[33] The reason for the universal ban on all political and religious discussion was the desire to create an enclosed milieu absent of 'profanity'. The social experience of cultism spawned its own *esprit de corps* among all those who felt socially or culturally impeded on the outside. The masons regarded themselves as equal brothers, not for the sake of any 'external' objectives, but in order that they might determine the course of their lives in the spirit of human fraternity. Last but not least, the masons professed their allegiance to the world of virtue introduced to them in the lodge by word of mouth, by images and by rituals in particular, and which was intended as their maxim of life.

The mason was to be trained in moderation, consistency, courtesy, fearlessness and confidentiality. In short, he was to graduate as a Bachelor of Enlightenment who subordinated all his passions to the law of reason and acted in the best interests of state and society.

> Freemasonry, so celebrated in these times, is a fellowship of reasonable men who, united by the bonds of fraternity, guided by the tenets of morality, strive towards the creation of a society of reason, to which each and every individual is to bring all the qualities at his disposal as his contribution to this useful and pleasant society . . .
>
> Should I wish to use the language of the masons, then I should have to say that secrecy, the law of morality and the benevolent society are the three pillars and flying buttresses which serve as the foundations of the splendid masonic edifice. In accordance with each of these three supporting pillars, special responsibilities are laid down to which we are bound by sacred bonds.
>
> In the case of secrecy, we are not only bound to protect the inviolability of everything we regard as secret, and for which I have already in part provided an explanation; we are also required to subject ourselves to a general self-analysis in order that we might be discreet in everything we say or do. You are well enough aware of the enormous benefit of the virtue of discretion, so I will not dwell any further on it here.
>
> The law of morality, the second supporting pillar, including the whole gamut of righteous virtues, not only requires consistency and decency of morals, but also an absence of any act which might offend against morality. This tenet might be regarded as the touchstone of a true mason. However great our consideration for persons who, by virtue of birth and high rank, are worthy of outside veneration, among ourselves, providing that he is of an agreeable

disposition, we only actually respect the man for himself. Since the spirit-level of nature is the only yardstick of our judgements, we regard all men as our brothers. The doctrines of the law of nature, the prime uniter of human society, do not permit us to enquire as to the religious beliefs of those we choose to be our brothers. It is sufficient for us that they bear the stamp of honesty. Our meetings expressly forbid the discussion of any religious topics in order to spare our members any annoyance and to avoid misunderstandings, which, as is well-known, tend to arise out of such discussions. Immoderate speech is equally as immoral; from this, it follows that we refrain from indulging in any kind of frivolous or indecent conversations which might offend chaste ears and are superfluous to pure hearts.

The benevolent society, the third supporting pillar, teaches us our obligations towards the brotherhood: everyone is obliged to make his utmost contribution to the usefulness and agreeableness of the brotherhood. As a result, we are obliged to refrain from everything which might lead to confusion and disturb the harmonious unity prevailing amidst our ranks. For this reason, it is expressly forbidden to discuss any political topics, which as a rule only spawn disunity and strife. (A speech by F. W. Steinheil in Frankfurt, 1742.)[34]

The attraction of the masonic lodges for the aristocracy and the middle class lay in the fact that they were the most enclosed and most isolated of all societies. In addition, they were the circles which most closely interwove conviviality and morality without demanding a complete break with everyday life. The rapid ascent of Freemasonry was due primarily to this openness. In this respect, the casual observer must be careful not to take the innumerable regulations, laws, rules, instruction booklets and moral addresses too much at face value or too seriously. There was a world of difference between the ideal and the reality.

Most lodge work concerned initiation and promotion ceremonies, though there were also readings from rulebooks and the catechism. At irregular intervals, speeches would be held on the spirit of Freemasonry, virtue and fraternity. The most important aspect of the lodge, however, was its carefully cultivated conviviality. Initially, the lodges held meetings in rented halls, in inns or in private quarters. Independent buildings, complete with spacious and representative function rooms and extensive grounds, and even libraries and private collections, appeared towards the end of the century.

Information on the spirit, the constitution and the inner soul of the lodge is provided by excellently preserved foundation statutes, statutes of lodges inscribed on plaques and basic laws.[35] To a large extent, three distinctive features characterized the lodge: the objective of the lodge was to establish equality and fraternity among the membership. However, the lodge did not regard a democratic structure as the guarantor of equality, and lodge activity was conducted within a framework which was unique to Freemasonry. This was best illustrated by the fact that the Grand Master was installed rather than elected: in line with the hierarchical system, he was empowered to determine and control activities within the lodge more or less as he saw fit. However, although the autocratic hierarchical system was, to some extent at least, very marked, it differed from the secular system of estates in that it was based on a moral entitlement to reward.

Very strict discipline was enforced during lodge conventions. 'Honourable' behaviour was an essential pre-condition of the conviction that the enforcement of a fair system of discipline '. . . can only be maintained on the basis of equality and the adoption of fair-minded policies'.[36] A member was expected to frequent the lodge on a regular basis wearing a pinafore and gloves. During the meeting, a member was forbidden to leave his seat, speak without permission, or, most of all, interrupt the Grand Master. Only the Grand Master could hear complaints as any public accusation was an offence against fraternity and harmony. All members were entitled to make a speech, but the speech had to be submitted for approval four days in advance. The members were subject to a set of rules during lodge repasts as well as during rituals. All guests at a lodge repast had to be suitably dressed, and it was forbidden to leave the table without permission. Any form of drunkenness, swearing and dishonourable behaviour, including religious baiting and utterances offensive to the state or morality, were especially taboo.

Any violation of the rules incurred a fine which was either payable to the lodge or could be donated as alms to the poor. A mason had to be financially well off: not only were there fines, but also contributions towards every repast and every banquet, and special donations to the poor at the end of every meeting. A member incurred greatest expense in attaining *grades* one to three. There were three reasons for this system of payments: increasing discipline, meeting lodge expenses and ostentation. It was good form to make donations to the poor, to show benevolence in accordance with the spirit of humanity. Avoiding these expenses was almost impossible, with the result that, generally speaking, only the wealthy middle class and the aristocracy were admitted as masons or, indeed, were in a position to accept any masonic social invitations.

The lodge did not concern itself with the realization of any abstract programme of Enlightenment, whether through didactic means or the discursory acquisition of knowledge. Neither was there any conscious attempt from within the lodge to reform society and impose upon it the maxims of morality. However, it is not the case that, in their own self-satisfied way, the Freemasons were interested only in their own affairs to the exclusion of the outside world. Too many lodge members were an integral part of the administrative apparatus of the absolutist state for this to have been the case. Indeed, around the turn of the century, most of the administrative elite of the absolutist German states were active both as masons and as champions of progressive ideas in the public arena. However, the principal distinction between the inner moral and the outer political worlds was never seriously questioned. Indeed, the coveted exclusivity of Freemasonry rested upon this very distinction. Nonetheless, the novel experience of Freemasonry was of central importance for society at large.

The primary achievement of the lodges was their *de facto* removal of the antagonisms between the middle class and the aristocracy. This still did not mean that there was political equality but, as revealed by the subsequent distribution of offices between the aristocracy and the middle class, there were some instances of exemplary cooperation. In the second place, the lodges reduced confessional and ideological antagonisms; Catholics and Protestants, at least in the upper echelons of society, learned to accept each other at face value and respect their common Christian origins. Lastly, the issue at stake was the abolition of traditional forms of behaviour based on the estates. On the one hand, such behaviour resulted in total immoderation and, to use a phrase of the masons themselves, fanaticism, and, on the other, it spawned snobbery and provincialism. It was to be replaced by a code of behaviour based on the tenets of reason and an order based on the principles of morality and the ideal of fraternal and responsible behaviour. This included a vigorous campaign against the use of 'unbecoming and immoral language' and the outlawing of mindless gossip, drinking and swearing. 'The true mason', according to one mason,

> is an enviable person. Virtue, moderation and wisdom are his guiding lights. Respectful towards his superiors, sociable and polite towards his peers, sympathetic and humane in his attitude towards those less fortunate than himself, he accords everyone the same degree of respect to which he himself is entitled. His first concern is the fulfilment of his responsibilities. Always seeking perfection, nothing disturbs his peace of mind. His ambitions are moderate, his behaviour modest, he is approachable, restrained in speech and true to his word; a loving brother and a loyal friend.[37]

Under the cloak of secrecy and in disregard of individual problems and cares, the lodges developed a society which was subject to its own laws of reason and morality. Thus, in spite of its 'irrational' lapses, Freemasonry was an important step along the road towards a civilized society. Politics remained unaffected for the time being: the principles of liberty and fraternity only applied to the citizen as a human being.

THE PATRIOTIC AND PUBLIC-SPIRITED SOCIETIES

The enlightenend journalist, Karl von Moser, wrote in 1786:[38]

> The histories of the existence, the deeds and the final moments of the German, economic, patriotic, agricultural, financial, scientific and all the other societies, and of the regional economic deputation, the regional commission, etc. would be glorious monuments to philanthropy and patriotism. However, they would also be humiliating and pathetic evidence of the eternal conflict between common sense and volition, between honesty and iniquity, envy, stupidity, egotism and selfishness, the cold ineptitude of most of the Regent's good intentions.

Initially, there was an extraordinary boom in the planning and founding of so-called patriotic and public-spirited societies, but such activity very soon subsided.

The enlightened self-image and concrete objectives of the patriotic societies were the antithesis of Freemasonry.[39] One crucial factor was their desire to reform external society. The patriots

wished to change society and serve the interests of the Enlightenment in a practical fashion. Associative and autodidactic factors
were only a means to an end. Another crucial factor was agreement on the nature of society's problems and a willingness on the
part of one group to solve these problems by their own means.
Patriotic societies evolved out of a widespread ambition to end the
monopoly of the Church and the state over society. They were
thus an expression of unwillingness to continue accepting the
status quo in a state of complete passivity and unwillingness to
continue tolerating a situation in which it was only possible to
work towards reform from within, as an official of the Church or
the state. Thus, the patriotic societies were ultimately the expression of the will of their members to assume responsibility for
the cause of the Enlightenment as mature citizens in their own
right. This did not mean that the patriots regarded themselves as
opponents of the absolutist state and the patrician town and city.
On the contrary, they regarded themselves as assisting and supporting state welfare provisions, particularly in those areas beyond
the reach of, or neglected by, the state.

The term 'patriotic society' embraces all those societies whose
goal, for reasons of patriotism or morality, was to engage in
practical activities of public benefit, that is, not the production of
wisdom but the furtherance and exploitation of practical knowledge and new scientific and practical discoveries; in other words,
putting such knowledge into practice in everyday life. Like Freemasonry, this form of society, another example of early middle-
class self-organization, originated in England, from where, during
the 1760s, via its bases in Northern Germany and Switzerland,
it quickly spread throughout urban and rural German-speaking
Europe. It became established under many different circumstances.[40] Some associations developed a multitude of practical
activities independent of any governmental support, while in the
principalities, others functioned almost as an instrument of benevolent absolutism; some preferred to forgo all forms of inter-
regional contact, others merged for the sake of increased effectiveness. Some attempted to accomplish comprehensive programmes,
others concentrated only on certain reforms. They never assumed
the air of professional organizations. The central issue was the
common good, societal activities in their entirety, but there was,
nevertheless, a great variety of regionally dependent priorities.

The patriotic societies were founded in waves, the most important of which occurred in the 1760s and the 1790s. Whereas the

first wave (including the societies founded at Weissensee in 1762, Celle and Leipzig in 1764, Zurich in 1764/5 and Karlsruhe, Kassel, Hamburg and Burghausen in 1765) was a consequence of the Seven Years' War and the urgent need for the reorganization of the agricultural structure, the second wave of societies (including those societies founded at Kiel in 1787, Nuremburg and Hamm in 1792, Lübeck in 1793 and Wetzlar in 1798) was a consequence of the replacement of ossified economic and social structures by new economic forces.[41]

In the main, the patriotic societies were not associations of professional scholars but of men from the public sphere; middle-class and aristocratic government officials, merchants and clergymen, most of whom belonged to the regional and urban salaried class. There was a strong aristocratic presence, but, as in the learned societies, they often played no official part in societal activities. As honorary members of the society, their main role was the bestowal of protection and prestige. Like the masons, the patriotic societies barred their doors to those lower down the social ladder; only towards the end of the eighteenth century did the numbers of artisan members begin to increase. The membership structure of the economic societies was as follows:[42]

Leipzig 1764–89

Total membership	281
State officials	41
Academics (professors, physicians, clergymen)	18
Merchants	13
Artisans (tradesmen)	11
Landowners	11
Factory owners	3
Aristocrats	184

Altötting-Burghausen 1765–78

Total membership	205 (including 36 aristocrats)
Court and government officials	76 (all in Bavaria)
Clergymen (theologians)	37 (24 in Bavaria)
Professors	14 (6 in Bavaria)
Physicians and pharmacists	14 (10 in Bavaria)
Officers	14 (9 in Bavaria)
Newspaper publishers	8 (1 in Bavaria)
Lawyers	6

On the whole, this is an indication that those directly concerned, namely peasants and artisans, were simply the objects of planning and education. This is one reason why, despite the initial desire for reform, the rapid increase in membership and the successful campaign of the founding societal fathers for official recognition, this forum for the exchange of views achieved only moderate success and sometimes degenerated to the level of a learned circle. The only patriotic societies to survive were those which received active official support. However, this did not mean that the patriotic societies were puppet institutions: the main source of their lifeblood was their commitment to the Enlightenment.

In structure, the patriotic societies were similar to the learned academies. There were full members and members from outside the society's catchment area. In addition, there were honorary members. They met once or twice a year as an act of solidarity and as a means of initiating joint undertakings (such as publications, open competitions and petitions). The academies of science always remained small in number, but the number of patriotic societies began increasing at the beginning of the 1760s. In the German-speaking territories, there were between fifty and sixty of them. While this did not rival the masonic lodges in terms of numbers, nevertheless, the patriotic societies, in influencing public opinion, represented the societal movement's first high-water mark. The societies varied in size and could comprise anywhere between twenty and several hundred members. There was dual membership, i.e. some members belonged to more than one society, and many members were only active for a short period of time. The total number of members of all the patriotic societies was somewhere between 4,000 and 5,000.[43]

Irrespective of the many different areas of emphasis of the patriotic societies, the 'purpose of [their] meeting' was, generally speaking, 'to discuss issues of public-spiritedness and, through closer relationships between reasonable men from different social backgrounds, age groups and professions, to forge and maintain closer bonds of friendship, patriotism and mutual exchanges of knowledge and views'.[44] When measured against its declared intentions and objectives, the individual patriotic society was ineffective. However, there are three reasons why the patriotic societies were still an important phenomenon: firstly, they were the first institution to endeavour to exploit the practical implications of theoretical knowledge. This practical approach to knowledge was to be of crucial importance in the successful introduction of technical innovations at the beginning of the capitalist era. Secondly, they activated middle-class virtues, civic commitment, the commitment of a local community, of a region, on behalf of the populace at large, to a greater extent than other, more established institutions. The objective was that the citizenry, at least the educated among their number, should actively participate in public life rather than simply remain chattels of the state. This sense of public duty helped to overcome feudal and absolutist structures. Lastly, they provided moral support to the awareness and consciousness of the need for social reforms, to the awareness and consciousness of society's ability to change for the better. This laid the foundations for a practical understanding of progress and the principle that active participation could provide the solution to society's problems. The dealings of the regional elite, who at the end of the eighteenth and the beginning of the nineteenth centuries were established in public office, were heavily influenced by their experience of the patriotic societies.

The patriotic societies also addressed special interests, of which one such example was agricultural problems. This emphasis was particularly evident in societies located in rural areas and in societies with a fairly large catchment area. Another area of concern was the improvement of urban trade and crafts. Areas of particular concern were health and poverty. High on the agenda of the patriotic societies was the promotion of all types of schools, particularly schools of industry, in order to create the pre-conditions for economic modernization. Finally, the societies were at pains to address and to educate the whole population in the spirit of Enlightenment. The Patriotic Society of Schleswig-Holstein proffered the following reason for publishing its writings: 'This might help to awaken an active interest in all that nature, the institutions of the state, morals and trade have to offer in our country, thus contributing to the creation of a community spirit, the citizen's soul, the ultimate goal of this society'.[45] This can be applied to all the patriotic societies. From the multitude of different societies in existence, particular attention is devoted below to three societies, each typical of one specific kind.

The Hamburg Patriotic Society

The best-known and most successful of the patriotic societies was

founded in 1765 in Hamburg.[46] Other societies modelled themselves on the 'Hamburg Society for the Promotion of the Arts and
Useful Trades', as it was officially called, but none of them attained similar prominence. There were no official ties with the
older Hamburg society founded for the purpose of publishing the
moral weeklies. The new society grew out of a private circle of
friends centred around the grammar school teacher, Hermann
Samuel Reimarus. It arose out of the post-war crisis in Hamburg
of 1763, which resulted in the stagnation, or at least the loss of the
competitive edge, of trade and commerce in Hamburg. In order to
tackle these problems, the jurist, K. J. Pauli, one of the members
of this circle, propagated the founding of a permanent forum for
communication and discussion open to everyone concerned about
the problems in Hamburg.

The outcome was a society with an executive committee of six
members, elected every two years, meeting once a fortnight. The
ordinary membership held its meetings every three months. This
patriotic society was organized along extremely pragmatic and
rational lines. The society's membership structure reveals the
central importance of the city's problems from the outset: in 1765,
the city's merchant class had 82 representatives among a total
membership of 96, and was thus the dominant force. There were
only twelve academic members. The admission of new members
confirmed and consolidated this trend. The society commenced
work in earnest once the Hamburg Senate had bestowed recognition. Its sphere of operation embraced a wide area of activities,
affecting potentially all the city's problems. Its contacts among
the city's political leadership (which between the years 1765 and
1792 consisted of twenty-two municipal senators) were such that
membership of the society became a factor in the election of new
senators and syndics. However, since the high membership fee
was a particular barrier to the broadening of the membership base
– although the high number of senate contacts was a consistent
contributory factor in the success of reform plans, the low level of
influx from below was a cause of concern – the constitution of the
society was amended in 1789. This amendment paved the way for
a large influx of new members. In 1790 154 new members were
admitted, including not only three of the four ruling mayors but,
for the first time, some artisans. Between the years 1790 and 1803,
total membership of the society was 514.[47]

The new constitution introduced permanent offices responsible for society affairs, and also three different types of meeting which typified the middle-class spirit of shared responsibility. Firstly, there was a weekly friendship meeting. The purpose of this was to discuss topics of a public-spirited nature as a means of cementing closer membership ties. In the second place, there was a monthly deliberative meeting for the conduct of societal business. Lastly, there were biannual general meetings at which public statements of account were produced. The new constitution had been introduced with the intention of 'arousing, increasing and promoting patriotism, industry and new forms of activity in order to generate an ever-increasing level of confidence and participation in the public-spirited purpose of this society on the part of all our well-meaning fellow citizens'.[48]

As part of this continual process of the exchange of ideas and experiences among the membership, all important aspects of urban life were now systematically identified and accorded the status of central themes of deliberation. Open competitions were organized as a means of prompting suggestions for improvements in particular areas. The society collected mountains of information, established a library and maintained close levels of contact with other societies. As a result of these measures, there was hardly any area of commerce or trade, including domestic and foreign policy, which remained unaffected by the society's proposals. Of particular note are the exhibitions (from 1790 onwards), the founding of schools (the school of drawing in 1767 and the school of navigation in 1785), and also the opening of the first fluvial public bathing facilities on the River Elbe and the marine baths in Cuxhaven, all of which were fruits of the society's labour. In 1769, the society also suggested equipping a fire station, and from 1767 onwards, it involved itself in urban street cleaning issues. It was also concerned with road surfacing and, above all, with the founding of the first public savings bank. The reorganization of provision for the destitute in 1778 was a significant and exemplary achievement. The Hamburg society manifested Enlightenment as a practical reform movement; philosophical and literary debate was a peripheral factor. Hence, the society endeavoured to encourage the liberation of the middle class from traditional forms of behaviour without crossing swords with established authority. Indeed, the society always regarded itself as a champion of the state's interests. As long as the society retained the status of a fee-paying club, its open-door policy in respect of the lower social classes did not affect the harmonious level of cooperation between the society and the city fathers.

> An independent public association comprising progressive citizens, including some government officials in the capacity of private citizens, who, as public-spirited men, pool their manifold resources of knowledge and experiences not, as is the case in France, out of any factional revolutionary interests, but for the benefit of the Fatherland as good German citizens, is of infinitely more importance and benefit to the state than anyone usually cares to admit. In such an organization, private citizens can debate, examine and attempt so much which is beyond the means of the state, can hear many a reproof and explanation which would otherwise never be brought to their attention. It is under these, more than under any other, circumstances that the baleful departmental mentality and narrow-mindedness is transformed into a spirit of citizenship and true public-spiritedness. I should be very much mistaken if the spirit of this society and these aspirations of public-spiritedness were not so apparent in the public endeavours of so many of its members, particularly when these endeavours are compared with the spirit of days past. (A 'Postscript' by J. A. Guenter, July 1792.)[49]

The society was, indeed, an independent association of 'private individuals' whose purpose, though they were quite at liberty to debate anything and everything, was to gather knowledge and experience for the improvement of the spirit of citizenship and the enhancement of public-spiritedness. The society made no demands for direct political influence as understood by the 'constitutional' movement. Nevertheless, in gaining sufficient influence to become a force in the shaping of urban life, the Hamburg society was almost unique among independent German urban associations. Only in Switzerland was there anything at all comparable.

The Helvetic Society

The Helvetic Society, which had its origins in a group of young patricians in Berne in 1765, was another autonomous association of patriotic and independent-minded young citizens.[50] The original intention of the Patriotic Society, as it was called, and its most forceful agitator, the Basle journalist, Isaak Iselin, had been to found a kind of international academy of social ethics which would concern itself not only with academic and socio-economic interests but also with reflection upon and debate about the intentions and foundations, advantages and disadvantages of legislature in various countries, and hence with socio-political problems. However, the Helvetic Society actually became a society which transcended the boundaries of cantonal authority and confessional divisions and strove to unite all the Swiss people. In 1773, Iselin wrote:

> There are many upstanding men here who are concerned for the common weal and the well-being of the Fatherland, but they are all operating on an individual basis. The unified enthusiasm, the social encouragement, the bonds of competitive zeal, the institutions, gatherings, meetings and occasions necessary for learned moral and political debate and action are lacking.[51]

The Helvetic Society, whose ultimate character had been settled at Schinzbach, adopted a simple organizational structure in keeping with its progressive programme. Its annual general assembly was presided over by a president, who served for a period of twelve months before being replaced, and a permanent secretary. A commission, whose members were constantly replaced, served the assembly in an advisory capacity. Central to the assembly itself were lectures and a general debate on particular proposals. The assembly, which often lasted for several days, devoted much of its programme of events to private debate and socializing.

There was a good deal of interest in the Helvetic Society, and its members came from all over Switzerland and from both religious denominations. By 1766, the society's membership had already reached a total of 82, and by 1798 it had risen to 386. A striking feature of the society was the significant number of its members who came from within the ranks of the municipal authorities, the patriciate and the clergy; professional scholars, preceptors and men of letters, on the other hand, were in a minority. Nevertheless, many of its members were leading figures in Swiss public life, such as, for example, Salomon Gessner, Johann Georg Ritter von Zimmermann, Isaak Iselin, K. Hirzel, Johann Kaspar Lavator, Heinrich Pestalozzi and Johannes von Müller. There were also some foreign members. It is revealing that the Helvetic

Society not only included representatives of the upper strata of Swiss society but also of most of the regional and cantonal reform groups, which had likewise founded economic and patriotic societies. In this respect, the Helvetic Society was a sort of umbrella organization for all the various cantonal societies.

The annual publication of the Helvetic Society's debates, including the president's speech and a varied selection of annual assembly lectures, gives a good insight not only into the way in which, from a patriotic and moral standpoint, the society saw itself, but also into the great variety of discussion matter, although, in contrast to the Hamburg Patriotic Society, it did not result in any practical reform movement. At the forefront were topics on political theory in general and problems of Swiss history in particular, including the delicate question of the liberty and equality of the Swiss people. Particular attention was devoted to social conditions, especially the puritanical Swiss way of life and schooling.[52] In spite of the society's cosmopolitanism, Switzerland remained the focus of its attention. The society's importance lay not in any tangible and practical reforms which it might have initiated; it lay solely in its status as a national forum for debate which was to create a new sense of Swiss national identity (the William Tell cult). The Swiss society, like that in Hamburg, made no demands for direct political influence. They justified the pursuance of their interests on the grounds of 'liberal' public-spiritedness without, however, either merging with or directly opposing the forces of state authority.

The Moral and Economic Society of Altötting-Burghausen

The Moral and Economic Society of Altötting-Burghausen managed to retain some degree of autonomy, despite succumbing to the reform programme of benevolent absolutism.[53] The society was undoubtedly a success. However, as the society was unable to realize its practical objectives, it concentrated on the debate of possible areas of reform: concrete achievements were not on its agenda.

The Moral and Economic Society evolved from an Altötting literary society whose main areas of emphasis were schools and language.[54] The bestowal of the privilege of the electoral prince in 1769 was coupled with the instruction from Munich to concentrate solely upon agricultural matters, especially since this field was neglected by the Munich Academy. In return, it was granted the maximum permissible level of academic freedom from censorship. The society had modelled its organizational structure on the learned academies; there were full members, members from outside its immediate catchment area and honorary members. However, the core of the membership was comprised of those members living in and around Altötting and, after 1772, Burghausen. Although the society was extremely self-important, it was never especially active. The members met only infrequently, and the most important event was the annual general meeting, the society's shop window to the outside world. The speeches made at these meetings were later reproduced in the 'Bair. ökonomischer Hausvater', the society's official publication. Most of the contributions to this publication concerned moral and economic themes in the broadest sense. Although the 'Hausvater' was targeted at the rural population, they accorded it a less than enthusiastic reception. Its target audience was, due to an absence of interest in what was essentially theoretical reflection, less than receptive. However, since the publication was neither intellectually nor academically superior to other publications, the learned world proved an equally unreceptive audience. The society's membership grew rapidly, despite the fact that its intellectual profile was, and always remained, uncertain. By 1772, that is, by the time it moved to the border town of Burghausen, the society had a membership of 130. By 1792, this had increased to 234. As a basic rule, anyone was eligible for membership 'who has an understanding of agriculture and is capable of using any agricultural improvement as a springboard for the discovery of further improvements to existing practices. Nobody is to be excluded from membership who has such a thorough and practical understanding'.[55] However, in matter of fact, membership remained restricted to the regional administrative elite. Groups directly affected by the problems central to the society, such as landowners and the rural population, were unrepresented. The teachings of the Altötting Society remained predominantly learned in character. In theory, the society was open to all social classes and religious beliefs, despite a strong Catholic presence. The society's membership selection criteria were essentially the same as those of the Bavarian Academy of Science.

Repeated attempts were made to set goals for the society. Plans were also forged for a school of economics, but ultimately, as is obvious from its outside contacts, such as the 'Hausvater' and its annual general meeting, the society pursued only the learned portrayal of the self. Following the discrediting of some of its members in the wake of the persecution of the Illuminati, the society went into decline. Its reorganization in 1782 into a Moral and Agricultural Academy of the Bavarian Palatinate in Burg-hausen was a last ditch attempt at the beginning of the nineteenth century to save itself from disintegration, a final ditch attempt to keep pace with contemporary developments. Ultimately, it was not simply the lack of middle-class forces which was responsible for the failure of the Burghausen experiment: other factors were, on the one hand, the isolation of Burghausen itself, which resulted in the absence of any intellectual milieu, and, on the other, the self-imposed social isolation of the membership committee. The society was unable to compete with the Munich Academy as a learned society, and, both in the case of its own membership and in that of the rural population, all the necessary conditions which would have enabled it to accomplish its goal of the practical education of the rural population in the spirit of the Enlighten-ment were completely absent. Revealingly, the society was ignored by precisely those circles which had a vested interest in the reor-ganization of agriculture, such as the true Bavarian agricultural experts, the legions of monastic clergymen.

There were various forms of patriotic societies. In the main, they concerned themselves with the interests of a single town, city or region, although they did also seek to establish inter-regional contacts. Accordingly, each society was an autonomous unit in itself. Only in Switzerland and in Austria were attempts made to unite all the practical and patriotic societies, in the latter case in order to create a broader rural basis for benevolent absolutism; in the former, in order to increase the Swiss sense of national identity. The activities of the societies were reported in their own publica-tions. In addition, some learned newspapers also made a particu-lar effort to report societal activities.

There are two phenomena deserving of a special mention: firstly, some societies founded their own societal publications in an attempt to establish an inter-societal communication network transcending regional boundaries. Secondly, during the last third of the century, some eminent intellectuals developed the notion of a patriotic society representing both regional and national in-terests, the interests of the whole of Germany.

In the first place, there was the 'Patriotic Society of Hesse-Homburg', founded in 1775 especially for the purpose of improving inter-societal communication.[56] The Frankfurt-based French writer, N. H. Paradis, and Landgrave Friedrich V. of Hesse attempted to establish a pan-European correspondence network and to create a central institute and an agency for academic exchanges in Homburg. The statutes reveal that there were both local and outside members. The outside members, who were subdivided into honorary, full and correspondence members, were to provide details of the results of the academic activities of all other societies. The local members came from Homburg and surrounding districts. Public meetings were to be held on a biannual basis, and working sessions for the scrutiny of the material submitted by outside members on a bimonthly basis. In addition to the secretary, the Homburg central committee was comprised of six other members. Learned circles displayed considerable interest in the Homburg project. By 1777, the society already had 143 members in 45 towns and cities in nine countries. The French contacts were particularly important. The French executive committee in Paris was also responsible for the society's official publication. The beginnings promised much, but quarrels and the excessive strain imposed upon the Homburg executive by the problems of coordination and correspondence evaluation led to its collapse.

A second, more modest attempt along these lines was made by the Gotha-based court tutor, Rudolf Zacharias Becker. He placed the 'Reichsanzeiger', upon which the Emperor had bestowed royal privilege, at the service of the learned and the patriotic societies.[57] In 1794, he published a 'Proposal for uniting the learned, economic and industrial societies of the German nation for the purpose of increasing efficiency', according to which all societal discoveries and knowledge were to be coordinated and published at the earliest possible date, for the particular benefit of 'the broad mass of the uneducated public at large'. The ambition was the creation of a national information centre, not a national academy: existing societies were to remain in being, but now they were to serve the national well-being and not simply regional interests. However, Becker's proposal met with no response.

The scope of the projects of two eminent progressive writers went beyond the creation of a regional information centre. In 1786, the pedagogue and initiator of the industrial schools movement, Joachim Heinrich Campe, propagated the creation of a

patriotic society encompassing the whole country.[58] This amounted
to a utopian plan, but it was by no means completely devoid of
realism. Economic and didactic interests coincided. Twelve men
in each capital of each principality, six (upstanding) representatives of means from each of the estates were to 'meet regularly
once or several times a week to enjoy a pipe together and discuss
matters of common interest'. The doors of the meeting place were
to be open to all, and all members were to be afforded the opportunity of reading the best available political, statistical, economic
and technical domestic and foreign periodicals. The patriotic society's main concern was the promotion of industry in the broadest sense. Competitions were to be organized and prizes awarded
for the best entries. The whole population was to be encouraged
to participate. However, for reasons of effectiveness, the society
was not autonomous of the state. On the contrary, in order that
external practical reforms might be introduced as soon as possible,
it was intended that the individual governments should exploit the
society's services.

Campe's plan concentrated on the enhancement of industrious-
ness and patriotic consciousness, but Johann Gottfried Herder's
'Idea for a first patriotic institute of the German intellect' of 1788
aimed at the creation of a National Academy as an umbrella for
all territorial and regional societies, with which it would also
cooperate.[59] As an 'umbrella organization of several provinces
serving general and practical intellectual and moral culture', the
German Academy had three tasks: firstly, the cultivation of the
German language. Since the language determines the thought
processes of a nation, German, which Herder described as a
written language, was to be transformed into a language of high
society and public speaking. Hence, the members were to create
linguistic models and disseminate writings serving this process of
refinement, and also awaken linguistic ambitions, particularly by
awarding prizes. The second task concerned German history.
What was now at stake was not the history of the German territories but a history of the whole fatherland. 'The sect mentality
of individual countries will wither and die, the age of darkness
prevailing in inaccessible crannies will be banished by the light of
man, reason, honesty and truth'. The third task, regarded as the
'ultimate and most noble aim of the academy', concerned everything 'which falls under the rubric of active philosophy in the
service of the creation of a sense of national identity and of

happiness'. This included everything which improved education and enhanced the public institutions of the state and the Church. The central issue was humane and wise government based upon the tenets of reason. 'Militating against injustice and barbarism . . . paving the way for the light of truth, the omnipresent expurgator, which in time will reveal itself as the gospel: such is the academy's task'.

These aims were reflected by the academy's organizational structure, whose purpose was not the abolition but rather the reorientation of the existing learned societies towards the pursuit of national objectives. Important tasks fell to the regional potentates: their job was to choose individuals from among their subjects, that is, release them from their state duties or commission them on an *ad hoc* basis to allow them to establish provincial deputations. The director of such a delegation had no direct authority, his job was simply the allocation of tasks. These provincial deputations sent representatives to the National Academy to report on their activities and enter their most important observations in the 'Yearbook of the German National Intellect'. The National Academy was to have full and honorary members. It was the full members who were to engage in the actual patriotic activities. The academy's main place of assembly was to be in central Germany, easily accessible and independent of any court influence. This was where the academy's annual assemblies were to be held, which were not just platforms for the representatives of the provincial deputations to report on their activities. It was open to every 'other receptive, patriotic thinking man' to offer a report of his activities to the assembly, the quality of which would then be scrutinized. Fair-mindedness was guaranteed. In addition, the academy assisted in the publication of the most meritorious essays. The academy was headed by a paid president and a secretary, who were the personification of unity.

Herder's conception was unique insofar as its objective was to promote patriotic intellectual activity and to commit the ruling princes to inter-territorial action on behalf of the 'German National Intellect'. Finally, it was intended that the academy should not only be an institution enjoying the protection of the state; it should be an institution of the ruling princes themselves, albeit an institution in which the individual members would be able to dictate the shape of the patriotic activities. Against this background, patriotism no longer meant openly supporting the cause of the common good of the 'regional' homeland and calling for public-spirited urban and rural activities. It meant supporting the cause of a unified German culture transcending regional and territiorial borders, a unified culture which was founded essentially on language, history and patriotism. Herder's notion of a National Academy was in the interest of the German cultural elite, but it met with as little positive response as other plans to establish national societies bridging regional divisions.

The patriotic and public-spirited society has a rich and multifarious history spanning the range from pragmatic agricultual societies and learned, patriotic societies to the notion of German cultural union.

The second phase of the eighteenth-century societal movement, between the years 1745 and 1750 and 1775 and 1780, was largely influenced by the expansion of the absolutist and bureaucratic state and, particularly following the end of the Seven Years' War, its permeation of all areas of social responsibility, from health to university education, which were formerly administered either on an autonomous or a cooperative basis. It was no longer mainly scholars but progressive advocates of the Enlightenment and officials of state, active in the public arena, who were now seeking to achieve their progressive ambitions in the shape of a society based on the tenets of reason and morality. This was achieved through the medium of Freemasonry, with its segregation of the moral inner world from the political external world, wherein it focused exclusively on the inner moral world. Or alternatively, it was achieved by founding patriotic and public-spirited societies which were either active in those areas where the citizen was beyond the state's reach, or which, by awakening a sense of patriotism, encouraged him to come of age, that is, to engage in public activities, to take matters into his own hands and organize the representation of his interests independent of the state. All those concerned focused on the external world without clashing with the forces of authority; on the contrary, they enjoyed the protection of those very forces.

The prototype of the Freemason was the cosmopolitan, that of the public-spirited society the patriot. Both groups recruited few scholastic members and both refrained from seeking to attain legitimacy through scientific and literary publications. Instead, they recruited 'civilized' men; men who were not simply active at the literary and scholarly level but who were also, on account of their education and social status, in positions of prominence. They included, for the first time, large numbers of government officials among their ranks, that is, exactly that class of men who were the standard bearers of government and political reform inside benevolent absolutism; their objective was the creation of their own society based on the tenets of virtue. In other words, as mature and self-confident citizens and patriots, their goal was to reform society by their own efforts, independent of the state, the Church and the estates.

Clubs of the Enlightenment and Political Associations

The third and final phase of the development of the societies of the Enlightenment occurred under the conditions of benevolent absolutism in crisis. The citizenry had grown in self-confidence and no longer blindly accepted that their socio-political aspirations could be fulfilled by a benevolent prince. They were progressive reformers in their own right, and, in order to uphold and advance the cause of the Enlightenment, they increasingly founded associations which were independent of, or co-existed alongside, established state institutions. Indeed, they even displayed a tendency to oppose the state's claim to be the sole legitimate source of authority. This phase was also linked to the development and expansion of the literary market and the consolidation of an autonomous public free of authoritarian constraints whose decision-making was influenced by the rational criteria of the middle class and who were on the verge of proclaiming a society of the middle class. The learned academies had developed within the framework of the authority of the court, and they functioned as state intellectual and academic authorities. The Freemasons and the patriots co-existed with the state, both in order to educate themselves as mature and responsible adults and in order to facilitate the furtherance of the Enlightenment. However, the new societies which developed after 1775/80 heralded the advent of associations of educated members of the middle class whose dual ambition was emancipation and enfranchisement, and the creation of a progressive and reformist platform independent of, indeed, even in opposition to, the feudal system of absolutism, in which there was equal status for all. Towards the end of the century, these societies had increased in number to such an extent that, despite the simultaneous growth of masonic lodges and patriotic societies, there was at least one in almost every town of any size (see map 3).

Three new types of society came into existence during this final phase, though this did not detract from the functions of the older societies. Firstly, various didactic associations appeared on the scene, a whole host of reading circles, ranging from loose reading associations to exclusive debating societies pursuing didactic aspirations and the displacement of traditional values and philosophies through collective reading and fraternal debate. In the second place, there were the secret societies of the late Enlightenment, particularly the League of Illuminati, whose objective was the projection of the Enlightenment to the seat of power. Lastly, the so-called people's societies, the German equivalent of the Jacobin clubs. Though short-lived, they were uniquely important in the period of the late Enlightenment. They were the most aggressive exponents of the Enlightenment in the quest to abolish feudalism and traditional behaviour, in the struggle for civil equality and freedom.

DIDACTIC SOCIETIES

Reading societies

The reading societies were perhaps the most prevalent form of society of the Enlightenment. They were the real didactic institutions of the eighteenth century, and to a certain degree they were rivals to the masonic lodges. However, in terms of their purpose and their structure, they bore more resemblance to the public-spirited societies. At the end of the eighteenth century, there were some 430 societies in existence in Germany.[1] What was the reason for the prolific growth of these societies and their increasing dominance among the societies of the Enlightenment during the 1780s and beyond? Throughout the eighteenth century, the mediation, reading and discussion of literature within the societal movement played a prominent role in the articulation of progressive, middle-class interests – examples of this are the German societies and the early reading circles, often operating in conjunction with patriotic societies and masonic lodges. However, the reading societies proper were special associations.

Two developments merged here: reading and debate provided
the new anti-traditionalist middle class with their first platform
for the articulation of their aspirations. In addition, these new
activities of study and debate provided the foundations for new
social attitudes on their part. This amounted less to an appro-
priation of the modern literature of the German Enlightenment,
Sturm and Drang and the classical period than to satisying a great
need for information, ranging from cultivating clover to ancient
history, from knowledge of overseas countries to reports from the
seats of royalty. This spawned a literary market which gradually
encompassed everyone with an interest in literature.[2] In terms of
the total population, this group was a small minority, but it still
represented a considerable improvement on the proportion of the
population with a literary interest at the beginning of the century.
Book publishing and the constantly increasing number of newspapers and periodicals are a sign of the change in outlook which
was underway. Religious and theological books written in Latin
made way for secular and practical books written in German,
which were intended as light entertainment for educated laymen.
This revolution in the book market both signalled and fostered a
revolution in the reading habits of broad sections of the population: reading many different books replaced the previous system
of reading and re-reading the same book.[3] This was particularly
evident in the reading societies which had been created to meet
the increasing need of the middle class for reading material and
the acquisition of knowledge, thus satisfying the social condition
that they should operate outside the norms of the schools and the
ecclesiastical and secular authorities. The Enlightenment as a
broad movement of the middle class is at its most palpable in the
reading societies, and, as a movement, these societies soon encompassed all social classes interested in the autodidactic process and
the Enlightenment.

Reading societies were societies of the Enlightenment comprising various forms of reading associations.[4] As books were relatively expensive and public libraries still unknown, the objective of all these associations was to be able to read the maximum
number of books and newspapers at the minimum cost. This was
only possible if several interested parties clubbed together to found
a library. The system of joint subscriptions was one of the earliest
examples of this; in such cases, for reasons of economy, the participating parties subscribed jointly to a periodical for private

reading on an alternate basis. In addition, there were the so-called reading circles and groups which acquired books and periodicals on a joint basis for common use. Although such circles often had no permanent home, they were still homogeneous groups with a common statute. Such reading circles were already involved in the dissemination of the moral weeklies.[5] There were also local libraries, organized for the most part by book dealers. For the participants, in addition to inexpensive access to books, these libraries often offered the possibility of literary debate. Finally, the most important type of didactic association was the reading cabinet, the reading society proper of eighteenth-century literature.

These reading societies had soon rented their own rooms, or had even bought their own premises complete with club rooms housing reading libraries. In order that reading might proceed without disturbance, reading and conversation rooms were segregated. Essentially, the reading society provided the opportunity for literary debate, regular meetings and the development of alternative forms of communication. Thus, the reading matter was supplemented by the institution of the literary society. This form of learned diversion and didactic collectiveness was a considerable factor in the consolidation and subsequent development, growth and attraction of the reading society as an urban centre of communication.[6]

The reading societies branched out quickly from their North German base. There were some fifty of them by 1780, seventy in the 1780s and 200 in the 1790s. All told, some 430 reading societies were actually founded before they went into decline: many disbanded, others aspired to fresh ambitions and still others concentrated on certain specialist areas. The predominant form of reading society became the social club; many associations adopted the designation 'reading and recuperation society' and pursued the social aspect to the exclusion of all else.[7] There are many reasons for this transformation. Firstly, in the wake of the persecution of the Illuminati and, later, in the wake of the French Revolution in particular, the reading societies were suspected of political, even Jacobin activities. Secondly, the disillusionment which followed the French Revolution and the social upheavals at the turn of the century resulted in a marked decline in passionate thirst for knowledge, enthusiasm for learning and for debate. In consequence, there was a marked increase in the desire for apolitical social clubs, both large and small.[8] The reading societies had approximately as many members as the masonic lodges. However, as many literary societies had between 150 and 200 members, it is not actually beyond the bounds of possibility that the literary societies had considerably more members than the masonic lodges. More accurate figures are not available, and thus, it is difficult to estimate the total membership number. It might have been as high as 15,000 to 20,000, a considerable number indeed for the late eighteenth century. However, compared both to the total population and to the total number of literate members of the population, this number is still surprisingly small. Ultimately, the reading societies encompassed only a small educated elite.[9] The geographical expansion of the reading societies is also interesting. They were founded first in Northern Germany, expanding mainly into Saxony and Thuringia and the Rhineland, in other words, into the heartland of the Enlightenment. In Bavaria and Austria, where the effects of the age of baroque Catholicism persisted the longest, they were surprisingly underrepresented. They were also scarce in Württemberg.

For the reading societies, their main function was 'the provision of a variety of political, learned and other interesting newspapers, reports and reading material at minimal expense'.[10] However, this practical function soon became coupled with the function of studying such material 'within a friendly and beneficial framework of debate'. In addition to the provision of inexpensive reading material and social intercourse, the reading societies had a third function, one which they shared with other contemporary societies: contributing towards Enlightenment through the acquisition of practical knowledge.[11] Thus was benefit to be combined with fraternity.

Our social association shall not be an end in itself. Rather, by exploiting that which has already been initiated, by continuing our own progress ever further along the road towards the discovery of the light, and through mutual assistance, it shall be a means of using our united strength to achieve the good that it is beyond the power of the individual member to achieve by his own efforts. Furthermore, armed with the knowledge of all the practical sciences, we shall be in a position to remedy the deficiencies of our times, in which falsehood is often clothed in the veil of truth, in which profligacy and immoderation of every kind besmirch the sacred name of the Enlightenment, in which spurious virtue is disguised as the splendour of true righteousness, in which bare-faced flattery and falsehood usurp the simple attire of politics, in which the sceptre of privilege still holds sway over the heads of the nation, in which blind superstition bars the path to the benign irradiation of reason and in which anarchy and despotism dispute the frontiers of freedom. If, through our intervention, reason is restored to its rightful place and the kingdom of truth is enlarged, if truthful concepts, the true assessment of values and their relevance to the happiness of mankind, and all knowledge of universal benefit are disseminated among the whole population, if all men recognize and experience the true nature of their existence, if deep-seated respect for the law is created among the people, if pernicious blindness ceases to impede the physical and moral perfection of mankind and if, finally, men acquire the degree of insight which is necessary for the recognition of their destiny, then we shall have remedied the most pressing deficiencies of our time. Then real, true, universally beneficial Enlightenment shall be a reality, the foes of which are the allies of darkness. Such Enlightenment improves and ennobles the spirit and the heart. Its progress is long and arduous, but following a lengthy process of ripening, it bears those most noble of fruits, the true virtues, the gift of enlightened reason and benevolent sensibilities. The outstanding example of our most gracious prince, whose devotion and whose paternal care for the physical and moral weal of his people was always so much in evidence, challenges us to assist in the creation of this so fortunate, so benevolent apparition for the good of our fellow men. (From the speech by K. A. von Mastiaux, 2 December 1789, to the Bonn Reading Society.)[12]

In keeping with this general objective, the reading societies adopted a democratic organizational structure which became the model for all subsequent associations. The highest authority was the general meeting, usually held on a monthly basis. The general meeting was responsible for settling any issue affecting the society. It was an assembly of the whole membership, and each member enjoyed the same right to air his opinions and put forward suggestions. For the most part, a majority vote, in many instances a three-quarters majority vote, was required to carry a decision. The general meeting took decisions affecting the statute and amendments to the statute, the establishment and funding of reading institutes, the selection of reading material and the admittance of new members. As a rule, in addition to the general assembly, there was also an elected committee consisting of a chairman, whose responsibility was the successful conclusion of current business, a treasurer and a secretary. The committee was answerable to the general assembly, and every member of the society had the right to be present during committee meetings. The policy of many reading societies was to enable every member to be on the committee at some time. The reason for this was twofold: to ensure that the decision-making authority always remained in the hands of the general meeting and to afford equal rights to the whole membership. At the heart of all these endeavours was the objective of creating a democratic structure which was in keeping with the principles of the society. The Karlsruhe Reading Society proclaimed: 'The principle of egalitarianism is the whole basis of the society: each member has exactly the same rights as his fellow.'[13] The patriotic and public-spirited societies had also adopted democratic principles, but the reading societies insisted upon the principles of democracy to a far greater extent than any other association. As is demonstrated by the surviving minutes of reading society meetings, the principle of equality did not remain simply a postulation of the statutes or the founding fathers. The membership structure of the reading societies was as follows:

Bonn 1787–99[14]

174 members (52 aristocrats)

Officials of state	42
Clergymen/theologians	32
Professors/teachers	30
Officers	16
Court musicians	12
Legal practitioners/notaries	6
Officials of the Teutonic Order	6
Merchants	2
Envoys	2
Court actors	2
Archivists	2
Court artists	2
Profession unknown	20

Ludwigsburg 1769/1796[15]

66 and 62 members respectively (35 and 12 aristocrats respectively)

Officers	48	(25)
Officials of state/public officials	8	(11)
Clergymen/theologians	2	(2)
Merchants		(2)
Physicians	1	
Professors	1	(1)
Profession unknown	6	(21)

Trier 1785/93[16]

134 members (18 aristocrats)

Officials of state	50
Theologians	32
Professors/legal practitioners	10
Officers	5
Physicians	3
Merchants	3
Profession unknown	31

Basel 1787/92[17]

123 members

Officials of state/public officials	29
Professors	14
Officers	8
Merchants	8
Artisans	5
Schoolmasters	4
Notaries	2
Profession unknown	53

As such, class and rank were supposed to be irrelevant as a criterion for the admittance of members. Membership was open to all, but as far as it is possible to ascertain, actual membership was restricted to a narrow section of the population. There were no women or middle- and lower-class artisans. Ultimately, only those with literary credentials or of 'higher' social origin were eligible for membership. In many instances, reading society membership contributions were beyond the means of all but a narrow section of the upper class, and anybody whose membership would destroy the homogeneous structure of the society would fail to achieve acceptance by the majority of the members. There was thus no real difference between the membership structure of the reading societies and that of other societies. As was the case with Freemasonry, in the seats of royalty, the majority of reading society members were government officials. In the free cities and centres of commerce, on the other hand, most members came from the merchant class, supplemented by professors, physicians and clergymen, among whom were many aristocrats. Like other societies, the reading society was the preserve of the higher classes, though the middle class was in the majority: the lower social classes were excluded from membership. The self-image of the reading society was that of a society of the educated. Thus, the reading society of the Enlightenment opened its doors only to those with intellectual or financial credentials. This bias operated in favour of the aristocracy, a phenomenon which the reading society shared with Freemasonry. However, there was still a strong middle-class ambition to establish associations which existed both parallel to, and independent of, the court. As was the case with other societies, the reading society's proclamation of equality amounted to little more than a plea for greater levels of contact between the aristocracy and the middle class, for a mutual process of familiarization in isolation. It was widely believed that the intrinsic value of the reading society lay in this very 'mixture of different social classes'.[18]

> However, it should be noted that it was the reading societies of the eighteenth century in which the German middle class, in full public view, took the first steps towards turning their egalitarian ambitions into reality instead of concealing them within the secretive confines of the lodge. For this reason, the reading society, despite its limitations, should be regarded as a positive step forward along the road to the realization of middle-class equality. The reading society was the arena in which members of the ascendant middle class were able to congregate and cooperate, both with each other and with representatives of the aristocracy, across the barriers of the estates, the professions and the religious denominations, a process which demonstrated that the middle class was the new dominant class.[19]

All the reading societies attempted to hire their own rooms or acquire their own premises in order to establish a library to which the members would have regular daily access. There were both reading rooms and conversation rooms. In the reading room, talking and noise of any kind was prohibited, as were loud noise and heated debate in the conversation rooms. Cultured social intercourse was expected of all the members; this stipulation was also behind the ban on gambling and smoking and 'offensive outbursts against religion, the state and morality'.[20] The statutes permitted only the following refreshments: tea, cocoa, coffee, almond-flavoured milk, lemonade and punch. This is an indication that the creation of an inn-like atmosphere was to be avoided at all costs. The premises of the reading society were for members only, but members were permitted to bring learned guests. The guestbooks of some of the reading societies reveal how often they were frequented by famous personalities on their travels.[21]

The most important events in the life of a reading society were the monthly debates of society lectures. The learned members were under particular pressure to structure the literary circles in an informative manner: for example, the list of the lectures of the 'Private Reading Society' of Elberfeld covers the whole gamut of issues connected with the late Enlightenment: the sciences, particularly those issues affecting morality and the Enlightenment, such as harmony, friendship, the betterment of the heart, happiness, the transience of time, obligingness, the problems of parenthood, self-knowledge, the benevolence of religion and philanthropy etc.[22] Heinrich Jung-Stilling, one of the founders of the Elberfeld society, noted:

> Several noble and progressive men founded a private society which met each Wednesday towards late evening for the purpose of improving their didactic horizons by means of studying interesting reading material and debating various subjects. Lectures could be delivered by anyone with the inclination and the ability. Fixed membership contributions funded the gradual establishing of a library of selected books for the benefit of the whole membership.[23]

The official, learned side of societal life was often followed by a social affair. Thus: 'an excellent evening meal, not unduly extravagant, and several choice wines were served at a well-laid table'.[24] Such conviviality was beyond the means of all but the financially comfortable: all members were required to pay for their own victuals.

The journals and books provided by the reading societies are well documented.[25] Surprisingly, these did not include any of the wide range of contemporary didactic literature and light fiction. Not surprisingly, in view of the predominance of government officials among the memberships of the literary societies, the staple literary diet was the many political and progressive periodicals, both German and non-German. Political journals were the most common reading matter, a contradiction of the widespread view that the educated German middle class was politically disinterested and retreated into domesticity and edification.

The study of reading matter was accompanied by literary debate, and while the maintenance of societal 'harmony' was important, this did not preclude the possibility that criticism might be voiced.[26] Any political or religious debate was a potential threat to this harmony, and was thus handled with care, as was the case in other societies. Nevertheless, the reading society was an unrivalled source of information and forum for debate. Thus, it comes as no surprise that, in 1797, some citizens of Cologne founded a reading society as a means of furthering their ambition for the introduction of a democratic constitution: the reading society was a forum for debate for the familiarization of the citizenry with the spirit and the content of a democratic constitution.[27] In addition to the study and debate of contemporary political issues, the reading societies also studied informed articles on the subject of the national economy, statistics, the legal system and agriculture. One member of a reading society in Bonn described the main aim of his society as 'exerting our joint strength to promote the spread and acceptance of the Enlightenment'.[28] Although every effort was made to exert outside influence by means of welfare and charitable initiatives and the founding of newspapers, the main concern remained the acquisition of knowledge and fraternal debate within a society which was essentially a middle-class and, to a lesser extent, aristocratic preserve.

The reading societies undoubtedly enhanced the political and social self-awareness, judgement and education of the cream of the middle class, even though this was accomplished solely against the backdrop of benevolent absolutism. Although there were strong fears in the wake of the French Revolution that the reading societies might propagate revolutionary ideas, democracy and anarchy among the population at large, the members of the reading societies generally displayed a very positive attitude towards the system of absolutism. Otherwise, they would never have so meekly accepted the official ban imposed upon many of the societies during the 1790s.[29] Obviously, this did not preclude the existence of links between the League of Illuminati and several of the reading societies, and nor did it prevent the Jacobin clubs from continuing the tradition of the reading societies. However, that section of the middle class involved with these societies had nothing to gain by the abolition of the system of benevolent absolutism and sharing their newly acquired privileges with the broad mass of the populace. The speeches delivered by the reading societies on the occasion of the death of Joseph II are evidence of[30] the extent to which the spirit of the old order persisted within the consciousness of the German middle class, even though they refused to withdraw their call for social emancipation. In this regard – and, ultimately, the reading societies did constitute a broad middle-class movement in which both deliberation of political and social issues and democracy were practised on a uniquely broad scale – the reading societies made a major contribution to the creation of the social and political consciousness of the ascendant classes during the phase of middle-class emancipation.

Literary friendship circles

A large number of minor literary and friendship associations appeared on the scene at the same time as the reading societies. Their structure was similar to that of the large public reading societies, but, due to their exclusivity and friendship links, they should be regarded as a separate entity. These associations – sometimes called after the day upon which their meetings were held – often assumed the character of private literary, or learned and philosophical, circles revolving completely around convivial conversation or philosophical debate but tracking them all down is an arduous task.[31] The dividing line between the large reading societies and the exclusive groups on the one hand, and the organized and informal circles on the other, is blurred. Only those groups with a formal structure will be examined in detail. These exclusive circles were also comprised of members of the political and social elite. They were not associations of intellectual outsiders, and, despite the many differences of emphasis between them, they all believed in the universality of the Enlightenment. Thus, they were not yet exclusive associations of the middle class. Four types will be examined in detail:

(1) The associations of poets. There were many different forms of these associations at the end of the century, of which the Göttinger Hainbund is particularly well documented.
(2) Those which were, in effect, reading societies with an exclusive fraternal culture. These were particularly prevalent in North Germany (Hamburg, Oldenburg and Bremen).
(3) Learned and literary circles specializing in the debate of particular topics. Examples of such circles are the Berlin Wednesday Society and Goethe's Friday Society.
(4) The philosophical and literary association of the League of Freemen in Jena.

(1) The 'Göttinger Hain' was founded by a small group of young students as an association independent of all the institutions of learning in the university town of Göttingen. All the founders were the sons of clergymen or students of theology. However, they soon turned their attentions exclusively to literature and poetry.[32]

The actual driving force behind this circle of poets was Heinrich Christian Boie (1744–1806), a young court tutor and the publisher of the Göttingen 'Musen Almanach'. He was an expert on modern literature, had a host of contacts among contemporary writers and was a sponsor of young talent. In Göttingen, he quickly gathered around him a circle of young lyric poets who were students at the university. The members of this circle were: Johann Heinrich Voss, the grandson of a Mecklenburg serf, who became famous for his translations of the literature of antiquity, and who later became the leading figure in the League of Poets; the clergyman's son, Ludwig Christian Hölty, a highly talented lyric poet; Johann Martin Miller, the son of an Ulm preacher who, as secretary, was responsible for the league's journal, and who later rose to prominence thanks to his popular novel 'Siegwart, the History of a Monastery' (1776). Finally, there was Johann Friedrich Hahn from Zweibrücken, a passionate admirer of Friedrich Gottlieb Klopstock. In addition, there were some other, less prominent, members who were also students at Göttingen. The group met frequently, discussing both their own poetry and the best known of the most recent literary publications. In addition, they also proclaimed their allegiance to Klopstock.

An enthusiastic vision transformed this loose friendship circle into a league of poets: six of the young poets spent the evening of 12 September 1772 in the open air on the outskirts of the town and formed a league of friendship by the light of the full moon.[33] Henceforth, the league met regularly every Saturday afternoon at a private house. The meeting was opened by the reading of a poem by Klopstock or Karl Wilhelm Ramler, which was then subjected to the critical judgement of those present. There then followed readings of members' poems, upon which first verbal and then written critical judgement was passed. This was accompanied by coffee. The poems thus scrutinized and revised were published in the league's journal. The league met 69 times between 13 September 1772, and 27 December 1773. The purpose of the league was the reciprocal fostering of literary talent by means of literary criticism, absolute candidness and honesty. Boie, who was not present at the founding ceremony, was appointed honorary chairman. However, Voss, the driving force behind the league, was elected league elder. Pen names were adopted, though they were not used openly. The league was soon extended to include the two Counts of Stolberg, Christian and the more eminent Friedrich Leopold, who were students at Göttingen University. There was a moving scene during their first Saturday attendance: the count embraced Voss, the grandson of an emancipated serf, sealing a League of Friendship.[34] At that time, this was a revolutionary gesture. The league united all enemies of tyranny and champions of freedom, irrespective of feudal origin.

The league's first loyalty was to Klopstock: he had gradually freed his poetry from the straitjacket imposed by the models of antiquity and now propagated patriotic German poetry set against the backdrop of an imaginary prehistoric age of darkness replete with Teutonic mythologies.[35] The literary cult of Göttingen united elements of poetry, religion, ethics and patriotism. The result was a cryptic whole comprising the notions of freedom and fierce patriotism, which expressly rejected the libertarian and cosmopolitan literature of Christoph Martin Wieland. The rivalry between Klopstock and Wieland was pursued with particular relish by the younger generation. Their close identification with Klopstock was predetermined by the league's choice of reading material, and this enthusiastic devotion was further fuelled by the enrolment of the Stolbergs: they had been personally acquainted with Klopstock since childhood, thus paving the way for personal contact between the league and the idol and revered master of his craft. The importance of Klopstock is revealed by a handwritten collection of poems of eight members of the 'Göttinger Hain' entitled 'For Klopstock', which Stolberg presented to the master in the spring of 1773. On 2 July 1773, the league celebrated Klopstock's birthday.

> We celebrated his birthday in fine style ... A long table was laid and decorated with flowers. There was a comfortable chair at the head of the table, for Klopstock, adorned with roses and stocks, upon which lay Klopstock's complete works. Beneath the chair, Wieland's Idris lay in shreds. Then Cramer read some passages from the Songs of Triumph, and Hahn some of Klopstock's odes to Germany. Then we drank coffee; the spills were made out of the works of Wieland. Boie, who didn't smoke, also had to light up and tread Idris into the dirt. Then we toasted Klopstock's health, the memory of Luther and Hermann, the health of the league, of Ebert, of Goethe, of Herder, etc. with Rhenish wine. Klopstock's ode to Rhenish wine was read, and a few others besides. Now the discussion grew livelier. We discussed freedom, the hats we were wearing, Germany, virtuous song and you can imagine what else. Then we ate and drank punch before finally setting effigies of Wieland and his Idris alight. (A letter from Voss to Brückner, 4 August 1773.)[36]

Klopstock, who at this time was in the middle of his 'German Republic of Scholars',[37] regarded the enthusiasm of the young men from Göttingen as a great honour, and he incorporated their objectives into his plans. Following a visit to Klopstock in Hamburg by Boie, Klopstock submitted a formal written request to be admitted to the league. This request met with enthusiastic approval, and when Klopstock visited Göttingen himself in September, he was besieged all day long by the whole membership. He gave them hope: 'He has great plans in store for the league, they have just not been finalized yet. All our writings have to be scrutinized in detail prior to publication to ensure that they are in keeping both with this plan and with good taste and morality. He willingly subjects himself to the league's judgement'.[38]

The affected patriotic behaviour of the Göttingen League, which propagated closer relations with England and greater emphasis on the merit and nobility of German as a counter to the predominance of French poetry, was not always warmly received. It also met with its fair share of derision and criticism. Wieland was not alone in denouncing the 'emasculated synovial' poetry of the young men from Göttingen: Göttingen professors also derided the league's poetic and patriotic activities.[39]

The 'Musen Almanach' of 1774 was the league's literary high-water mark. It contained a selection of the league's poems and those of the league's influential supporters. However, close co-operation was short-lived. By 1774, the league had disintegrated, despite its central importance in the lives of all its members. All the members had gradually moved away, and while they did maintain ties with Göttingen, they never returned to the fold. In 1776, Boie became the last to leave Göttingen, and Hölty died. The importance of the League of Poets was twofold: firstly, it was an association of young poets who concluded an eternal pact of friendship across social barriers. Secondly, patriotic nonsense not-withstanding, its social criticism later resulted in the support of the majority of its former members for the French Revolution. Such support was an exception to the rule of German political culture at the end of the eighteenth century.

(2) An eminent example of an exclusive literary society was the so-called Klopstock and Büsch Society in Hamburg which came into being during the period 1777–9. It remained the cultural centre of the Hamburg Enlightenment for two decades.[40] The

society met every Thursday at half past four at the house of Professor Johann Georg Büsch in order to hold readings of German writings 'suitable for, and worthy of, public readings'. In contrast to other societies, literature was the focal point of the Klopstock and Büsch Society. This was not only due to its fixation with the highly acclaimed figure of Klopstock, who had been resident in Hamburg since 1770, but also to the interests of the private membership. But this was not the only unusual feature: there were also women members, and they were not simply passive listening fodder; they were instrumental in selecting the reading material. Secondly, the ritual of public reading, during which talking was prohibited, formed only one part of the convivialities. The public reading of a literary piece, for which a minimum of seventy-five minutes was reserved, was followed by parlour games and an evening meal. The statutes dictated the course of the meetings in minute detail. Unfortunately, none of the minutes of any of the reading societies have survived, and thus, there are no records of their reading material. Fortunately, however, the society's guests, who were permitted to attend meetings in the company of a member, provide colourful records of this learned circle, which played such an important social role. The great attraction of the society lay in the combination of public readings, parlour games and female participation. However, this also attracted criticism from some quarters, which regarded this very combination as the downfall of the reading society as a circle of the Enlightenment.[41]

Gerhard Anton von Halem, an advocator of the Enlightenment from the town of Oldenburg, learnt from this experience. His literary society, founded in Oldenburg in 1779, barred both women and all forms of games. This is the only literary society still in existence today. According to his own account, von Halem long toyed with the idea of founding an 'intimate literary circle'. However, not until after his visit to Hamburg did he actually realize his ambition, in conjunction with 'some young men of approximately my own age' who had an interest in literature. 'The idea met with approval, and thus, the Oldenburg literary society was founded . . . to which I owe the most noble, most pristine pleasures of my life.'[42] The association was an exclusive society limited to a membership of twelve. The members were scholars, officers and government officials, in other words, representatives of the educated elite of this administrative centre and seat of royalty. 'Literature and art, friendly, cheerful conversation and respite from serious debate'[43] provided the subject matter for their convivial discussions, not politics or learning. The main purpose of von Halem's society was the same as that of the Hamburg society, namely, social recuperation from the stresses and strains of professional life. Only the parlour games were absent.

Lastly, the Hamburg society was also an inspiration to A. G. Deneken, a senator from Bremen. His literary society, founded in 1797, an unfavourable period for new associations, was intended as the 'beginning of a new form of social existence'.[44] Deneken also gathered around him men from all walks of professional life, mostly representatives of the Bremen elite: senators, clergymen, jurists, teachers and one merchant. The purpose of their meetings was not simply reading and conversation: they held didactic and friendly debates on learned subjects, and lectures 'for the Socratic and pure enjoyment of true fraternal companions'.[45] The society had ambitious goals: it met once every fortnight, held readings and debates on the philosophy of Immanuel Kant, Johann Gottfried Herder and Fichte and the theology of Heinrich Eberhard Paulus and Johann Kaspar Lavater and read philologians such as Christian Gottlob Heyne, as well as classical literature. They also debated scientific and political essays. The members were united by the bonds of a cult of friendship. The Bremen society, like those in Hamburg and Oldenburg, did not aspire to external influence, though it did cherish a self-image as the 'seed of humanity' and 'the centre of public education'.[46] In aspiring to this self-image, the Bremen society was similar to the 'League of Freemen' in Jena.

(3)   The root cause of the third type of society was not personal friendship but the desire for more detailed knowledge of particular contemporary literary and academic problems and for conversation in the intimate surroundings of a small circle. The purely social aspect was less important than the institutionalization of certain private professional interests. The most important of these societies was the illustrious 'Berlin Wednesday Society', a 'private society of friends of learning', which existed between the years 1783 and 1797.[47] There were a great many exclusive clubs in Berlin, but the Wednesday Society was the most prominent. The society not only included the elite of Berlin's champions of the Enlightenment: it was also the breeding ground of initiatives for

the reform of Prussian absolutism. The Wednesday Society was a secret society, and only the members were aware of its existence. Originally, there were twelve members, but this was increased to twenty-four. They devoted their attentions to all the issues of the Enlightenment. The members included the minister of state, Johann Friedrich Graf von Struensee, and the Prussian state officials, Karl Gottlieb Suarez and Ernst Klein, who rose to prominence as the reformers of the Prussian legal system. The society secretary was the publisher of the *Berlin Monthly Journal*, Johann Biester. Friedrich Nicolai and Christian Dohm were members of long standing, and Moses Mendelsohn was an honorary member. Without exception, the members of the Wednesday Society were academics, physicians, clergymen and theologians.

> The objective of the members was the civilized debate of interesting subjects, particularly scientific subjects. The purpose of these debates was the reciprocal broadening of the mind by means of the amicable exchange of ideas, thus shedding some light on a whole host of concepts and subjecting them to impartial scrutiny. All the members were true philanthropists; thus, they all strove to base their interpretation of the truth upon facts rather than upon vacuous phrases or intuition.[48]

Although the topics of debate did include subjects of a learned and scientific nature, most of all they were political. It was usually the case that an article which appeared in the *Berlin Monthly Journal* had been debated by the Wednesday Society prior to publication.

The society held regular meetings at the home of one of the members. During the winter they met every second Wednesday, during the summer every fourth Wednesday. A treatise was presented, 'mostly concerning governmental or financial administration, law and speculative and practical philosophy, very rarely literature'. The treatise then became the subject of general debate.[49] Finally, copies of the contributions were circuated among the members so that everyone had the opportunity of submitting written comments. Strict secrecy was essential, not least because senior government officials spoke freely and openly during these meetings. All the members were advocates of the Enlightenment, though the considerable differences of opinion between them was a characteristic feature of the Wednesday Society. The Wednesday

Society's debate on Klein's essay, 'Freedom and Property', prior
to publication in 1790 was particularly revealing.[50] This debate
seems to have brought the supporters and the opponents of the
French Revolution into open conflict: nevertheless, as a result of
its policy of outright rejection of arguments, which could not hold
water under impartial scrutiny, the society remained intact. However, the intensive debating style of the Wednesday Society was
exceptional: its high standards of criticism and debate remained
second to none.

The second society in this section, Johann Wolfgang von
Goethe's Friday Society, probably founded in Weimar in 1791,[51]
also focused on scientific and learned subjects. Goethe himself speaks of 'a society of highly educated men' in which each
member had the opportunity of lecturing on any subject of his
choosing from the realm of his 'business and professional dealings,
his love affairs – anything at all'.[52] The original members came
from Weimar: Goethe, Herder, Wieland, the officer and tutor,
Karl Ludwig von Knebel, the jurist and man of letters, Friedrich
Johann Bertuch, publisher of the *General Journal of Literature*, the
art critic, Johann Heinrich Meyer, the pharmacist, Wilhelm Buchholz, and the high-ranking government official, Christian Voigt.
Other members were the painter, Georg Kraus, the court physician, Christoph Hufeland, and the government official, von Fritsch.

During the first meeting, agreement was reached on the society's statutes and the procedure for the admittance of members,
whereby all decisions required a three-quarters majority. The
society met on the first Friday of every month between five and
eight p.m., first at the home of the mother of the duchess, later at
Goethe's house. Goethe was the first chairman. All members were
permitted to bring guests. Women, however, were rarely in attendance. The Friday Society had particularly close links with Jena.
The meetings were very informal, and they were sometimes held
in the presence of the duke and duchess. The opening lecture, for
which a maximum of thirty minutes was reserved, was followed
by a general debate. Although Goethe himself had been the driving force behind the foundation of the society and was instrumental in shaping the circle during the early days, the meetings
soon became less frequent. This situation persisted until, in 1795,
Goethe rekindled enthusiasm with his invitation to the society to
meet at his home on a weekly basis.

Goethe himself is our main source of information on the society.

He made the inaugural speech on 9 September 1791, and had high expectations of the society's activity: 'The personal experiences, thoughts and achievements of the individual shall redound to the benefit of the society. The prior assurance of the active interest of universally respected individuals in our endeavours will result in each of these endeavours being pursued with greater vigour.'[53]

Surviving records provide an informative insight into the society's first meetings: during the inaugural meeting, Buchholz demonstrated the effects of coal dust on foul water, Bode held a lecture on the tendencies of human strength, Voigt on the most recent discoveries on the West Coast of America, Goethe himself read extracts from his 'Farbenlehre' and Knebel posed the question: 'Why has Minerva apparently taken an owl as her companion.' A broad spectrum of problems was also debated during the second meeting: Buchholz continued his experiments, Goethe presented an essay on the subject of pholades, Voigt on the volatility of basalt. In addition, reports were presented on successful physical and chemical experiments which had been conducted abroad.[54] The spectrum of scientific and learned discussion embraced problems of the history of art, philology and literature in addition to the natural sciences. In contrast to other reading circles, anything which was 'entertaining and useful' was a subject for debate: the members' first priority was to increase their knowledge of those modern contemporary issues which might be of benefit to the country at large. There is nothing to indicate that the society also fulfilled a social function, possibly because the members already knew each other from elsewhere. The society was a mirror image of the intellectual horizons of a group of educated citizens of the royal seat of Weimar who had founded their own association independent of all the existing institutions of both the court and the Church.

(4)   The last of the societies of the late Enlightenment were the Leagues of Friendship, most of whose members were young men whose dream was co-existence as brothers and human beings on the basis of free self-determination. A perfect example of the Leagues of Friendship was the 'Society of Freemen' in the university town of Jena between the years 1794 and 1799. It consisted of a group of highly talented students, most of whom were followers

of the philosophy of Fichte, who at that time had just begun his career in Jena.[55]

> Imbued with the most profound love of good and truth, aware of the inadequacy of the strength of the individual in isolation and infused with the best intentions of serving the cause of humanity, we join together in unity in order to commit our combined strength to the propagation of truth and to endow the principles of truth with universal validity – truth is our sole and most noble aim.[56]

The League of Friendship met at set times each week. The management of the league's affairs and the chairmanship of its ordinary and extraordinary meetings were shared among the members on a rota basis, and, as elsewhere, all issues were settled by consensus. Unfortunately, the league's statutes are unknown, but the records of its meetings have been preserved. The league met 123 times. In general, a lecture was delivered by the chairman. This was followed by a general debate or a debate on specific topics. On occasion, other topics were proposed for debate. There then followed readings of extracts from the works of some eminent writers, including Lessing, Goethe, Friedrich Schiller, Klopstock and Blaise Pascal. Finally, there was a debate on the admission of new members. The meeting did not usually conclude on a social note, though this did occasionally happen. 'Then the society sat down to dine. Dinner over, punch was served. Freeman Krüger entertained those present with his own music to Goethe's 'Bundeslied', and the whole society joined in. Everyone was cheerful and in good spirits, and at 2 o'clock in the morning, we went our separate ways.'[57] In contrast to Goethe's society, the league debated only a limited number of subjects. 'The subject had to be related to the field of applied practical philosophy.'[58] Both politics and the practical sciences were taboo. The league debated topical social, political science, philosophical and aesthetic questions of universal relevance. The league explicitly identified with the philosophy of Fichte, who also made the occasional guest appearance.

Topics of a general nature, such as the achievements of mankind, freedom, the destiny of mankind, egoism, true enjoyment of life and the knowledge of mankind were accorded high priority. However, other topics were also debated: the decline of statehood, the obligation of the citizen to improve his inherited constitution, the civil responsibility of the scholar, the improvement of civil rights and, last but not least, the rights of women.

The members of the league came from the student elite. A candidate could only be accepted for membership if two members vouched for his 'morality' and he submitted an essay reflecting the aims of the league. At one stage, the league did contemplate a large-scale increase in membership, not least to lend it some external clout, but self-preoccupation prevented the realization of any such plans. The league had a total of thirty-four student members, mostly from Northern Germany, the Baltic states and Denmark. At times, the membership fluctuated widely, but even when a member moved away, the society endeavoured to maintain contact. In addition to the exchange of information and the pursuit of education through the medium of debate, the league also cultivated fraternity and friendship, and thus, its influence outlasted its short-lived existence. The Jena league always retained a special place in the heart of its members.

I am indebted to those times, and I shall always be indebted to those times, for my unshakable faith in the spiritual dignity of man, for my practice of setting high standards and for my firm conviction that all secular relationships are predetermined by a higher destiny. They have all been my sheet anchor and my constant companion through the wildly fluctuating fortunes of this life, through the good times and the bad.[59]

Although the league produced no philosphers or writers of any importance, it did produce a considerable number of influential scholars and government officials: Johann Friedrich Herbart, Johann Erich von Berger, Friedrich Muhrbeck, Johann Erichson, Karl Schildner and Friedrich Köppen all became professors; Johann Smidt became mayor of Bremen, Claude C. Perret Napoleon's private secretary, and Paul Wilhelm von Pomian-Pesavovius and Martin E. Reimers senior government officials in Russia.

The various groups of literary and social societies might have had much in common with the reading societies, but their exclusivity, leading to a rather limited membership, their preoccupation with general questions of philosophy and Enlightenment and their intimate social atmosphere set them apart. On the

whole, they were very much a manifestation of the 'public' societies as, with the exception of the Wednesday Society, none of
the societies discussed or debated anything which was not common knowledge. However, as exclusive societies, they were not
readily accessible, even for men of learning, and were unknown to
the general public. Nevertheless, it is a fair assumption that they
existed in large numbers and were established by the intellectual
elite throughout Germany.

POLITICAL SOCIETIES

Secret societies: the League of Illuminati

'These days, regardless of social class, there are few people whose
thirst for knowledge, adventure and good company, and whose
curiosity will not have led them to join one secret society or
another at some time'. Thus wrote Adolph Freiherr von Knigge,
one of the leading experts on the secret societies of the late
Enlightenment, in his work 'Social Intercourse', which appeared
in 1788.[60] And, indeed, secret societies blossomed to such an extent
towards the end of the eighteenth century that discovering and
documenting the traces of their multipartite existence is an almost
impossible task. Little is known about either the activities of the
secret societies or their respective individual structures, though
many of their names are well known. Some were undoubtedly
figments of the imagination with no foundation in reality, and
some were no more than eccentric fantasies. However, there were
many more, short-lived or no, which generated great excitement.[61]
Most of them had connections of one sort or another with Freemasonry, but they cannot all be counted among the supporters of
the cause of the Enlightenment. Indeed, it is almost a characteristic of the period of the late Enlightenment that anti-Enlightenment
groups also exploited the medium of independent organizations in
imitation of Freemasonry and the learned societies in order to
assert themselves more forcefully. The most famous secret society of the Enlightenment was the League of Illuminati. To
some extent, the Goldicrucians and Rosicrucians were their anti-
Enlightenment counterparts, though in the eighteenth century,
they did not assume anything like the same importance.[62] Although the League of Illuminati was short-lived – it was banned

by the authorities after only eight years and disbanded many years before the onset of the French Revolution – its history exerted a strong influence upon late eighteenth-century German society. However, the conspiracy theory propagated by the incipient forces of conservatism, according to which the Illuminati were accessories to the French Revolution, was of little relevance:[63] the Illuminati were not at all inclined towards conspiracy. Of greater significance were the first visible signs of an attempt on the part of some of the advocates of the Enlightenment to use the League of Illuminati as a means of politicizing the Enlightenment, with the ultimate objective of abolishing absolutism.

The League of Illuminati was founded in 1776 in the university town of Ingolstadt by the twenty-eight year old Professor of Church Law and Practical Philosophy, Adam Weishaupt (1748–1830). The origin of the anti-Jesuitism which exercised so powerful an influence over both Weishaupt and the League of Illuminati was to be found in Weishaupt's social background, which was typical of Catholic supporters of the Enlightenment. However, anti-Jesuitism did not prevent the League of Illuminati from adopting many of the structural aspects of their foe.[64] Weishaupt himself was an ambitious scholar of unusual unworldliness who, in contrast to many of the other leading figures of the League of Illuminati, lived in modest circumstances and acquired the majority of his knowledge from books. He devoted all his efforts towards the creation of a secret organization, which would provide him with a platform for exerting power and influence. However, he was not unduly renowned in Ingolstadt for his originality, although his open support for radical French Enlightenment was exceptional in the Germany of the 1770s and 1780s.

Weishaupt had no definite plan for the creation of the League of Illuminati. It was rather a case of developing the league during the recruitment of the first batch of members, not least in order to tailor the organization to suit contemporary needs and requirements. Certain principles at the core of the early statutes and directives were to remain of central importance: the hierarchical structure of the league, the emphasis on secrecy, the equality of the membership and protection against external influences. Weishaupt regarded these principles as the only possible route towards the attainment of perfection. Weishaupt recruited the first members from among those of his students to whom he was particularly close. However, it was not until he became a member of a masonic lodge in Munich and established contacts and connections among some of the regional capital's influential government officials, academics and secular priests, including a large number of aristocrats, that his organization made any really significant advances. From the end of 1778 until the middle of 1779, the number of members increased from 29 to 45. Munich apart, there was also a high degree of interest in the league in the religious centres of Eichstätt and Freising, which were early Illuminati bastions.[65]

The recruitment of men of influence in Munich not only secured that city the status of the league's headquarters, it also had other important consequences. A permanent structure and binding statutes and directives had long been lacking, and it now became imperative to remedy these deficiencies as soon as possible. This led to the first serious disagreements between Weishaupt and the incipient Munich leadership. Whereas Weishaupt envisaged a hierarchical, ultimately monarchical, society organized along strict lines, Munich, which was soon no longer prepared to play second fiddle to Weishaupt, advocated the idea of a more mature, aristocratic structure. In other words: Munich demanded leadership participation and initiation into the secret of the league's ultimate objectives. In 1779, as a form of compromise, the leading forces in Munich created a so-called 'Areopagus', the 'highest collegiate of the league', which actively participated in the consolidation of the league and the development of its statutes.[66]

In 1781, the 'General Statutes of the League' were inaugurated.[67] This document, like those which followed, unmistakably bore Weishaupt's stamp. After gaining a strong foothold in Munich between the years 1779 and 1781, the league rapidly began to gain ground, initially throughout the whole of Bavaria. The change of seat of government, that is, the move of the electoral prince, Karl Theodor, from Mannheim to Munich, worked as equally to the league's advantage as the outside contacts and connections of the Munich Illuminati. Masonic lodges proved to be ideal meeting places, particularly the lodge of 'St Theodor zum guten Rat' in Munich, which was soon under complete Illuminati control.

However, the League of Illuminati did not truly blossom until the conversion of the journalist and North German champion of the Enlightenment, Adolph Freiherr von Knigge (1742–90), to the cause, in which he discovered a suitable arena for his activities.[68] Von Knigge united the previously rather heterogeneous league on the basis of Weisheit's designs and established the league's initial links with Northern and Western Germany, and thus, he is regarded as the league's second founding father. Von Knigge was the complete opposite of Weishaupt: a sophisticated man of democratic principles, he had grown up in the liberal climate of British Hanover and was very well acquainted with contemporary German life, from both the literary and social points of view. He was a prolific writer of novels, moral essays, philosophical treatises, political tracts and utopian dreams. As a result of his open support for the French Revolution and his links with German Jacobins, he was considered as belonging to the more radical wing of the German champions of the Enlightenment, and was one of the early victims of the campaign of vilification waged by the incipient forces of German conservatism. Von Knigge possessed unrivalled knowledge of the secret societies of his day, and maintained an ambivalent attitude towards Freemasonry. Weishaupt completely washed his hands of Freemasonry, and only availed himself of masonic facilities in order ultimately to undermine and convert the movement to the Illuminati cause. Von Knigge, however, especially following the collapse of the doctrine of Strict Observance at the Convention of Wilhelmsbad in 1782, endeavoured to use the League of Illuminati as a vehicle for the regeneration of Freemasonry.[69] After becoming acquainted with the league's actual condition during his visit to Munich, his every directive urgently called for the completion of the hierarchical structure. He assumed responsibility for the deadline himself, though he did not interfere with the basic concept of Weishaupt's principles. Cooperation with the Munich Areopagus blossomed, though this was accompanied by a proliferation of disagreements with Weishaupt. Von Knigge was as unwilling as Munich to subordinate himself to Weishaupt.

Von Knigge was not only instrumental in finalizing the league's structure – the most important stages of which, however, were not completed until the league was in the process of disbandment – but also in extending the league's influence into Northern and Western Germany. He met with great success, though he did not apply strict standards. The Catholic Rhineland, Mainz and Bonn were particularly fruitful areas for the League of Illuminati, and important centres were also established in Neuwied, Wetzlar and Aachen. In Northern Germany, by way of contrast, the recruitment campaign focused almost exclusively on individual masons, rather than on whole lodges.[70]

Von Knigge's recruitment campaign resulted in a consistent

growth in the number of aristocratic members joining the league. The first signs of this development had already been evident in Munich: Count Costanzo and Count Savioli were influential figures in the Bavarian capital, and in 1780, the young Count Maximilian Joseph von Montgelas, who later became Bavarian Minister of State, also joined the ranks of the Illuminati.[71] In Northern Germany, even princes joined the league: Duke Ernst von Sachsen-Gotha, who later afforded sanctuary to Weishaupt, Landgrave Karl von Hessen-Kassel, who was an active Freemason, and Duke Ferdinand von Braunschweig. There were also Count Stolberg-Rossla from Neuwied, who became national leader of the League of Illuminati following von Knigge's departure, and Karl Theodor von Dalberg, who later became *primus inter pares* of the ruling princes. Equally as revealing as this increase in aristocratic membership is the fact that, although von Knigge's campaign did not attract the literary intelligentsia to the league, a great many eminent literary figures were committed sympathizers, at least for a short time. Among them were the philosopher, Friedrich Heinrich Jacobi, the journalist, Friedrich Nicolai, Anton Dorsch, who later joined the Jacobins, and the pedagogue, Heinrich Pestalozzi. The recruitment campaign in Austria was also a success; the reign of Joseph II had created the belief among many of the Illuminati that Austria might provide a particularly happy hunting ground for the activities of the league.[72] The Austrian connections became especially active when the Chancellor of Bohemia, Count Kollowrat, was admitted to the league in 1782 while passing through Munich. The Viennese lodge, 'Zur wahren Eintracht' is regarded as the centre of the League of Illuminati in the Habsburg Empire. All contacts from Austria to Northern and Western Germany were maintained through Freemasonry to a much more marked extent than was the case in Munich and the rest of Bavaria. Von Knigge found willing accomplices in the junior judge at the Imperial supreme court, Franz von Ditfurth of Wetzlar, the founder of the Eclectic League of Freemasons, and the Viennese Hofrat, Christian Bode.

The League of Illuminati attained the height of its influence around the year 1783: a reasonable assumption is that it had no more than a total of 600 members, even including those whose interest was only of a short duration. The league made most headway among middle-class and aristocratic government officials, journalists, professors and clergymen; merchants and artisans were almost completely absent, but the aristocracy was well represented. The membership structure of the league was as follows:[73]

Known by name: 454 members (including 162 aristocrats)

Court and administrative officials	103
Clergymen/theologians	64
Officers	51
Merchants	31
Professors	25
Physicians/apothecaries	12
Musicians	7
Urban physicians	5
Councillors	3
Judges	3
Writers	3
Envoys	3
Innkeepers	2
Book dealers	2
Governors	2
Tutors	2
Archivists	2
Vice-chancellors	2
Librarians	2
Court tutors	2
Profession unknown	128

Following the editorial activity of von Knigge during these years, ideologically, the League of Illuminati, despite its mounting difficulties at every turn, especially in Munich, revealed itself to be remarkably determined to resolve internal conflicts, even though many of its regulations were simply ignored: in addition to the unresolvable conflict between the league's founder and the Munich Areopagus – Weishaupt's main charges against Munich were imprudence and fanaticism, while Munich accused him of authoritarian posturing and inflexibility in the face of change – there were also repeated clashes between Weishaupt and von Knigge, whom Weishaupt distrusted and whose authoritarian behaviour caused him extreme annoyance. As a result, von Knigge soon resigned, and at the end of 1783 he left the league altogether, though he never denied his erstwhile commitment to the cause or rejected the league's basic philosophies. But von

Knigge's departure was not an isolated case: it heralded a rapid decline. The league as such had ceased to exist even before the official ban of 1785. The documents of the League of Illuminati, confiscated and published by the electoral prince of Bavaria, were proof to the sceptics and the foes of the Enlightenment of the latent danger to the state posed by the radical wing of the Enlightenment as represented by the League of Illuminati. The advocates of the Enlightenment, on the other hand, viewed the state's action against the League of Illuminati as a campaign against the Enlightenment itself. For their part, many of the Illuminati themselves were astounded at the plans nurtured by Weishaupt, plans of which they had had no inkling. However, the history of the demise of the League of Illuminati belongs more to the history of the conspiracy theory of the conservative reaction than it does to the history of the organization of the middle-class champions of the Enlightenment.[74]

The aims of the League of Illuminati are stated in the 'General Statutes of the League' of 1781, which were readily accessible to most Illuminati:

> All the efforts of the league are directed towards the arousal of a passionate interest in the improvement of moral character; the propagation of a humane and socially acceptable philosophy of life; thwarting malicious intent; the protection of troubled and unhappy virtue from injustice; the support of the worthy and the dissemination of beneficial truths which are mostly concealed from general consciousness.[75]

> The sole intention of the league is education, not by declamatory means, but by favouring and rewarding virtue. The order of the day is to put an end to the machinations of the purveyors of injustice, to control them without dominating them. In a word, universal moral standards should be introduced, a form of government which shall spread throughout the world without losing touch with the people, a form of government in whose footsteps all other forms of government shall follow, in which all things shall be possible except neglect of the ultimate goal of contributing to the triumph of good over evil.

> A more powerful weapon than didacticism will be necessary to attract the material world to the quality of virtue. Passions cannot be extinguished. What is required is the knowledge of how passions might be exploited for the cause of righteousness. It must be revealed to the ambitious that the true nature of the respect that

they seek is to be found in virtue and can most readily be attained through the practice of virtue: to the ungenerous that those who crave the possession of everything in truth possess nothing; the hedonists that overindulgence will spoil their enjoyment. In short, it must be revealed that each and every ambition born of pure heart can be fulfilled within the framework of virtue, and that the league is the provider of the means of fulfilment.

Therefore, we must all strike the same chord, stick together, have but one objective in our sights and offer each other support and encouragement in order that the Word should spread throughout the world. The order of the day is to besiege the powerful on this earth, to assemble a legion of warriors who shall never tire of exploiting all ways and means of serving the noble cause, of serving the good of mankind, of converting the whole country: then force shall be superfluous. The day shall soon come when the rulers of the world open their eyes and recognize that the practice of virtue shall bring them its just rewards, the practice of injustice its just deserts. The pure of heart shall soon triumph over the wicked who are unsurping the role of masters, and all those who oppose them shall meet a sorry end ... It is the first duty of each and every constitution to ensure that honourable men are at the helm, to reward merit, to honour virtue. If the league can achieve this end through word of mouth, through inspiring the hearts and minds of men; if, within the shelter of its walls, the league prepares the most loyal, the best, the most reliable of men to serve the state; if the league is at pains to promote such men, to reward their diligence, then the league shall fulfil all the obligations incumbent upon the most loyal of subjects, and at the same time, the purpose of those who joined forces to form a social bond. (General insight into the whole system of the Order, 1782).[76]

Weishaupt had devoted a great deal of time and effort to drafting the league's platform. He was assisted by the Munich Areopagus, and subsequently by von Knigge in particular. From the very beginning, Weishaupt's conceptions were characterized by three fundamental premises, which distinguished him from all his contemporary presagers: in the first place, he was no longer of the opinion that the Enlightenment, once proclaimed, would be able to rely upon the power of language and propaganda alone to consolidate its position. For Weishaupt, the self-realization of virtue dashes against the rock of real benevolent absolutism: the Enlightenment can only triumph if it shelters under the protective cloak of secrecy and offers the carrot of personal gain. Secondly, in

order to pave the way for the eventual triumph of the Enlightenment, Weishaupt did not consider it necessary for everyone to join
the ranks of the Illuminati, not even all those who satisfied the
essential requirements and were thus potential candidates. Weishaupt did not wish his league to become an open house. His only
objective was to raise the intellectual *niveau* among a selected elite,
those who were in a position to subvert existing institutions and
promote the spirit of the Enlightenment at all levels, so that all
vestiges of repression and superstition might be banished and man
thus free to determine his own destiny without outside interference. From this standpoint, the League of Illuminati exercises a
didactic and a political function, but never replaces civilized society. Lastly, Weishaupt considered that only secret societies were
in a position to realize the moral objective of the Enlightenment,
the triumph over power and ignorance, because, according to
Weishaupt, they did not have their origins in any human plan.
Rather, they were innate to human nature, whose ambition to
create a world based upon the tenets of reason and morality, of
freedom and justice, was in grave danger of being thwarted by the
forces of evil. Therefore, secrecy was essential to the realization of
a moral society. In his 'Address to the New Illuminatos Dirigentes'
in 1782, Weishaupt revealed the historical and philosophical
foundations of his concept.[77] Despite the unreserved and universal
acclaim with which this was received by the leadership, the question concerning exactly what kind of society should be established
remained unresolved, and this point proved to be a contentious
issue. This was the equivalent of the more general question concerning which form of constitution would do justice to the tenets
of reason. This was also a contentious issue; a democratic model
was out of the question, but the elite was still faced with the
choice between a monarchy and an aristocracy.

Initially, the League of Illuminati, following the example of the
radical wing of the Enlightenment, set itself the task of creating an
elite band of supporters ignorant of its true objectives. The lifeblood of the plan was the conflict between autodidacticism (the
independent acquisition of all sources of knowledge, the study of
contemporary writings and the processes of self-observation and
the observation of the outside world) and absolute subordination
to a leader. The purpose of this autodidactic process, which was
subject to the control of the leader, was the preservation of in-
dividuality and the homogeneity of the order. The ideal Illumi-

natus was a self-sufficient advocate of the Enlightenment who was a submissive tool in the hands of the league. The league also strove to collate all available knowledge, both academic and practical and scientific and political, in order to be able to place the whole gamut of human learning at the disposal of the Enlightenment.[78] Thus, the League of Illuminati was both a didactic establishment and a learned society. The objective proved unattainable, but it was still one of the league's original fundamental aims.

Finally, it was also the objective of the League of Illuminati to secure public victory for morality. In other words, in addition to the creation of an exclusive learned and fraternal society, the league cherished ambitions of wider external influence. To this end, it was the deliberate intention of the league that existing societies should be systematically undermined and all important religious, governmental and, not least, didactic institutions should be infiltrated by Illuminati sympathizers in order that they might operate in the best interests of reason. The plan was sufficiently audacious to include surrounding the ruling princes with a network of Illuminati sympathizers so that they would be left with no alternative but to govern in the spirit of Illuminism. In Weishaupt's opinion, this was the only way of realizing the dream of the kingdom of reason, in which equality before the law, freedom of thought and freedom from violence would reign supreme, while avoiding turbulent change and the abolition of feudal and absolutist institutions.[79]

Similar to Freemasonry, only with a different objective in mind, this general programme corresponded to a three-tier structure which, although subject to fluctuating plans and often beyond realization, nevertheless reflected the many and varied ambitions of the league. The young Illuminati were educated in the novitiate, the 'League's nursery', each under the individual supervision of a leader. They were taught to lead a moral life, to educate themselves, to read a particular canon of books, view everything in a critical light and write short tracts. In order to rise through the ranks and make steady progress towards the league's fount of wisdom, it was essential to display both absolute obedience to the leader and discretion.[80] The middle tier, the 'minerval' tier, was the 'league's foundation', a type of learned society, meeting in lodges and providing 'minervals' with all the help they required. 'These are places of study, of personalities past and present, of antiquity, of the art of observation, of tracts and of prices. Basically, I turn them into spies, of each other and of everyone else.'[81] Each month, fresh objectives were set. The study of the sciences and the works of important writers of the ancient world, humanism and the Enlightenment was recommended. The third and final tier was comprised of the arcana, the foundations upon which the whole edifice stood, into whose ranks only the most able were admitted. Within this tier, the arcana were afforded a 'complete insight into the politics and maxims of the league. This is the body which plans our campaigns against the enemies of reason and humanity and decides upon the procedure for initiating the membership into these plans, upon the members to whom these plans should be entrusted'.[82] The creation of the league's own moral code, theories of education and political science and religion was intended as the ultimate perfection of the system. Later, the hierarchical system was strengthened even further by the introduction of a masonic grade. However, in general, the three-tier system remained intact. The upper grades were never realized, and thus, the 'minerval' tier exercised the decisive influence. The secrets of the league were to be revealed stage by stage. The leadership believed that this would provide them with the best possible protection against those of inferior calibre, while at the same time safeguarding the development of an elite guard who would one day implement the policies of the Enlightenment on the league's behalf. There were only limited channels of communication between the novices and the 'minervals'. The creation of a spirit of solidarity played second fiddle to the complete realization, the complete accomplishment of the plans and objectives of the leadership.

Left to Weishaupt, the League of Illuminati would have been a strictly hierarchical, even monarchical, organization – a sort of mirror image of the arcane practices of absolutism – in which all channels of information converge at the centre. The enthusiasm of the individual was fired by a system of gradual promotion through the ranks, leading ultimately to the revelation of the league's secrets, and by the furtherance of his career in the 'middle-class' world outside. Ultimately, the differences of opinion between Weishaupt and the Areopagus in Munich, that is, von Knigge, concerned the structure of the leadership rather than the structure of the league. Von Knigge also favoured a system of the gradual acquisition of knowledge and the exclusion of any elements uncommitted to the Enlightenment. In this respect, there was a marked difference between the League of Illuminati and both public societies and masonic lodges: the public societies and the lodges assured all members of equal status or, at least, they did not resort to any such instrumentalism.

Details of many Illuminati plans have survived, and thus there is much more information available concerning the League's objectives and projects than the concrete form that Illuminati Enlightenment might have assumed. It is known that the upper tiers never materialized, and it is also certain that 'life' in the lower tiers did not conform to the ideal. Weishaupt complained vociferously.[83] The League did not possess its own organizational model: its classic breeding ground was the network of masonic lodges, which were gradually undermined until they were completely under Illuminati control and then converted into 'minerval' churches. Thus, it can be assumed that the lodges in Ingolstadt, Munich, Freising, Eichstätt and Burghausen, and subsequently in Vienna, Mainz, Bonn, Neuwied and Aachen, were almost completely in Illuminati hands.[84] However, the actual Illuminati infiltrators always remained in the background. Records of lodge meetings reveal that rituals were reduced to a minimum, which had always been one of Weishaupt's objectives,[85] but otherwise, there is no evidence that the practices of these lodges differed to any great extent from the practices of non-Illuminati lodges. Once the meeting had formally been declared open, new members were admitted and existing members promoted. Official announcements were made, guests welcomed, passages read from the works of antiquity, and an address held concerning masonic issues. A collection for the poor concluded the official part of the meeting.[86] This was often followed by an unofficial, fraternal, part and a formal dinner. Illuminati ideas were never publicly discussed. It was the ultimate objective of the League of Illuminati to enlarge the network of Illuminati centres in both established and newly founded lodges. One extant expansion plan reveals that the territory covered by the Reich was subdivided into provinces, prefectures and districts. Count von Neuwied was earmarked to assume the national leadership.[87] In contrast to the established system of Freemasonry, the new lodges were not intended to be autonomous bodies. They were to be controlled by the leadership of the league in order to ensure a unified policy. Thus, the activity of the lodge was of less importance than the activity of the individual. As a consequence, it was not always possible for the member to differentiate between his activity on behalf of the league and his professional activity, and he was subject to the control and instructions of the leadership. This ultimately reduced masonic meetings to the status of an instrument of verification of, and control over, masonic activities.

In line with the league's strategy of creating an educated elite for the purpose of placing the religious, didactic and governmental institutions in the service of the Enlightenment, only educated men from the sphere of public service were considered for membership. This resulted in the almost complete exclusion of artisans and merchants.[88] Indeed, their admittance was never even considered. On the other hand, there was disagreement as to the worth of aristocratic members. Weishaupt himself was vehemently opposed to the presence of aristocrats in the leadership, even though he was well aware of the prestige and protection a prince could afford. In contrast, neither the Munich Areopagus nor von Knigge had any qualms whatsoever on this issue. On the contrary, they regarded the number of aristocratic members as a direct reflection of the extent of their influence. Thus, ultimately, there was a very strong aristocratic presence in the league. The most active members in Munich were the two counts, Count Costanzo and Count Savioli-Corbelli, and both Counts Seinsheim and Törring were proud of their membership status. There was not only a strong aristocratic presence in Munich. According to those membership records which have survived, the league's membership structure was not radically different from that of other societies. It was mainly comprised of government officials, professors and clergymen, that is, the representatives of the intellectual elite. It is remarkable that the aristocratic members were not troubled by the league's middle-class didacticism. It was mainly the new functional elite of the territorial state who recognized in the League of Illuminati the fulfilment of a programme which mirrored their own ambitions, both from the standpoint of the Enlightenment and from a professional standpoint.[89]

This standpoint also explains the league's attitude towards public order and politics. The league's strategy was to surround the absolutist prince with Illuminati sympathizers to such an extent that he had no alternative but to govern in accordance with their concepts. In other words, the objective was to occupy the state from within, and the ultimate goal the abolition of government altogether. However, this did not mean that the league aspired to the overthrow of the political system. On the contrary, the league's objective was the 'perfection' of benevolent absolutism, the transformation of the despotic state into one based on the rule of law. This was more than simply wishful thinking: despite the league's often amateurish political strategy, attempts were actually undertaken to infiltrate certain institutions. The extent of the influence exercised by the Munich Illuminati on the Ecclesiastical Council and the Censorship Council, and in the department of literature of the Academy of Science is well documented, even though no change of policy was achieved in any of these institutions. This strategy did not present a political threat. The strategy of infiltration was not unusual: other groups, such as the Rosicrucians, were using the same method in an attempt to gain a degree of social influence.

The League of Illuminati, despite the presence of many prominent members within its ranks, was unable to exercise any effective public influence. However, the very notion of using a secret society of advocates of the Enlightenment as a means of creating an internal didactic institution and exerting external political influence was remarkable *per se*. That this should result in a double contradiction is not surprising. The league provided assurances that, on the one hand, religion and politics and, on the other, the state and the Church, would remain inviolable. At the same time, the league attempted to ensure that the process of development within the framework of benevolent absolutism proceeded in the spirit of the Enlightenment. Similarly, while it adopted a didactic methodology based upon critical observation as a means of transforming the Illuminati into independent-minded members of society, the league pursued this policy only insofar as it suited the plans of the leadership. For the Illuminati, individualism and instrumentalism were as much part and parcel of the whole as independence of mind and the veil of secrecy. It is not surprising that upon publication of the league's plans and documents, these contradictory notions were greeted with incredulity and criticism by advocates of the Enlightenment and non-Illuminati alike.[90]

The League of Illuminati was not a self-contained system and it did not pose a conspiratorial threat to the state. On the other hand, neither can the league be branded socio-culturally ineffective and unimportant simply because of its failure to achieve its major objective. One reason why the league was able to recruit a considerable number of members in a very short space of time – members who were motivated to join neither by curiosity nor boredom – was probably the fact that, in general, secret societies along the lines of the Freemasons were regarded as an important forum of the Enlightenment, offering the possibility of exerting effective influence under the securest of conditions. A further reason was the fact that the League of Illuminati offered much greater didactic potential than any other institution of its time, even for younger members. From both the autodidactic and the didactic standpoints, this was an extremely attractive proposition. This is the only possible explanation for the fact that men such as Pestalozzi, Christian Gotthilf Salzmann, Jacobi and Herder could ever have taken to the ideas of the Illuminati at all. No former Illuminatus ever denied his membership of the league. Indeed, testimonies have survived in which many former members confess that they found their erstwhile membership extremely stimulating and look back upon it with gratitude. The Jacobin, Anton Dorsch, from Mainz, wrote in 1791: 'The League of Illuminati, which has the education of numerous young men to its credit, included amongst its ranks the most noble men in Germany.'[91] Ritter von Lang stressed the fact that:

> The 'Obervoigt' was an Illuminatus, and he made every effort to lick me into shape during my days as a league apprentice, or novice. I willingly submitted to this treatment because I was attracted by the way the young men were encouraged to exercise self-criticism and rise above mediocrity. In my experience, all aspects of the league very much resembled a Socratic or Platonist school.[92]

The people's society: the Society of the Friends of Freedom and Equality in Mainz

At the end of the century, another short-lived societal form appeared on the German scene. The secret political societies attempted to gain influence through the exposure of a social elite to the process of Enlightenment, while retaining the contemporary political system. Although this new form of society was built on the experiences of previous secret societies, it was a new phenomenon with political aspirations far in excess of those of the League of Illuminati. This new form of society was the people's society, the so-called Jacobin club, and it went under several different names: the 'Society of the Friends of Freedom and Equality', as in Mainz, the 'Patriotic Society of Universal Education and Enlightenment', as in Cologne, or the 'Society of the Friends of the Constitution', as in Landau. These were societies of radical political Enlightenment. They demanded, and actively campaigned for, the amendment of the political constitutions of the day.[93]

Two conditions were responsible for the development of the Jacobin clubs between the years 1792 and 1795/7: firstly, the existence of a radical wing of the Enlightenment, that is to say, radical to the extent that this wing debated and propagated a reasoned legal system, democracy, equality and the development of the political self, albeit from multifarious standpoints. Many of the speeches at the Mainz club are classic products of the radical Enlightenment. Secondly, the Jacobin clubs were exposed to the conditions and expansive force of the French Revolution. Without the French conquest and occupation of the territories on the left bank of the Rhine, and without the propaganda efforts of the French occupation forces, the Jacobin clubs would never have evolved. They were guaranteed both French protection and active French support.[94] An important point is the fact that German Jacobinism adopted both the political and ideological experiences and ideas of the French Revolution and the programmes and objectives of the German Enlightenment.

There is a further important point: from the point of view of their mission, their organizational structure and their support, the Jacobin clubs were unique. However, the Jacobin clubs not only maintained close links with the reading societies and the League of Illuminati, at least to the extent that the Jacobin elite in Mainz were members of both these associations: the Mainz reading society and the Illuminati lodge actually facilitated the transition to Jacobinism, particularly for the champions of the Enlightenment in Mainz.[95] On the other hand, it should not be overlooked that the Jacobin club adopted elements from other societies of the Enlightenment: the notion of a medium of communication untrammelled by the constraints of absolutism long propagated by the learned academies, the notion of friendship and fraternity propagated by the Freemasons and the notion of a public patriotic consciousness propagated by the patriotic societies were also common to the Jacobin club, albeit with a different social dimension. Thus, Mainz Jacobinism was not the product of 'foreign domination': it was supported by political men steeped in experience, acquired to some extent through literary and political debate in other societies, and refined through a process of the critical analysis of benevolent absolutism.

The objective of the Association of the Friends of the Constitution was, according to the Mainz Jacobin and professor of philosophy, Anton Dorsch, 'to assist the craven people back onto their feet, to familiarize them with the eternal rights of men and citizens, and to disseminate the sacred principles of freedom and equality throughout the land'. It was his 'dearest wish' that 'the inhabitants of this city and this region should, as is right and proper, attend the meetings of this patriotic society and enlighten themselves as to their true interests, then going forth and acting in accordance with these interests with courage and resolution'.[96] Thus, the central issues of German Jacobinism concerned morality and the Enlightenment, the familiarization of the population with the notions of the Enlightenment and assisting them to obtain their rights. Hence, the Jacobin clubs did not directly encroach upon the interests of the state anymore than did the patriotic and public-spirited societies: their objective was simply the creation of the mental pre-conditions for the creation of a society of the middle class. Georg Christoph Wedekind, also a member of the Jacobin club in Mainz and a professor of medicine, places the Jacobin club midway between actual authority and the family:

> Places where the public weal, politics, the legal system and morals, etc. can be discussed are essential: places where it is possible for someone to agree with something today only to reject it tomorrow without incurring any disadvantage, places where people can reach a common consensus, thus preparing the way for legislation. These places are the Jacobin clubs.[97]

Following the example of the French Jacobin clubs, the society possessed a distinctly democratic organizational structure. At the head stood a president, elected on a monthly basis, whose responsibility was to ensure that 'order' reigned. He possessed no privileges. On the contrary, he was subject to 'the will of the whole society'. This was also true of the vice-president. In addition, secretaries were elected. As the scope of the tasks increased, committees appeared alongside the general 'public meetings'. These committees had the task of addressing certain issues; thus, there was an economic committee, a charitable committee, a watchdog committee, a correspondence committee and a didactic committee. The nucleus of the club's activities was the general meeting, which in Mainz during the early days was held almost every evening. Both the club members and the population of Mainz were welcome. During the short lifetime of the Mainz Jacobin club, between October 1792 and March 1793, 103 meetings were held, first at the castle and then in the Comedy House. The records which have survived provide a revealing insight into the atmosphere of the meetings, the club's self-appointed tasks and the arguments and debates among the membership. The scope of the tasks was comprehensive indeed. In the main, particularly during the early days, a prominent club member delivered a speech. This was followed by the reading and debate of every conceivable kind of petition. A selection of quotations reporting the successes of the French Revolution was then read from among the club's voluminous correspondence. The Mainz Jacobin club had concluded pacts of friendship with numerous constitutional circles, and this created a unique communications network. An important topic of debate was the club statutes, which had originally been adopted from Strasbourg.[98] Due to its short lifetime, the club never finalized its own set of rules and regulations. Herein lies one of the reasons why the club presented a disunited front and was never able to develop a definite plan of campaign. Initially, the public at large showed considerable interest in the club, but this soon ebbed away.

The implement which fate wields in the execution of its judgements is often a simple tool without any special value or inherent worth. If we strip the Mainz Jacobins of the glamorous façade bestowed upon them by the brilliantly illuminated assembly hall, and if we remove from their midst the noteworthy merits of those few upright and enlightened men at its core, then what is left is a confused mass which is encumbered with all the weaknesses generated by its precipitate emergence and which falls far short of living up to the noble ideal of the educated and well-bred man. Several capable professors of jurisprudence, whose impartiality has been honoured with the Regent's disfavour and repression, several respected merchants and decent citizens whose honesty is universally recognized, some professors of the university sponsored and favoured by the electoral prince and, last but not least, some astute, virtuous priests, professionally trained and true teachers of men, have sided with these local friends of the people, and they would bestow honour upon any society they chose to enter. A bunch of loutish students and other somewhat ill-mannered young men, together with some people of rather dubious repute, are the only recruits which have so far been admitted, willy-nilly, with no form of prior scrutiny, partly to generate a rapid increase in the membership numbers, and partly as a means of invoking the principle of equality to the utmost. The noble cause of freedom will soon reap more in the way of harm from the youthful smugness and arrogance of the one, and the selfishness and dubious intentions of the other, than it will gain in the way of recognition from the wisdom and passions of the respectable among its ranks. Up to now, the fire of the republican agitators has only inflamed an enthusiasm for the cause itself among the spectators, who flock in their thousands to heap the most deafening, most thunderous applause upon this first manifestation of innate, inalienable human rights. There are signs which give grave cause for concern about the suitability of this society's activities. It will, after all, depend solely upon the purity of its patriotism, and upon its usefulness, whether or not this passionate, whole-hearted approval of the population will, with the passing of time, develop into veneration and faith, or into some other passion of a directly opposite nature. (Georg Forster's 'Depiction of the Revolution in Mainz', 1793.)[99]

The society set itself three main tasks: firstly, to explain to the members who attended its meetings the aims of the French Revolution, that is to say, to create the mental pre-conditions for the realization of a middle-class democracy on the basis of liberty, equality and fraternity through the abolition of the old system of privilege and the adoption of the French constitution. Most of the society's speeches were devoted to this theme.[100] In the second place, the society felt responsible for the political Enlightenment of the illiterate urban and rural populations. Speakers were sent out into the countryside, the speeches were published and symbolic acts, such as the planting of liberty trees, were afforded support. The planting of the liberty tree in Mainz was one of the most important acts of the 'Society of the Friends of Liberty and Equality'.[101] Lastly, the society attempted to act as mediator between the military administration and the population, conveying messages of complaint to the French, and making every effort to contribute towards the improvement of the material and cultural environment.[102]

To this extent, the Jacobin club was by no means a 'management committee of radical change'.[103] It attempted to use only the means at its disposal, usually those of instruction, to disseminate the principles of the Enlightenment both within and without, and to mobilize the population. The leaders of the club did not play at politics. They acted in the capacity of champions of the Enlightenment, without, it should be said, any elitist pretensions, and based their hopes solely upon the changing power of reason. The Mainz club undoubtedly possessed a learned and intellectual habitus. This is ascribable both to the intrinsic nature of associations of the Enlightenment, for which very reason the Jacobin club ranks alongside all the other constitutional societies as a society of the Enlightenment, from Landau to Aachen, and to the club's membership structure and leadership.[104]

It had been proclaimed, and so it was in practice, that membership of the Jacobin club was open to every German to 'whom the fortune of the Fatherland and that of enslaved and despairing mankind is a sacred cause'.[105] Every member swore a public and solemn oath 'to live in freedom or die'. All the members were expected to participate in the public meetings and actively to support the society's aims. Few people responded to the first appeal, not even Forster, who only became a member late in the day. But then the numbers mushroomed, only to drop off again. Considering that the club existed for only 150 days, for a city the size of Mainz with a population centred very much on the court, its final membership total of some 492 was very impressive in comparison with that of other societies. Although the club refused admittance to young people and, especially, women, no other social groups were excluded. In terms of numbers, artisans, tradesmen and merchants were the backbone of the Jacobin movement, not government officials or professors.

Although the Jacobin club was thus much more representative of the city's overall social structure than of the upper classes alone, the intellectuals among the membership were still an influential force. They were not only frequently in evidence as orators and argufiers (of particular importance in this respect was Georg Wedekind, a professor of medicine): they also counted the office of president among their exclusive possessions. In addition to Wedekind, Dorsch, the well-known writer and university librarian, Georg A. Forster, the mathematics professor, Matthias Metternich and the Strasbourg journalist, Friedrich Cotta, were

Table 5.1 The membership structure of the Jacobin clubs*

	Mainz 1792			Speyer 1798		Koblenz 1798			Cologne 1798		
	Total	A in % Aristocrats	B in % Middle class	Total	A and B in % Aristocrats and Middle class	Total	A in % Aristocrats	B in % Middle class	Total	A in % Aristocrats	B in % Middle class
Clerics	14	3.0	3.3	1	2.3	4	1.7	1.8	1	0.5	0.6
Jurists	35	7.4	8.3	3	6.9	42	17.4	19.1	17	8.3	10.8
Free professions (professions teachers, physicians, artists writers)	81	17.0	19.2	3	6.9	20	8.3	9.1	7	3.4	4.6
Merchants	11	2.3	2.6	6	13.7	4	1.7	1.8	21	10.3	13.4
Traders, bookdealers, innkeepers	62	13.0	14.6	6	13.7	41	17.0	18.6	26	12.8	16.7
Artisans	170	35.8	40.0	15	34.1	78	32.4	35.5	60	29.5	38.7
Public officials (policemen, postal service officials, court ushers) and officers	23	4.8	5.2	2	4.5	28	11.7	12.7	17	8.3	10.8
Peasants	2	0.4	0.5	5	11.4	–	–	–	–	–	–
Foreign nationals (French)	26	5.5	6.2	2	4.5	3	1.2	1.4	6	2.9	3.8
Profession unknown	51	10.8	–	1	2.3	21	8.8	–	48	23.6	–
Total	475			44		241			203		

	Clerics	Jurists	Professors	Merchants	Traders	Artisans	Public officials	Peasants	Foreign national
Mainz 1792	3.3	8.3	19.2	2.6	14.6	40.0	5.2	0.5	6.2
Speyer 1798	2.3	6.9	6.9	13.7	13.7	34.1	4.5	11.4	4.5
Koblenz 1798	1.8	19.1	9.1	1.8	18.6	35.5	12.7	–	1.4
Cologne 1798	0.6	10.8	4.6	13.4	16.7	38.7	10.8	–	3.8

*Column A shows the percentage distribution using the key 'total membership number = 100'. Column B shows the percentage distribution using the key 'number of members whose professions are known = 100'.

Source: Kuhn, *Jakobiner im Rheinland*, p. 185.

all temporarily president of the Jacobin club at one time or an-other.[106]

The public inauguration of the club was one of the two most decisive factors in its history. The other was its radical objective of democratic Enlightenment. The reform of the existing system, a process of gradual change, and the realization of a purely spiritual and intellectual self-determination in a state of isolation were now no longer at stake. The issue now was the abolition of the feudal system and the establishment of a constitution based upon the tenets of reason and the principle of political self-determination. Liberty and equality were to be guaranteed to the whole popu-lation, as citizens of an enlightened society in whom all authority was invested. Thus, these patriots and champions of the Enlighten-ment campaigned for a democratic system which guaranteed both freedom of conscience and economic freedom, protected private property, imposed a universal obligation of labour and practised the principle of equality before the law. Even so, the society was anything but a political party; it was more akin to a 'preliminary parliament'. The Jacobin club aspired to nothing more than the status of a forum for 'mutual instruction and Enlightenment on the inalienable rights of man', and thus, it was a typical society of the Enlightenment. It has been described as a place 'where the spirit of solidarity is fashioned and consensus reigns, and thus, where the way is smoothed for the acceptance of the rule of law'. In other words, a place where, through the process of the Enlight-enment of the people, the ground is prepared for the establish-ment of a civil constitution which also 'guarantees the (tangible) perfection of man'.[107]

Thus, the Jacobin clubs were the first to wield the Enlighten-ment as an instrument of the political will for change. The En-lightenment became a reality on the left bank of the Rhine thanks to the French occupation. The demise of the Jacobin club is evidence of the powerful influence that this area exerted upon Jacobinism. Ultimately, the history of the Jacobin club was but a small episode in the development of democratic movements. German Jacobinism was the product of champions of the Enlight-enment who broke with tradition, propagated morality and reason and aspired to the emulation of the French Revolution. But it was only of brief duration.

During the final phase of the societies of the Enlightenment, their numbers increased so dramatically that it can reasonably be assumed that most of the late eighteenth-century champions of the Enlightenment established societies, associations and clubs. The Enlightenment was no longer the concern of a small educated elite: it was the concern of a broad spectrum of a middle class on the verge of political maturity who adopted the objectives of the Enlightenment as a means of self-realization. The range of interests had grown to such proportions that it now catered for the most diverse needs. The fact that alongside the new secret societies of the late Enlightenment, the various reading societies and political clubs, the older forms of Enlightenment, that is, the learned society, Freemasonry and the public-spirited society, also remained on the scene, and even flourished, is evidence of the interest that practical reform, learned fraternity and political Enlightenment attracted, going far beyond learned debate. Despite the existence of conflicting areas of priority, particularism was never an issue: every form of association remained true to the universality of the Enlightenment. This did not change even as the influence of learned circles began increasingly to decline, and intelligent, educated citizens began to seek the realization of their didactic ambitions within the ranks of the societies of the Enlightenment. The educated middle class were beginning to establish themselves as a social class in their own right.

6

SOCIETIES OF THE ENLIGHTENMENT AS MEDIA OF EARLY MIDDLE-CLASS CULTURE

The eighteenth century produced a wealth of societies of the Enlightenment. They developed in three distinct stages, which clearly indicates that their development was wedded both to the general socio-cultural process of the Enlightenment and to the development and emancipatory *niveau* of the educated German middle class. The development of the societies derived its significance from this combination of factors. A certain socio-political situation favours or creates certain opportunities for social articulation. In the same way, certain social needs and interests of the nascent middle class spawned particular manifestations of the Enlightenment. No single society was the 'true' society of the Enlightenment: rather, there developed several different forms for the articulation of interests, and these were often related to actual social models. Similarly, some societies pursued the twin goals of Enlightenment and middle-class emancipation differently from others. The interests of the new social elite were best represented by Freemasonry and the reading societies. Although the learned academies and the League of Illuminati were typical manifestations of the process of 'intellectual' Enlightenment, from a social standpoint, their influence was marginal.

This study of the societies of the Enlightenment does not concentrate on a single model, but rather on their common objectives and structure.

All the societies, from the early learned academies to the Jacobin clubs, regarded themselves as free associations of men. To some extent, this was also true of both the pre-Enlightenment societies (the language societies) and those societies which proliferated towards the end of the century and which pursued patently anti-Enlightenment objectives (such as the Rosicrucians). A free association was not an association of peers (a guild), which awarded membership on the basis of trade and profession and was the sole spokesman of the interests of the membership. Neither was a free association an ideological community (a sect) of birth to which the member was bound by virtue of faith. A free association was a society which anyone with aspirations of championing the Enlightenment was free to join and leave as they pleased. The voluntary decision, the conscious act, was the basis of the free association, and this distinguished it from the guild and the religious association.

The societies wished to be accessible to all proponents of the Enlightenment, but, in reality, only learned and educated men were accepted for membership. Thus both the vast majority of the middle and lower classes and women were excluded. Women were occasionally admitted to membership, but mainly as the wives of existing members. It was a widely accepted fact that there were many learned and educated women, but the male champions of the Enlightenment apparently thought them incapable of independent decision-making and of championing science, virtue and the Enlightenment on the public stage. Lastly, an independent role for women was not in keeping with the serious, stern and chaste character of the societies. Freemasonry and the reading societies, in particular, excluded women *expressis verbis*. Although discourses on female emancipation were making their first appearance at this period, this ban appeared so natural that female membership was never even discussed. The issue at stake was the attempt of men, mainly from the public sphere, to acquire a new social status independent of the court and the Church, and thus, mutual recognition, free association and commitment to the Enlightenment were regarded as male preserves. There was little disagreement on this point between any of the societies, from the learned societies to the Jacobin clubs.

Although the societies of the Enlightenment had different areas of emphasis, two objectives were common to them all: firstly, the pursuit of learned and moral autodidacticism within the framework of an association, culminating in the moral perfection of the self as defined by the tenets of enlightened reason. This is particularly true of those societies without any ambitions of exerting an external influence, in other words, the exclusive reading societies and friendship circles, the esoteric and secret societies and, most of all, Freemasonry. The individual was to broaden the horizons of his knowledge by study, attending lectures and addressing theoretical and practical problems in collaboration with his peers. Generally, this process occurred not at the occupational, but at the human and intellectual level, and served the purpose of the education of independent and virtuous men whose ambition it was to act solely in accordance with the tenets of reason and morality, independent of external didactic influences, the state and the Church: they graduated as erudite and civilized members of society. The creation of a secular morality transcending the barriers between the estates was not achieved by theoretical Enlightenment alone: compulsory rituals imposing a new mode of behaviour upon the initiated were also a contributory factor. The societies were self-centred institutions, though links with the outside world were never wholly absent; this is reflected in the notion that the pursuit of autodidacticism and the moral perfection of the self would reform society as a whole.

The second objective which the societies of the Enlightenment shared was the 'propagation' of the Enlightenment. They sought the improvement of state and society and the enlightenment of the population at large through public lecture and debate, founding newspapers and organizing open competitions. All the societies believed in the universal benefit of the Enlightenment, and they appealed to both the public at large and the state. The programme of the public-spirited society revealed that there was a broad spectrum of reform proposals, ranging from schools to agricultural reform, from welfare provisions to the practical application of technical innovations. The administration and the improvement of the common good was traditionally the preserve of the Church. Generally speaking, the societies did not challenge the competence of the Church in this area, even though the Church did not pursue this task in the spirit of the Enlightenment and was often found wanting. However, the calls for reform from members of the societies of the Enlightenment were the first instances of claims to the rights of co-determination and co-responsibility on the part of worthy 'citizens' and private individuals who had not been commissioned by, and did not act on behalf of, the authorities. Furthermore, these private individuals went beyond appealing to the secular and ecclesiastical authorities for the bestowal of these rights: they urged all their fellow subjects and citizens, as patriots and cosmopolitans, not to leave matters affecting them solely to the discretion of 'alien' institutions, but to assume the responsibility for the improvement of their own lives. Although the literary societies placed less emphasis on social responsibility than the Jacobin clubs, this was a concern shared by all the societies of the Enlightenment. The societies might have been esoteric and self-oriented institutions, but all sought to legitimize their activities by calling for individual action and the creation of a society founded as far as possible upon morality and reason, and thus, for the reform of society. All the societies believed both in the ability of society to change for the better and in reforms.

Although the realization of practical reforms and ritual fraternity were the ultimate objectives, central to all the societies were learned debate, the pursuit of autodidacticism through the discussion of literary and philosophical and secular and social issues within the framework of the Enlightenment, the exchange of information, the dissemination of knowledge and the encouragement of reform. To a certain extent, the primary objective of the societies of the Enlightenment was to facilitate the formulation, articulation and propagation of common interests through the creation of a societal framework. The societies concerned themselves with detailed literary and scientific questions, general philosophical and political problems and practical projects. Surviving records of societal lectures suggest that they all addressed similar topics: true patriotism and true cosmopolitanism, friendship and philanthropy, the common good and the necessity of reform and, finally, repeatedly, the furtherance of science, the improvement of morality and the initiation of the Enlightenment. The problem of the definition of the common interest and the establishment of the primary objective was tackled from omnifarious standpoints.

In principle, providing that it was of equal learned or intellectual concern to the whole membership, any problem regarding the philosophy of nature, political theory, morality and aesthetics was a potential subject of debate. However, religion and the Church and politics and the state were taboo. In other words, there was a blanket ban on the debate of objects of established secular and ecclesiastical monopoly. This was often enshrined in the statutes. The only possible explanation for this ban is the fact that any interference in affairs of state or Church could have been interpreted as a conspiracy and would thus have jeopardized the

society's very existence. As many societies enjoyed state privilege
and were supported by men in important government and ecclesiastical offices, most societies adhered to this arrangement. However, perhaps a more important factor than this precaution was
the inclination common to all the societies of the Enlightenment to
preserve harmony and unity by excluding potentially highly controversial subject matter. It was necessary from the very outset to
disallow any potentially troublesome and controversial subject
upon which agreement would be impossible in order to facilitate
communication, often between men of many different nationalities
and religious beliefs, and in order to protect the moral unity of the
societies in whose name the new reality of reason was to be
achieved. At the same time, this also showed the societies in a
more positive light in comparison to the court and the Church,
and afforded them independence from these two socio-political
fulcra of the age.

In addition, there was also a ban on any subject matter which
might endanger the dignity and the solemnity of the meeting.
Upon entering the societal premises, the member was expected to
discard both his religious and political beliefs and all his private
and professional problems. This was not simply in order to ex-
clude specifically professional interests and idle gossip, but also to
ensure that the meetings were congregations of men, champions of
the Enlightenment and literary connoisseurs, not government officials, professors and physicians. The society was to comprise
only the unifying factor of the common interest.

Every society had a complex set of statutes by which each and
every member was bound and whose aim was to ensure that life
within the society conformed to the tenets of reason, served the
interests of the Enlightenment and morality, safeguarded informal
communication and guaranteed each member equality of status.
These statutes, the result of collaboration between the membership, laid down strict guidelines for the admission of new members, the election of the president and the course of official meetings. All proponents of the Enlightenment were agreed that
societal life and social agitation required a regulatory framework.
This is significant in that such 'agreement' was absent elsewhere
in feudal society and was therefore without precedent. Thus, the
importance of this process and this conviction should not be
underestimated. However, a statute did not guarantee an absence
of conflict, oligarchical tendencies or a restrictive membership
policy. The central role of a rational statute, which also dictated

that any structural alteration, and even the dissolution of the society required the agreement of the whole membership, was nevertheless significant. However, most important of all, the statute guaranteed equality of status for all members. In other words, estate, social origin and religion were of no societal consequence. Thus, the societies were the first forums of communication in which the members of the various estates had an equal voice, in which they enjoyed freedom of speech and in which aristocrats and members of the middle class could treat each other as social equals. However, an equal voice and equal status as an agitator on behalf of the Enlightenment did not signify equality of social status. Fellow members were only greeted as a brother or a friend in the shelter of the lodge or the literary circle. The quest for equality of status not only disregarded social status but also religious denomination. Catholics, Lutherans, Calvinists and even Jews, mixed freely within the secluded confines of the society in an atmosphere uniquely free from prejudice. Religious prejudice was so alien to the societies that they were able to spread evenly throughout both Catholic and Protestant regions. The open-mindedness of the Rhineland Catholics was matched by that of, for example, the Protestants in Saxony-Thuringia. This also applies to Freemasonry and to the reading societies, both of which existed in Catholic and Protestant regions alike.

A discursive social atmosphere was common to all societies. This was different from the social atmosphere in courtly circles, where it was centred around the ruling princes, and from the liturgical atmosphere prevailing in the various churches. The individual societal member was still, in many ways, wedded to the court and the Church. However, the new middle class of society members increasingly drew their self-image and self-awareness from their belief in modern science, the Enlightenment and middle-class moral values, and from their membership of a rational, non-denominational community based on the tenets of reason and transcending the divisions of the estates, and not from the social status accorded to them by feudalism. The role of the society was to secure universal well-being, self-education, moral behaviour and a society founded on reason through self-determination alone. Thus, for the emergent middle class, self-education and social reflection were a civil responsibility. In this sense, the 'learned' society and 'moral' Freemasonry were indeed prototypes of middle-class society.

This basic structure is common to all the societies of the Enlightenment, from the learned academy to the Jacobin club. Even Freemasonry, in other words the secret societies, conformed to this pattern, albeit less obviously. However, by the end of the eighteenth century, the secret society had undergone a transformation, due in equal measure to both external and internal factors. This is revealed by the interdependence between social structure, the programme of Enlightenment and public relations.

Firstly, there was a change in the supporters of the societies, clubs and organizations, though a distinction should be made between social origin, profession and self-estimation. Initially, associations were founded by scholars who, although middle class in origin, emancipated themselves from the urban middle class in order to join the ranks of ecclesiastical and government administrators. They included many professors and members of the clergy, some government officials and a few aristocrats, though the latter occupied no positions of influence within the learned and literary societies; their role was to increase the social prestige of the scholars. Next to rise to prominence were middle-class and aristocratic government officials. Regardless of their commitment to the state, these officials either felt excluded from court society or purposely excluded themselves. In addition, there were some merchants, though they had a stronger presence in commercial centres than in the residential towns and cities and were never able to rival the large numbers of middle-class government officials. Although there were no major differences between the membership structure of the public-spirited societies and that of Freemasonry, the aristocracy were more heavily represented among the leading circles of the latter than the former, one indication of the particular attraction of Freemasonry for the aristocracy. Conspicuously few members were jurists or physicians, and their numbers only gradually began to increase towards the end of the century. In contrast, the number of priests, theologians and professional scholars declined. The middle class, the educated middle class, rose to prominence among the supporters of the society of the Enlightenment during the final phase, in which elements of feudalism were markedly less apparent than previously. Public servants continued to predominate: government officials in administrative centres, and merchants in centres of trade and commerce. However, both in the reading society and in the League of Illuminati, aristocrats played a leading role, though their motive was no longer to seek compensation for their decreasing influence at court, but rather to demonstrate their solidarity as proponents of the Enlightenment with the educated middle class. The interests, disposition and commitment of aristocrats, most of whom were government officials, were very much akin to those of the middle class. Generally speaking, the number of secular scholars, professors and clergymen declined drastically during the course of the eighteenth century, whereas aristocratic and middle-class public servants attained a majority among the membership. However, the former continued to set the tone. On the other hand, the number of members from the merchant class and the freelance professions not employed in the public sector was on the increase. It was not until the onset of the Jacobin clubs, the mainstay of which was also the educated middle class, that representatives of the non-academic and uneducated social classes, such as artisans, appeared on the scene in any numbers. Men of letters and writers were also represented, though, strangely enough, not in leading positions. However, they were more likely to be Freemasons than members of a reading society, perhaps because of the lodge's stronger aristocratic presence and more marked intellectual character. There was a total absence of students and teachers among the societies, that is to say, the societies were bastions of men of social status. Thus, the development of societies, clubs and organizations reveals itself as a process of the emergence of an educated elite. As in other countries, the German educated elite was not socially isolated. On the contrary, during the latter phase of feudalism, they occupied powerful positions of state.

The aims of the Enlightenment and the aspirations of the societies also underwent a tranformation. Initially, the aims were of an exclusively learned nature: the establishment and development of the modern sciences, the new natural sciences and the historical sciences. Learned activity was based upon the perception of a need for explanation; there was not an absence of practical and moral interests, but these were of wholly secondary importance. The autonomy of scholars was declared to be an essential requirement for the acquisition of intellectual and learned knowledge, for they were answerable to truth and reason alone. This autonomy was achieved through the institutionalization of informal communication in the learned societies. Increased activity on the part of middle-class and aristocratic government officials then heralded the arrival of practical and patriotic and moral and fraternal interests. On the one hand, the central objectives were the realization of the practical implications of knowledge for the benefit of all of society, the propagation of social reforms emanating from the spirit of the Enlightenment and the practical realization of the Enlightenment. On the other, the objective was the creation of a moral environment outside the court and the Church, within the confines of which the disciples of the Enlightenment were secure among their own kind: here, they were transformed into paragons of morality. From the middle of the century onwards, the Enlightenment ceased to be the concern of a privileged class and became the concern of each and every individual who acknowledged the maxim of reason. Practical initiative and moral self-determination were proclaimed as the duty of any 'autonomous' person whose self-awareness and practical existence were increasingly based on the normative influence of reason and morality, and who thus elevated social responsibility and moral perfection to the status of the hallmark and objective of emergent middle-class society. Ultimately, Enlightenment was regarded not as the social realization, the achievement, of the general principles of morality and reason, but as the subjectivization of the self and the social foundations of existence. It was not simply a case of reforming existing institutions or of achieving true morality within the safe confines of a moral institute such as the lodge. It was also a case of education and information, of recognizing relationships and perceiving social conditions, of displaying reason and morality in the secular world. Admittedly, the Illuminati approached the task of self-scrutiny differently than the elitist reading circles and the Jacobin clubs, but central to all the societies of the late Enlightenment was middle-class self-determination whose sense of social responsibility was not spawned by state or ecclesiastical edict.

This generated a change in the attitude of the societies of the Enlightenment and their members towards both society at large and the state. Initially, since the scholars were reliant upon the support of the state, which, indeed, was their sole means of attaining social recognition, a truce existed between the two sides. The learned societies were able to determine their societal character more or less without interference, but they were completely dependent upon the state. Indeed, some of them even regarded themselves as state institutions. Then, however, the relationship between the society and the state became weaker. The public-spirited societies were hopeful that they would receive the privilege of the state, and some state forces actively encouraged the population to engage in patriotic activities. But, on the whole, the societies existed outside the sphere of state authority and were wholly dependent upon the commitment of their members, whose foremost goals were to support any necessary reforms and to lend assistance wherever the state failed to discharge its obligations, or discharged them unsatisfactorily. The patriots strove for reform in areas which had previously required state legislation. This reveals the existence of a new sense of civic responsibility, not of representatives acting on behalf of the state, but of citizens who had reached maturity.

More ambivalent was the attitude of the Freemasons towards public order. The reason for this was not simply their secretiveness but also their essential openness towards both the court and the middle class. Providing that the new territorial administrative elite used the lodge as a meeting place for themselves and their ruling princes (as in Bayreuth), then ultimately, the lodge assumed the character of a special court institution. However, if the lodge operated outside the world of the court, it could indeed constitute a 'state within a state' in which citizens were able to exercise moral self-determination independent of the state, thus undermining the state's claim to be the sole custodian of the common good. While this did not entail a rejection of absolutism, emancipation from the absolutist state as the arbiter of social standards began in earnest. Although the exclusion of political and religious topics from fraternal debate enhanced the moral claims of cosmopolitanism, there was no opportunity for political agitation in either the lodges or the patriotic societies. The ban on societies imposed in 1785 was without any objective foundation.

A conscious rejection of, even latent antipathy towards, the particularist interests of the state did not develop until the final phase of the Enlightenment. Benevolent absolutism had not been able to deliver all the many reforms which it had promised, foremost among which were tolerance and freedom of expression. The resulting disillusionment with benevolent absolutism fuelled middle-class reflection on political and social processes and sparked a will for change. The state would have been able to assimilate this development without any problem had the French Revolution not lent grist to the mill of the reaction, that is, brought the libertarian aspirations of the new middle class into disrepute. The societies were neither anti-state nor anti-Christian. In the final analysis, the societal classes had such close ties with the administrative elite that a complete rejection of the traditional forces of authority was out of the question. For the Enlightenment, the transformation of benevolent absolutism into a constitutional state based on the rule of law was a necessary step. Insofar as they declared that liberty and equality were not simply provinces of the intellect but also those of human co-existence, the Jacobin clubs were alone in politicizing the Enlightenment. The Jacobin club was the only society of the Enlightenment to reject the feudal and absolutist state. On the whole, only a minority of German champions of the Enlightenment supported the abolition of the monarchy. The ultimate goal of the societies was not the removal of benevolent absolutism. The major factors in their evolution were the dawning of consciousness *vis-à-vis* socio-political processes during the late eighteenth century and the formulation of radical and progressive reforms which laid the foundations for the separation of state and society. The development of the societies of the Enlightenment from the learned society into the fraternal and literary club and the political association is a clear indication of the fact that the process of Enlightenment and moralization was part and parcel of the process of the self-discovery of a nascent middle class, which was regrouping outside the feudal order and court society.

It is difficult to assess the socio-cultural importance of the societies of the Enlightenment. However, it did not lie in any measurable intellectual or practical and reformist achievements. There are six areas of particular emphasis.

Firstly, membership of a society ended the social isolation of those few scholars and intellectuals whose needs and activities set them apart from traditional society. They joined forces, formulated common interests, founded societies and, where possible, engaged in public agitation. In so doing, they established a supra-regional union in the shape of a Republic of Scholars which exercised the most formative influence upon the intellectual development of the individual. The societies stimulated and encouraged their members, and, above all, heightened their sense of self-awareness in a world which was still unable to appreciate modern achievements and concerns. Lastly, joining forces with or without the approval of the authorities and irrespective of proximity to the court, they helped scholars, champions of the Enlightenment and educated citizens to endure their often difficult social position at the court, in the universities and schools and in the administrative apparatus. They recognized the new opportunities for combining individual interests with social objectives, and thus, for creating a new sense of identity, which were offered by working and communicating together.

Most importantly of all, the society was often the first arena in which the member was able to discuss his interests and deliver talks outside his professional milieu, among like-minded contemporaries and across all social barriers, requiring him to formulate ideas, which would be subject to the criticism of the whole society. At that time, this was an unusual phenomenon: university lectures, lectures delivered in the presence of the ruling princes and sermons were delivered under completely different conditions. The opportunity not only for reading but also for attending and debating lectures with like-minded contemporaries was a significant experiential boon. Learned and progressive debate in the modern sense was not cultivated at all levels. However, where discussion did take place, this was regarded as a unique asset whose course required strict control. The fact that speaking was forbidden during lectures and that the sequence of contributors to the subsequent discussion, who were required to speak loudly and clearly, was strictly regimented is an indication of the difficulty of pursuing uninhibited communication even against this backdrop. The importance of what was said within the society was often enhanced by the fact that minutes were kept and the speeches organized into anthologies, sometimes for publication. The art of conducting learned discussion was first taught and practised on a large scale within the society, and thus, the society was the originator of learned debate *per se*.

One of the fundamentally novel experiences for many societal members was democratic association. The majority of state and ecclesiastical, and, to some extent, also guild and feudal, institutions were characterized by hierarchical structures. In contrast, the societies – albeit mainly the public rather than the secret societies – often provided the membership with their first experience of democratic principles, which were frequently enshrined in writing. The admission of new members, all issues affecting the society as a whole and the appointment of a 'committee' were decided, in accordance with the majority principle, by all registered members, all of whom had the same rights and obligations. Just how serious a matter the principle of egalitarianism was is revealed by the efforts of many societies to elect each member to the committee and working parties in turn in order to forestall any oligarchical development. All decision-making authority was invested in the general assembly. Certainly, aristocratic members were accorded superiority, and founder members always possessed particular influence in the decision-making process. However, such influence was, or could be, cancelled out by committed activity on the part of ordinary members, and thus, each member was able to exercise an influence on societal life commensurate with his commitment. Democratic association among societal members was one of the most important experiential backgrounds to the development of middle-class society.

There occurred a process of *rapprochement* between the middle class and the aristocracy, which went beyond mutual respect. This was not due simply to the fact that the principle of equality among members was enshrined in the statutes but also to the fact that members of the middle class and the aristocracy engaged in the debate of common interests and agitated for reform and for the Enlightenment shoulder to shoulder. Although this did not affect extra-societal association, nevertheless, the old gulf was bridged. This process was facilitated on the one hand by the fact that increasingly, throughout the course of the eighteenth century, the aristocracy became less and less averse to assuming governmental posts, and hence to competing with the middle class. And on the other hand by the fact that, as a result of their education and ability, some members of the middle class were afforded unimagined opportunities for upward social mobility, even elevation to aristocratic rank, by the absolutist state. Members of the middle class and the aristocracy joined forces in the societies as a means of achieving their social aspirations, and they engaged in enlightened debate and practical and enlightened activity side by side, mixing freely together, all of which represented a qualitatively new phenomenon. Although they practised social apartheid *vis-à-vis* the lower classes, this was a by-product of the self-view of the champions of the Enlightenment, to whom equality meant equality between the middle class and the aristocracy rather than equality between all men. The process of mutual acquaintance and acceptance, joint societal activity and the common clarification of social functions consolidated the existence of an educated middle class, consisting mainly of middle-class government officials, a few merchants and freelancers and also some aristocrats. These classes kept their distance from both the feudal court and the feudal ruling classes in the towns and cities, although court and feudal influences long continued to make their presence felt. They propagated a new society, a middle course between these two worlds as it were, bound by its own laws and the principles of humanity, reason, liberty and morality.

The societies were more than simply centres of learning. They were also moral institutions of the educated middle-class elite, which not only preached morality but also taught their members a standard of civilized behaviour that was in keeping with their moral claims transcending the culture of the court and feudalism. This implied not only practising reasoned speech but also a form of social intercourse free from hubbub, suggestiveness and coarseness as well as frivolity, play and eroticism.

An atmosphere of solemnity prevailed, and this was the reason for the prohibition of alcohol and parlour games. As long as the societies were forced to hold their meetings in inns or at court, the prevention of dishonourable behaviour proved a difficult undertaking. However, upon the acquisition of their own premises, whose location and furnishing were a reflection of their autonomy and reserve, the societies were successful in banishing all vestiges of an inn-like atmosphere and all forms of parlour games, though not until after the official proceedings and the social aspect had become more sharply segregated. This resulted in a refined and cultured society which elevated middle-class forms of intercourse to the status of paradigms of communication and association.

Finally, going beyond enlightened debate, the societies developed social activities, which were fundamentally different from those of both the absolutist state and the churches. On the one hand, the members held the conviction that the Enlightenment should be more than simply a theory, that it should achieve realization in the shape of social improvement and reform. The extraordinary willingness of the champions of the Enlightenment to engage in social commitment and assume social responsibility, even to dedicate their whole lives to the cause, was rooted in their belief that as champions of the Enlightenment rather than as servants of the state, they had an obligation to the common good. On the other hand, their objectives were to place the Enlightenment in the service of the moral improvement of man and, as men of education and morality, not only to speak in learned and enlightened tones but also to act in accordance with the demands imposed upon all men by the tenets of reason and morality. The members of the societies never used their experience of internal societal morality as a yardstick for their outside lives – which was the fundamental difference between the societies of the Enlightenment and sects. This was the reason that they had no difficulty in functioning now as compliant cogs in the administrative wheels of the state and now as mature adults in the society. However, their societal experience taught them that only common thought and action can further the cause of the common good, that the Enlightenment and education must be organized independently of state authority, that democratic behaviour is dependent upon the existence of binding regulations and that the means of generating middle-class self-determination is the common debate of social problems. The repercussions of these realizations reverberated far beyond the confines of this privileged elite, carrying practical implications for society at large.

APPENDIX

LIST OF SOCIETIES* IN THE SEVENTEENTH AND EIGHTEENTH CENTURIES

This list has been compiled from: Dolzauer, Winfried, Freimaurer-geaollschaften am Rhein, 1977. Eulen, Focko, Vom, Gewerbefleiss zur Industrie, 1967. Geppert, Ernst, Die Freimaurer-Logen Deutschlands, 1974. Müller, Kurt, Zur Entstehung und Wirkung der wissenschaftlichen Akademien und gelehrten Gesellschaften im 17. Jahrhundert, 1970. Prüsener, Marlies, Lesegesellschaften im 18. Jahrhundert, 1972. (See Select Bibliography). The list includes only the following main types of society: learned, literary and public-spirited societies, masonic lodges and reading societies.

SEVENTEENTH-CENTURY SOCIETIES

Die Fruchtbringende Gesellschaft	Weimar-Köthen	1617
Aufrichtige Tannengesellschaft	Strasbourg	1633
Deutschgesinnte Genossenschaft	Hamburg	1643
Neunständige Hänseschaft	Hamburg	1643/4
Pegnesischer Blumenorden	Nuremberg	1644
Elbschwanenorden	Wedel	1658
Poetisches Kleeblatt	Strasbourg	1671
Der Leopolden-Orden	Dresden	1695
Görlitzische Poetische Gesellschaft	Görlitz	1697
Die Oettinger Blumengenossen	Oettingen	–
Ister-Gesellschaft – Nymphen-Gesellschaft an der Donau	Lower Austria	–

ACADEMIES AND LEARNED SOCIETIES

Berliner Akademie	Berlin	1700
Academia Taxiana	Innsbruck	1741
Societas Eruditorum Incognitorum	Olmütz	1746
Göttinger Gesellschaft d. Wissenschaften	Göttingen	1751
Societas Litteraria Germano-Benedictina	Kempten	1752
Gesellschaft d. freien Künste. Kaiserl. Franziscische Akademie der freien Künste und Wissenschaften	Augsburg	1753
Kurfürstlich-Mainzische Akademie der nützlichen Wissenschaften	Erfurt	1754
Kaiserlich-Franziscische Akademie der freien Künste	Augsburg	1755
Akademie der freien Künste und Wissenschaften	Bayreuth	1756/63
Gelehrte Gesellschaft	Duisburg	1759
Churbayerische Akademie der Wissenschaften	Munich	1759
Kurpfälzische Akademie der Wissenschaften	Mannheim	1763
Fürstlich Jablonowskische Gesellschaft der Wissenschaften	Leipzig	1774

* The following abbreviations appear in the list: RL = reading library; RG = reading group; RC = reading circle; UL = unofficial lodge (a lodge which has no formal recognition as such, editor's note); UOL = unofficial officers' lodge

LITERARY SOCIETIES (GERMAN SOCIETIES)

Literary Society	Halle	1701–3
Society of Close Neighbours on the River Isar for Engendering Usefulness and Willingness	Munich	1702/3
Society for the Practice of German	Hamburg	1715–17

German Society of Painters	Zurich	1721
Patriotic Society	Hamburg	1724
German Society of Jena	Jena	1728/30
German Society of Leipzig	Leipzig	1731
Confidential Society of Speakers in Thuringia	Weimar	1732
German Society	Göttingen	1738
German Society	Halle	1738
German Society	Berne	1739
Blithe German Society	Berne	1740
German Society	Greifswald	1740
Society of Triers	Thorn	1740
Growing Society	Zurich	1740/1
German Society	Königsberg	1741
German Society	Basle	1743
German Society	Berlin	1743
German Society	Strasbourg	1743
German Society	Helmstedt	1746
Society of Fine Sciences	Basle	1747
German Society	Rinteln	1750
German Society	Bremen	1752
German Society	Danzig	1752
Society of Fine Sciences and Liberal Arts	Leipzig	1752
Society for the Improvement of the Fine Sciences	Tübingen	1753
Kiel Society of Fine Sciences	Kiel	1754
German Society	Erlangen	1755
German Society	Altdorf	1756
Society for the Practice of German	Wittenberg	1756
German Society of the Principality of Anhalt	Bernburg	1761
German Society	Vienna	1761
German Society	Giessen	1763
Literary Society	Marburg	*c.*1772
German Society	Mannheim	1775
German Society	Duisburg	n/a
German Society	Kassel	n/a
Society of Fine Sciences	Oettingen	n/a
German Society	Zittau	n/a
German Society	Frankfurt/Oder	n/a
Literary Society	Nordhausen	n/a

PUBLIC-SPIRITED SOCIETIES

Society of Physics and Economics	Zurich	1757
Swiss Agricultural Society	Berne	1758
Economic Society (with branches in Emmental, Simmental, Aarau Nidau, Aigle, Avenches, Lausanne, Nyon, Payerne, Vevey and Yverdon)	Berne	1759
Economic Commission of the Society of Natural Research (with a branch in Kyburgeramt)	Zurich	1759
Economic Society	Biel (Switzerland)	1761
Economic Society	Freiburg (Switzerland)	1761
Economic Society	Solothurn	1761
Royal Danish Academy of Agriculture (Glücksburg Economic Society)	Flensburg	1762
Thuringian Society of Agriculture	Weissensee	1762/3
(Royal British) Society of Agriculture of Brunswick and Lüneburg (with branches in Uelzen, Hanover, Nienburg, Dannenberg and Stade)	Celle	1764
Imperial and Royal Society of Agriculture and Useful Arts in Steyermark	Graz	1764
Imperial and Royal Society of Agriculture in Kärnten	Klagenfurt	1764(1765)
Economic Society (with six district societies)	Leipzig	1764
Agricultural or Economic Society in the Kingdom of Bohemia (later: Imperial and Royal Bohemian Patriotic and Economic Society)	Prague	1764

Moral Society	Zurich	1764
Franconian Society of Physics and Economics	Ansbach	1765
Imperial and Royal Society of Agriculture	Görz	1765
Society for the Promotion of Manufacturing, the Arts and the Useful Trades (later: Patriotic Society)	Hamburg	1765
Society of Useful Sciences for the Promotion of the Common Good (Society for the Improvement of Agriculture)	Karlsruhe	1765
Royal Society of Agriculture and the Arts of Hessen-Kassel	Kassel	1765
Society of Morality and Agriculture of the Electorate of Bavaria (founded in Altötting)	Burghausen	1765
Oberlausitz Apicultural Society of Physics and Economics	Bautzen	1766
Imperial and Royal Society of Agriculture and the Arts for Tyrol and Vorarlberg	Innsbruck	1766
Imperial and Royal Society of Agriculture	Linz	1766
Imperial and Royal Society of Agriculture and the Useful Arts in the Duchy of Krain	Laibach	1767
Imperial and Royal Society of Agriculture of Upper Austria	Freiburg (Breisgau)	1768
Economic Society	Gotha	1768
Imperial and Royal Society of Agriculture (Lower Austria) (in Vienna for the crown lands of Lower Austria)	Vienna	1768
Society of Agriculture of Siebenbürgen	Hermannstadt	1769
Society of Physics and		

Economics of the Electorate of the Palatinate	Kaiserslautern	1769/70
Imperial and Royal Society of Moravia and Silesia for the Promotion of Agriculture, Natural History and Regional Studies	Brünn	1770
Imperial and Royal Society of Agriculture	Troppau	1770
Patriotic Society in Silesia (9 district societies)	Breslau	1771/2
Economic and Patriotic Society of the Principalities of Schweidnitz and Jauer	Jauer	1772
Economic Society of Magdeburg and District	Magdeburg	1772
Imperial and Royal Society of Agriculture	Debrecen	1775
Imperial and Royal Society of Agriculture	District of Tolna	1775
Imperial and Royal Society of Agriculture	Ödenburg	1775
Imperial and Royal Society of Agriculture	District of Pressburg	1775
Society for the Promotion of Good and Public-spiritedness	Basle	1777
Society of Friends of Agriculture in Bünden	Chur	1778
Royal Patriotic Society for the Promotion of Knowledge and Morals of Hessen-Homburg	Homburg	1778
Society of Physics and Economics of the Electorate of the Palatinate	Heidelberg	1784
Patriotic Society of Schleswig-Holstein	Altona	1786
Patriotic Society of Schleswig-Holstein	Kiel	1786
Society for the Promotion of Public-spiritedness	Lübeck	1789
Seefeld Society of Agriculture and Hunting in Bavaria	Seefeld	1789

Westfalian Society in the Mark for the Economic Promotion of Factories, Manufacturing, Trading, Industry and the Arts	Hamm	1791
Society of Physics and Economics of Mohrungen	Mohrungen, later, Königsberg	1791
Patriotic Society of Emulation	Neuenburg (Switzerland)	1791
Royal Economic Society of the Mark	Potsdam	1791
Imperial Public-spirited and Economic Society of Livland	Dorpat	1792
Society for the Promotion of National Industry	Nuremberg	1792
Economic Society	Basle	1796
Public-spirited and Economic Society of Liefland	Riga	1796
Patriotic Society of Mecklenburg	Güstrow	1798
Agricultural Society of Mecklenburg	Rostock	1798
Public-spirited Society of Wetzlar	Wetzlar	1799
Economic Society	Strasbourg	1800

Year of foundation not known:

Economic Society of Holstein	Eutin
Patriotic Society	Giessen
Royal Society of Agriculture	Hanover
Economic Society	Wittenberg
Society for the Arts, Manufacturing and Trade	Danzig

MASONIC LODGES

Name not known	Frankenthal	reputedly 1737(?)
Absalom	Hamburg	1737/40
Name not known	Heidelberg	reputedly 1737(?)

Name not known	Heilbronn	reputedly 1737(?)
Name not known	Mannheim	reputedly 1737(?)
Zu den drei weissen Adlern	Dresden	1738
La Première	Rheinsberg (Berlin)	1738
Zu den drei Schwertern	Dresden	1739
Aux trois globes	Berlin	1740
Provinzialloge von Hamburg und Niedersachsen	Hamburg	1740
Großloge Zur Sonne	Bayreuth	1741
Eleusis zur Verschwiegenheit	Bayreuth	1741
Zu den drei Todtengerippen	Breslau	1741
Aux quatre Quarreaux	Breslau	1741
Zu den drei Todtengerippen	Dresden	1741
Zum aufrichtigen Herzen	Frankfurt/O.	1741
Zu den drei goldenen Schlüsseln	Halle	1741
Minerva zu den drei Palmen	Leipzig	1741
Aux trois Boussoles	Meiningen	1741
Lodge with no name	Altenburg	1742
L'union	Berlin	1742
Zur Einigkeit	Frankfurt/M.	1742
Aux trois Canons	Vienna	1742
St. Georg zur grünenden Fichte	Hamburg	1743
Zu den drei Rosen	Rüssdorf/ Sachsenfelde	1743
Aux trois Planches à tracer	Altenburg	1744
Jonathan	Brunswick	1744
Zu den drei Ankern	Bremen	1744
Schottische Loge	Hamburg	1744
Zu den drei Rosen	Jena	1744
Zion	Jena	1744
Zu den drei Winkelmassen	Nossen	1744
Aux trois Colonnes d'Aivain	Wesel	1744
Name not known	Wittenberg	in existence 1744
Schottenloge	Halle	1745
Judica	Hamburg	1745
St. Jean aux trois Compas	Leipzig	1745
St. Barbara	Lübeck	1745
Zu den drei Löwen	Marburg	1745
Zu den drei Säulen	Glogau	1746
Zu den drei goldenen Hammern	Halberstadt	1746

Friedrich (zum weißen Pferd)	Hanover	1746
Minerva (zu den drei Palmen)	Leipzig	1746
Universitätsloge	Trier	1746
Loge und templarisches Capitel	Unwürde	1746
Friedrich	Göttingen	1747
Afrikanische Loge	Hamburg	1747
Gideon	Hamburg	1747
Apollo	Leipzig	1747
Auguste	Celle	1748
Zum helleuchtenden Stern	Celle	1748
Zu den drei Hammern	Naumburg	1749
Zu den drei Kompassen (Aux trois Boussoles, Aux trois Globes)	Gotha	1750
Aux quatre Pierres cubes	Altenburg	1751
Zu den drei Bleiwagen (Aux trois Niveaux)	Danzig	1751
Minerva zu den drei goldenen Hammern	Jever	1751
Zu den drei Säulen (moved to Görlitz in 1764)	Kittlitz	1751
Zu den drei Zirkeln	Kniphausen	1751
De la fidélité	Cologne	1751
La sincérité	Frankfurt/M.	1752
Zum goldenen Hirsch	Bad Harzburg	1752
Caroline zu den drei Pfauen	Neuwied	1752
Abel	Oldenburg	1752
Zu den drei Zahlen [UL]	Leipzig	1753
La petite Concorde (Zur Eintracht)	Berlin	1754
Aux trois Colombes	Berlin	1754
St. Michael	Schwerin	1754
Aux trois cœurs (unis)	Vienna	1754
Zu den drei Palmen	Dresden	1755
Bund der Treue und Wahrheit zu den 3 Rosen Weiß, Rot und Gold [UL]	Frankfurt/M.	1755
Ernestus	Hildburghausen	1755
Augusta zu den drei Flammen	Göttingen	1756
Schwedische Armee-Loge	Greifswald	1756
Große Provinzial-Loge v. Hannover	Hanover	1756
Afrikanische Bauherren-Loge	Berlin	1757

Französische Militärloge Zu		
den drei Lilien [UL]	Brunswick	1757
Libanon zu den drei Cedern	Erlangen	1757
La Concorde	Strasbourg	1757
Drei Sterne	Ansbach	1758
Alexander zu den drei Sternen	Ansbach	1758
Fidélité	Berlin	1758
L'Harmonie	Berlin	1758
Aux trois Lys	Brunswick	1759
Arkadische Gesellschaft zu		
Phylandrin	Darmstadt	1759
Zum goldenen Apfel	Eutin	1759
Hochcapitel von Jerusalem	Berlin	1760
Zu den drei Hügeln Zions	Halberstadt	1760
Zu den drei Kronen	Königsberg	1760
Capitel von Jerusalem	Königsberg	(?) – 1764
Zum Palmbaum	Offenbach	1760
Zum Thale Josaphat	Pritzwalk	1760
Zu den drei Sternen	Rostock	1760
Zur Sonne	Rostock	1760
L'Union	Stettin	1760
Capitel von Jerusalem	Stettin	1760–4
Purita	Brunswick	1761
De la Félicité	Magdeburg	1761
Zur Einigkeit	Nuremberg	1761
Zu den drei Hügeln Zions	Aschersleben	1762
Capitulum Hierosolymitanum	Brunswick	1762
Zu den drei Granatäpfeln	Dresden	1762
L'Union militaire du		
Régiment Royal Deux Ponts	Frankfurt/M.	1762
Zu den drei Greifen	Greifswald	1762
Zum funkelnden Nordstern	Greifswald	1762
Salem	Halle	1762
Capitel von Jerusalem	Halle	1762
Capitel von Jerusalem	Hamburg	1762
Au temple	Hildesheim	1762
Zur Pforte zur Ewigkeit	Hildesheim	1762
Loge (L'Union désirée)	Koblenz	extended 1762
La parfaite Union	Königsberg	1762
Zur Beständigkeit	Magdeburg	1762
Schottenloge	Magdeburg	1762
La parfaite Union [UOL]	Magdeburg	1762
Zur unverfälschten Weisheit		
[UOL]	Magdeburg	1762

Zur Einsamkeit [UOL]	Magdeburg	1762
Capitel von Jerusalem	Rostock	1762
Eintracht	Stralsund	1762
Zur Eintracht (La parfaite Union)	Stuttgart	1762
Capitel von Jerusalem	Stuttgart	1762
Drei-Schlüssel-Loge Zum Winkelmaß	Wetzlar	1762
Veritas	Brunswick	1763
Zu den drei Pyramiden	Danzig	1763
Pax et Concordia	Emden	1763(1764)
Zu den drei Felsen	Hirschberg Silesia	1763
Capitel von Jerusalem	Jena	1763
Zu den drei Säulen	Magdeburg	1763
La Candeur	Metz	1763
Zu den drei Quellen	Bad Pyrmont	1763
Zum funkelnden Morgenstern (Zu den 3 Zirkeln)	Stettin	1763
La Charité	Stralsund	1763
St. Charles de l'indissoluble Fraternité	Brunswick	1764
Zur weißen Taube	Darmstadt	1764
Zur gekrönten Schlange	Görlitz	1764(1765)
Josua (zum Korallenbaum)	Hadersleben (Silesia)	1764
Zum Tempel der Pflichttreue	Krotoschin	1764
Victoria zu den drei gekrönten Thürmen	Marienburg	1764
L'Amitié [UL]	Weimar	1764
Loge der gerechten und vollkommenen Amalia	Weimar	1764
Modestia	Basel	1765
Etrangère	Dresden	1765
La parfaite Amitié	Düsseldorf	1765
Zur goldenen Himmelskugel	Glogau	1765
Carl zum Purpurmantel	Hanover	1765
Zu den drei Disteln	Mainz	1765
Zu den drei Kronen	Marienburg (West Prussia)	1765
Mutterloge zur goldenen Himmelskugel	Nistiz	1765
St. Charles de la Constance	Regensburg	1765

St. Jean de la bonne harmonie	Saarlouis	1765
Loge des Kapitain Smith	Bremen	1766
Zum Thale Josaphat	Kassel	1766
St. Jean des Voyageurs	Dresden	1766
Provinzial-Loge von Franken, dem Ober- und Niederrhein	Frankfurt/M.	1765
Zu den drei Triangeln	Glatz	1766
Zu Bethlehem	Marburg	1766
La paix de Bas-Rhin	Düsseldorf	1767
Zu den drei Disteln	Frankfurt/M.	1767
Wilhelm zu den drei Rosen	Frankfurt/M.	1767
Zu den drei Säulen	Guben-Triebel	1767
Capitel von Jerusalem	Leipzig	1767
Zu den drei Helmen	Wetzlar	1767
Zu den drei Löwen	Wismar	1767
Gustav zum goldenen Hammer	Wismar	1767
Loge des heiligen Ludwig	Darmstadt	1768
La juste et parfaite Loge de St Louis des braves maçons	Jägersburg, near Neunkirchen	
Zur vollkommenen Einigkeit	Ludwigsburg	1768
Minerva	Potsdam	1768
Josua zum Korallenbaume	Rendsburg	1768
Salomon zum goldenen Löwen	Schleswig	1768
Zu den drei Zedern	Stuttgart	1768
Zu den drei Disteln von Wolfsgarten	Wolfsgarten-Langen	1768
Zu den drei goldenen Schlüsseln	Berlin	1769
Indissolubilis	Berlin	1769
Zur Freundschaft [UL]	Halle	1769
Andreas zur goldenen Leuchte	Königsberg	1769
Zu den drei Rosen	Marburg	1769
La parfaite Union	Marburg	1769
Der flammende Stern	Berlin	1770
Toleranz-Loge	Berlin	1770
La Candeur	Berlin	1770
Zu den neun Sternen	Brunswick	1770
Zum silbernen Schlüssel	Bremen	1770
Zum blauen Löwen	Kassel	1770
Zu den drei Sternen	Danzig	1770
Sincera Concordia	Erfurt	1770
Zur goldenen Kugel	Hamburg	1770
Zu den drei Rosen	Hamburg	1770

Zu den drei Herzen	Marienburg	1770
Herkules	Potsdam	1770
Herkules	Schweidnitz	1770
Drei goldene Anker zur Liebe und Treue	Stettin	1770(1769)
Zum Pelikan	Altona	1771
Zum goldenen Schiff	Berlin	1771
Zum Pegasus	Berlin	1771
La Bienfaisance	Buchsweiler (Alsace)	1771
Johannes der Evangelist zur Wohltätigkeit	Buchsweiler (Alsace)	1771
Des Zêles du Bas-Rhin (Die Eifrigen am Niederrhein) (Zur Eintracht am Niederrhein)	Cleve	1771
Pour la Vertu	Freiberg	1771
Zum rothen Löwen	Berlin	in existence 1772
Cherub von Eden	Glogau	1772
Provinzial-Loge von Schlesien	Glogau	1772
La Candeur (Zur Redlichkeit) [UL]	Hamburg	1772
Zum Todtenkopf	Königsberg	1772
Loge der echten Maurerei	Leipzig	1772
Zum Füllhorn	Lübeck	1772
De l'Union et de l'Amitié	Aachen	1773
Friedrich von der Freundschaft	Kassel	1773
Zur Bruderliebe	Kassel	1773
Carolina	Eisenach	1773
Constantia zur gekrönten Eintracht	Elbing	1773
Le compas d'or	Göttingen	1773(1772)
Carolina zu den drei Kellen	Marktsteft	1773
Zur weißen Taube	Neisse	1773
Minerva zu den drei Lichtern	Querfurt	1773
Herkules	Reichenbach	1773
Friedrich zu den drei Seraphim	Berlin	1774
Carl zur gekrönten Säule	Brunswick	1774
Zur Säule	Breslau	1774
Zum goldenen Ring	Glogau	1774
Kosmopolit	Gotha	1774
Emanuel zur Maienblume	Hamburg	1774

Zum rothen Adler	Hamburg	1774
Elise zum warmen Herzen [UL]	Hamburg	1774
Zum schwarzen Bär	Hanover	1774
Zum Krokodil	Harburg	1774
Libanon	Hirschberg	1774
Zum gekrönten Löwen	Marburg	1774
Charlotte zu den drei Nelken	Meiningen	1774
Zum gekrönten Greif	Neubrandenburg	1774
Zum glänzenden Siebengestirn	Nieder-Zaucha	1774
Augusta zur goldenen Krone	Stargard (Pommerania)	1774
Zur Eintracht	Belgard	1775
Zur Beständigkeit	Berlin	1775
Zur Verschwiegenheit	Berlin	1775
Präfektur Templar in Castello Catorum	Kassel	1775
Zur Hoffnung	Cleve	1775
La double Union	Diedenhofen	1775
Ferdinand zur gekrönten Säule	Hildesheim	1775
Friedrich zum Tempel	Hildesheim	1775
Carl zur guten Hoffnung	Husum	1775
Phönix	Königsberg	1775
Zur goldenen Traube	Lüneburg	1775
Zur Maximilianischen Eintracht	Munich	1775
Zur goldenen Krone	Stendal	1775
Zur strahlenden Sonne an der Ostsee	Stolp	1775
Zur Eintracht	Treptow	1775
Zum goldenen Schwerdt	Wesel	1775
Loge Juliane zu den drei Löwen	Altona	1776
Julius zu den drei empfindsamen Herzen	Anklam	1776
Zum Pilgrim	Berlin	1776
Zum goldenen Pflug	Berlin	1776
Zum Widder	Berlin	1776
Großes regierendes Ordens-Capitel der großen Landesloge der Freimaurer von Deutschland in Berlin	Berlin	1776
Rudolf zu den drei Schwänen	Bonn	1776

Loge der strikten Observanz	Bonn	1776
Friedrich zum goldenen Zepter	Breslau	1776
Zur Glocke	Breslau	1776
Zum Kranich	Danzig	1776
Zum goldenen Apfel	Dresden	1776
Ordenskapitel der strikten Observanz, Großkomturei Creuznach, später Errichtung des Kapitels Neu-Kreuznach	Frankfurt/M.	1776
Ferdinande Caroline zu den drei Sternen	Hamburg	1776
Zur Ceder	Hanover	1776(1777)
Louise zur gekrönten Freundschaft	Kiel	1776
Le Secret des trois Rois	Cologne	1776
Balduin (zur Linde)	Leipzig	1776
Memphis	Memel	1776
Adolphe zum Ritterringe	Neubrandenburg	1776
Zu den drei vereinigten Wassern	Passau	1776
Rother Löwe	Rinteln	1776
Zu den drei Felsen	Schmiedeberg	1776
Rother Löwe	Stolp	1776(1775)
Zu den drei Kleeblättern	Aschersleben/ Magdeburg	1777
Rudolf zu den drei Schwänen	Friedberg (in Taunus)	1777
Wilhelmine zu den drei Buchen	Gersfeld	1777
Fidelis	Hamburg	1777
Maria zum goldenen Schwert	Köslin	1777
Bergloge	Marienberg	1777
Zur goldenen Leier	Marienwerder	1777
Zum goldenen Löwen	Marienwerder	1777
Zur Behutsamkeit	Munich	1777
Zum guten Rat	Munich	1777
Zur wahren Treue	Neustrelitz	1777
Zum großen Christoph	Stade	1777
Provinzial-Loge für Pommern, Neumark und Uckermark	Stettin	1777
Templarisches Capitel	Wetzlar	1777
Kapitel Alt-Kreuznach	Wetzlar	1777
Zum goldenen Apfel	Zwickau	1777

Zur Beständigkeit	Aachen	1778
Zur vollkommenen Freundschaft	Basle	1778
Zum goldenen Becher	Breslau	1778
Zum gekrönten Löwen	Kassel	1778(1774)
La Concorde	Colmar	1778
Ludwig zu den drei goldenen Löwen	Gießen	1778
Zur königlichen Eiche	Hameln	1778
Wilhelmine Karoline	Hanau	1778
Maximilian zu den drei Lilien	Cologne	1778
Armeeloge Nr. 1	Landeshut	1778
Zum goldenen Becher	Leer	1778
Fridericia zum Todtenkopf	Lüben (Lübben)	1778
Zum Wegweiser, Armee-Loge Nr. II	Magdeburg	1778
Lodge with no name	Mainz	1778
Karl zur Einigkeit	Mannheim	1778
Zu den drei Balken	Münster	1778
La Sagesse	Potsdam	1778
Zum Tempel der Tugend	Schwedt	1778
Zur beständigen Einigkeit	Wiesbaden	1778
Zu den drei königlichen Adlern	Aurich	1779
Friedrich zur Tugend	Brandenburg	1779
Minerva zu den drei Pfeilern	Jever	1779
Zur Weltkugel	Lübeck	1779
Zur wahren Hoffnung	Neuwied	1779
Die guten Maurer von St. Ludwig–Des braves maçons de St. Louis	Saarbrücken	1779
Des braves maçons de St. Jean	Saarbrücken-St Johann	1779
St. Heinrich	Saarbrücken	1779
Aurora	Bielefeld	1780
Zum heiligen Johannes	Kammin	1780
St. Alban zum echten und wahren Feuer	Hildesheim	1780
Zum silbernen Schlüssel	Jever	1780
Name not known	Langensalza	1780
Aurora	Minden	1780
Wittekind zur Westfälischen Pforte	Minden	1780

Die gekrönte Standhaftigkeit	Posen	1780
De St. Jean des vrais amis à l'Orient de Sarreguemines en Lorraine allemande	Saargemünd	1780
Ludwig zum rothen Löwen	Stargard (Pommerania)	1780
Constantia zur Freundschaft	Brandenburg	1781
Johannes zur brüderlichen Liebe	Worms	1781
Friedrich Wilhelm zum goldenen Szepter	Küstrin	1782
Ferdinand zur goldenen Krone	Hanover	1782
Carl August zu den drei flammenden Herzen	Kaiserslautern	1782
Zur goldenen Harfe	Salzwedel	1782
Ferdinand aux neuf Etoiles	Strasbourg	1782
Ludwig zum halben Mond	Augsburg	1783
Friedrich zur aufgehenden Sonne	Brieg	1783
Pallas (Pollux) zu den drei Lichtern	Eichstätt	1783
Zum weißen Adler	Frankfurt/M.	1783
Zu den drei Rosen	Halberstadt	1783
Flammender Stern	Hamburg	1783
St Alban zum ächten Feuer	Hoya	1783
Zur Linde	Leipzig	1783
Westphalia	Minden	1783
Zum weißen Adler	Posen	1783
Zur Schule der Weisheit	Posen	1783
Zum goldenen Schwert	Wesel	1783
Friedrich zur Beständigkeit	Zerbst	1783
Aurora	Belgard	1784
Zur echten Aussicht	Freiburg (Breisgau)	1784
Zu den drei Rosen	Bromberg	1784
Zum Tempel der wahren Eintracht	Kassel	1784
Zur Hoffnung	Duisburg	1784
Zur freien Einigkeit	Esslingen	1784
Zur schottischen Beständigkeit	Grünstadt	1784
Constantin zu den drei Kränzen	Rothenburg (Hanover)	1784

Ludwig zum flammenden Stern	Bentheim-Steinfurt	1784
Zu den drei Rosenknospen	Bochum	1785
Ludwig zum flammenden Stern	Burg-Steinfurt	1785
Union	Ebersbach	1785
Zum preußischen Adler	Insterburg	1785
Carl zur Einigkeit	Karlsruhe	1785
Leopold zur Treue	Karlsruhe	1785
Günter zum stehenden Löwen	Rudolstadt	1785
Aurora	Treptow	1785
Zur Bundeslade	Zerbst	1785
Sympathie	Altona	1786
Eugenie zum Löwen	Stolzenburg near Danzig	1786
Zu den zwei Zahlen	Duisburg	1786
Capitel von Zion	Hanover	1786
Charlotte zu den drei Sternen	Kaufbeuren	1786
Zur Aufrichtigkeit	Leipzig	1786
Zur Reinigkeit des Herzens	Leipzig	1786
Zum Zirkel der Eintracht	Weißenfels	1786
Carl zu den drei Rädern	Erfurt	1787
Melchisedek (Israeliten)	Hamburg	1787
Karl zum Rautenkranz	Hildburghausen	1787
Zur aufgehenden Sonne	Kempten	1787
Friedrich zur wahren Freundschaft	Konitz	1787
Vrais Amis	Metz	1787
Des beaux Arts	Strasbourg	1787
Zum Ölzweig	Bremen	1788
Drusis zur Mutter Natur	Elbing	1788
Pax Inimica Malis	Emmerich	1788
Wilhelm zu den drei Nelken	Halle	1788
Ferdinand zum Felsen	Hamburg	1788
Zur Vollkommenen Gleichheit	Krefeld	1788
Zur wahren Eintracht	Schweidnitz	1788
Friedrich Carl Joseph zum goldenen Rade	Aschaffenburg	1789
Zur Eintracht	Danzig	1789
Zur wahren Treue	Emden	1789
Caroline zum gekrönten weißen Löwen	Grünstadt	1789
Carl zum entfesselten Löwen	Hamburg	1789
Zum goldenen Rad	Mainz	1789

Zu den drei Pfeilen	Nuremberg	1789
Quartalsgesellenloge	Nuremberg	1789
Toleranz und Einigkeit	Hamburg	1790
Zur Beständigkeit	Königsberg	1790
Zur gekrönten Unschuld	Nordhausen	1790
Carl zum rothen Thurm	Regensburg	1790
Charlotte zur gekrönten Tugend	Stade	1790
Astraea zu den drei Ulmen	Ulm	1790
Zum stillen Tempel	Hildesheim	1791
Zu den drei Zahlen	Ruhrort	1791
Zum goldenen Löwen	Hagen	1792
Zum hellen Licht	Hamm	1792
Zur Morgenröthe	Memmingen	1792
Zum Tempel der Eintracht	Osterode	1792
Zum westfälischen Löwen	Schwelm	1792
Quelle zur Wahrheit	Nuremberg	1793
Zum Bienenkorb	Thorn	1793
Zu den wahren vereinigten Freunden	Brünn	1795
Zur aufgehenden Sonne	Küstrin	1795
Zum goldenen Löwen	Emper	1795
Zum Wegweiser	Löwenberg in Silesia	1795
Zur Wahrheit	Prenzlau	1795
Zur Einsicht	Salzburg	1795
Zur allgemeinen Harmonie und Eintracht	Triest	in existence 1795
Carl zum Felsen	Altona	1796
Johannes zum Degen	Hanover	1796
St. Johannes zum Degen	Hoya	1796
Zur deutschen Redlichkeit	Iserlohn	1796
Castor und Pollux	Rawitsch	1796
Zum Brunnen in der Wüste	Cottbus	1796
Georg zu den drei Säulen	Einbeck	1797
Zum hellen Löwen	Hamm	1797
Feldloge	Hanover	1797
Gustav Adolph zu den drei Strahlen	Stralsund	1797
Friedrich Wilhelm zur gekrönten Gerechtigkeit	Berlin	1798
Zur siegenden Wahrheit	Berlin	1798
Urania zur Unsterblichkeit	Berlin	1798
Pythagoras zum flammenden		

Stern	Berlin	1798
Innerster Orient	Berlin	1798
La Paladienne	Erfurt	1798
Zu den drei Bergen	Freiberg	1798
Zur Vaterlandsliebe	Iserlohn	1798
Zur grünenden Eiche	Leipzig	1798
Zu den drei Flammen	Plauen	1798
Zu Harmonie	Chemnitz	1798
Victoria zu den drei gekrönten Türmen	Graudenz	1799
Zum Morgenstern	Hof	1799
Harmonie	Hohenstein	1799
Pythagoras zu den drei Strömen	Münden (Hanover)	1799
Louise zum aufrichtigen Herzen	Tilsit	1799
Zum Tempel der Wahrheit	Rostock	1800
Quatuor Elementa	Stralsund	1800

Year of foundation not known:

Acacia	Bamberg
Augusta	Augsburg
Friedrich zur Bruderkette	Berlin
Anker der Eintracht	Bremen-Vegesack
Zu den drei Aufrechten	Krefeld
Zu den drei Disteln	Darmstadt
Zur grünen Flagge	Hasenpoth
Zur fränkischen Treue	Kulmbach
Philipp zur Wiedervereinigung	Landau
Friedrich zur Eintracht	Lörrach
Zu den drei gekrönten Schwertern	Mietau
Acacia	Munich
Trois flammes vivifantes	Neustadt
St Kund zum goldenen Lindwurm	Nyeborg
Zur brennenden Granate	Pirmasens
Zum Schwerdt	Riga
Schottische Großloge der strikten Observanz der Grafschaft	Saarbrücken

Zur bergischen Freiheit	Solingen
Brudertreue an der	Wunsiedel/
Luisenburg	Marktredwitz
Royal York zur Freundschaft	Berlin

READING SOCIETIES

Reading Society (Private Association for the Study of English Language and Literature)	Bremen	*c.*1750
	Stralsund	1750
Reading Society (for teachers)	Saulgau	1760
Reading Society (for a number of journals) [RC]	Leipzig	1763
Journal Society [RC] (Society for the Joint Subscription to 'Avant-Coureur')	Berlin	1764
	Leipzig	1765
Reading Society (plan)	Mainz	1766
Reading Society [RC]	Ludwigsburg	1769
Reading Institute [RG]	Coburg	1771
Reading Society	Lübeck	1771
Reading Society [RC]	Lüneburg	1772
Reading Society (four in existence in 1778)	Oldenburg	1772
Reading Society [RC]	Oberpahlen/ Estonia	1772
Reading Society [RL]	Bayreuth	1773
Reading Society	Saarbrücken	1773/4
Historical Reading Society (for collecting travel memoirs)	Bremen	1774
Reading societies (several)	Schweinfurt	1774
Reading Society	Buchsweiler (Alsace)	1775
Theological Reading Society	Grossrudestädt	1775
Reading Cabinet [RG]	Stuttgart	1775
Closed Reading Society	Elberfeld	1775
Reading Society (literary)	Zweibrücken	1775–7
Reading Society (of Protestants)	Cologne	1776

Reading Circle (for learned newspapers) [RC]	Görlitz	1777
Reading Society (3)	Heilbronn	in existence 1777
Reading Circle (medical journals)	Leipzig	1778
Literary Society	Oldenburg	1779
Reading Society [RC]	Stralsund	1779
Journal Society [RC]	Stralsund	after 1779
Reading Circles (several)	Lausitz (Bautzen)	in existence 1779
Reading Society 'Museum' (emerged from a reading society founded in 1774)	Bremen	c.1780
Reading Society [RC]	Bremen	c.1780
Reading Society	Glückstadt	c.1780
Reading Society (for medical students)	Göttingen	1780
Reading Society (not developed)	Bonn	1781
Theological Reading Society	Gehren/ Thuringia	1781
Learned Reading Society [RG]	Mainz	1782–90
Literary Society [RG]	Marburg	1782–93
Reading Society (of young daughters) [RC]	Speyer	1782
Reading Society [RG]	Aschaffenburg	1783
Klopstock-Büsch Reading Society (literary)	Hamburg	in existence 1783
Reading Society [RG]	Koblenz	1783
Reading Society [RG]	Regensburg	1783
Reading Society [RG]	Trier	1783–93
Reading Society [RG] (later: Casino Society)	Worms	1783
Reading Cabinet	Göttingen	1784
Reading Society [RC]	Grünstadt	1784
Reading Society	Gumbinnen/ East Prussia	before 1784
Reading Society [RC]	Hermannstadt	1784
Reading Society [RG]	Karlsruhe	1784
Ladies' Reading Society	Leipzig	in existence 1784
Reading Society [RG]	Stuttgart	1784
Reading Society	Baden (the town)	1785
Reading Society	Frankenthal	1785
Reading societies (4)	Frankfurt/Oder	in existence 1785

New Reading Society [RC]	Glückstadt	1785
Reading Society	Goslar	c.1785
Agronomic Reading Society	Grossflintbeck	1785
Reading Society [RG]	Heidelberg	in existence 1785
Reading Society [RL]	Insterburg	1785
Reading Society [RG]	Landshut	1785
Reading Society	Lippstadt	1785
Learned reading societies (2) [RG]	Magdeburg	in existence 1785
Reading Society (for medical students)	Marburg	1785
Reading Society [RL]	Öhringen	probably before 1785
Reading Society [RG]	Pforzheim	1785
Reading Society [RG]	Würzburg	1785/6
Reading Society	Bamberg	dissolved 1786
Forest Reading Society [RC]	Breitenbach	1786
Reading Society	Calbe (Brandenburg)	1786
Journal Society	Hanover (the town)	1786
Reading Society [RG]	Hildburghausen	1786
Village Reading Society	Leuna	in existence 1786
Village Reading Society	Spergau	in existence 1786
Reading Cabinet	Nuremberg	1786–1805
Reading societies (several)	Schweidnitz	in existence 1786
Reading societies (several)	Schweinfurt	in existence 1786
Reading Society (for students)	Bamberg	1787
General Reading Society	Basle	1787
Reading and Recuperation Society	Bonn	1787
Reading Society [RG]	Dillingen	1787
Reading Society	Hadersleben	in existence 1787
Academic Reading Institute [RG]	Jena	1787
Reading Society [RC]	Neuburg/Danube	banned 1787
Reading Institute [RC]	Oranienburg	1787
Reading Society for the Promotion of Good, Truth, Usefulness and Beauty	Rostock	1787
Reading societies (2)	Wittenberg	in existence 1787
Reading Society	Bochum	in existence 1788
Large Reading Society [RC]	Celle	1788
Reading Society [RG]	Frankfurt/Main	1788

Reading Society (for periodicals) [RC]	Göttingen	*c.*1788
Reading societies (several)	Halberstadt	in existence 1788
Reading Society	Kremmen Brandenburg	in existence 1788
Reading Society	Langenburg	in existence 1788
Reading Society	Lindau	1788
Reading Society (for journals and learned newspapers)	Mulhouse/Alsace	in existence 1788
Reading Society	Neubrandenburg	in existence 1788
Social Reading Institute [RC]	Nuremberg	1788–1804
Journal Society [RC]	Upper Silesia	dissolved 1788
Reading Society	Ravensburg	in existence 1788
Reading Society	Schwelm	in existence 1788
Reading Society	Wunstorf	in existence 1788
Reading societies (3) [RC]	Brandenburg	in existence 1789
Reading societies (4)	Eisleben	in existence 1789
Reading Society [RG]	Hermannstadt	1789
Reading societies (several)	Kassel	in existence 1789
Corresponding Reading Circle (literary society)	Mainz	1789
Reading Society [RG]	Mannheim	planned 1789
Reading Society [RG]	Müllheim (Breisgau)	1789
Reading Cabinet	Nuremberg	in existence 1789
Reading societies (5)	Rügen	in existence 1789
Ladies' Reading Society	Rügen	authorized 1789
Reading societies and reading libraries (several)	Schweidnitz	in existence 1789
Reading Society (probably a reading circle for journals)	Teschen	1789
Reading Society [RG]	Teterow	1789
Reading Society [RG]	Ulm	1789
Reading societies [RC] (closed society)	Berlin	1790
Journal societies (several) [RC]	Coburg	*c.*1790
Journal Society [RC]	Göttingen	*c.*1790
Second Reading Society [RG]	Mainz	*c.*1790
Reading circles (2)	Prenzlau	in existence 1790
Reading societies (several)	Reval	in existence 1790
Reading societies (for journals and travel memoirs)	Riga	in existence 1790
Reading societies (3)	Speyer	in existence 1790
Closed reading societies		

(several)	Stolpe	in existence 1790
New Reading Society	Teschen	1790
Reading societies (several)	Zerbst	in existence 1790
Reading Society [probably RG]	Arnsberg	1791
Reading societies (36, both large and small)	Bremen	in existence 1791
Citizens' Reading Society [RC]	Erlangen	1791
Society for Learned Newspapers (several) [RC]	Giessen	in existence 1791
Theological Reading Society	Goslar	in existence 1791
Reading Institute	Gotha	in existence 1791
Journal Society	Hanover	1791
Reading Society	Krefeld/ Uerdingen	1791
Reading Society	Lauban	1791
Reading Cabinet	Mannheim	1791
Reading Society	Mannheim	in existence 1791
Reading Society [probably RG]	Rheinberg	1791
The Karl School Academic Reading Society	Stuttgart	1791/2
Reading Society	Apenrade	in existence 1792
Reading societies (several, incl. one ladies' society)	Aurich	in existence 1792
Reading Society (for journals) [RC]	Bamberg	1792
Legal Reading Society [RG]	Bamberg	1792
Ladies' Reading Society	Greiz	authorized 1792
Reading circles and societies (several)	Harburg	in existence 1792
Reading Cabinet	Memmingen	1792
Reading societies (3)	Mitau and Libau	in existence 1792
Reading Library	Pirna	1792
Reading Society [RC]	Ebersgrün	in existence 1793
Journal Society [RC]	Greiz	in existence 1793
Theological Reading Society [RC]	Greiz	in existence 1793
Journal societies (numerous)	Königsberg	in existence 1793
Reading Society (Citizens' Reading Society)	Mittweida	in existence 1793
Reading Society	Mühlbach	in existence 1793

Reading societies	Münster	banned 1793
Reading societies (8)	Neustrelitz	in existence 1793
Journalistic Reading Society [RC]	Reichenbach	in existence 1793
Reading Society (for priests) [RC]	Szassregen	1793
Reading societies	Tilse/East Prussia	in existence 1793
Reading Society	Zeulenroda	in existence 1793
Reading Cabinet	Brunswick	1794
Theological Reading Society [RC]	Breslau	in existence 1794
Reading Cabinet	Dresden	1794
Reading societies	Düsseldorf	banned 1794
Reading societies	Eisenach	banned 1794
Teachers' Reading Society [RC]	Grünberg	in existence 1794
Museum [RC]	Leipzig	1794
Reading Institute	Passau	in existence 1794
Teachers' Reading Society	Rellingen	before 1794
Reading societies (2) [RC]	Wunstorf	in existence 1794
Reading societies	Erfurt	in existence 1795
Reading Cabinet	Erlangen	1795
Reading Institute [RG]	Frankfurt/Main	1795
Reading Society [RG]	Heidelberg	1795
Reading Society (for medical students)	Jena	in existence 1795
Reading Society [RC]	Lipprichhausen	in existence 1795
Reading Society [RG]	Ludwigsburg	1795–7
Reading Institute	Mannheim	in existence 1795
Reading Society	Regensburg	in existence 1795
Theological Reading Society	Schweinfurt	1795
Reading Society	Barth	in existence 1796
Journal Society [RC]	Bremen	1796
Reading Rooms [RG]	Breslau	1796
Society [RG]	Crailsheim	in existence 1796
Private Reading Society	Detmold	in existence 1796
Reading Society	Ludwigsburg	1796
Educational Reading Society	Regensburg	1796
The Reading Convent	Rundhof	in existence 1796
Reading Society (for aristocrats and dignitaries)	Stroppen	in existence 1796
Theological Reading Society	Stroppen	in existence 1796
Reading Society [RC]	Bernburg	1797

Reading Society [RC]	Bremen	1797
Literary Society	Bremen	1797
English Reading Society	Bremen	c.1797
Reading Museum [RG]	Göttingen	1797
Reading Society [RG]	Cologne	1797
Reading Society [RG]	Köstritz	1797
Reading Institute [RG]	Nuremberg	1797
Teachers' Reading Society	Wilster	in existence 1797
Medical Reading Society [RC]	Brunswick	1798
Economic Reading Society [RG]	Cismar	1798
Museum [RG]	Dresden	1798
Reading Cabinet	Giessen	1798
Reading societies (2)	Glückstadt	1798
Reading Society [RC]	Göttingen	1798
Reading Society [RG]	Neuwied	1798
Ladies' Literary Society	Oldenburg	in existence 1798
Reading Society	Oldesloe	in existence 1798
Reading Society [RC]	Rastatt	in existence 1798
Specialist Reading Society (for teachers)	Berlin	1799
Reading Institute (for periodicals)	Elmenhorst	authorized 1799
Reading Society [RC]	Göttingen	before 1799
Journal Society [RC]	Bremen	1799
Museum	Hamburg-Altona	1799
Large Reading Society [RG]	Hanover	1799
Reading Society	Kaiserslautern	1799
Reading Society [RC]	Köthen	1799
Reading societies (approx. 20)	Mark (county)	in existence end of C18
Reading societies (6–8)	Meissen	in existence 1799
Reading Society [RC]	Rellingen	1799
Reading Society	Unna	in existence 1799
Reading Society [RL]	Waldkappell	1799
Citizens' Reading Institute	Bayreuth	1800
Specialist Reading Society (for merchants)	Berlin	1800
Reading Cabinet	Dresden	in existence 1800
Reading Society	Eckernförde	in existence 1800
Journal Society [RC]	Göttingen	authorized 1800
Reading Circle (for periodicals)	Gotha	in existence 1800

Theological Reading Society [RC]	Hoya	in existence 1800
Literary Society	Cologne	1800
Village Reading Society	village near Leipzig	in existence 1800
Teachers' Reading Society	Lüdenscheid	in existence 1800
Ladies' Reading Cabinet	Nuremberg	planned 1800
Reading societies (3)	Sonderburg	in existence 1800
Reading Society	Stargard/ Pommerania	in existence 1800
Artisans' Reading Society [RC]	Ulm	in existence 1800
Reading Society	Lahr	in existence 1801
Reading Society	Ravensburg	in existence 1801
Reading societies (for periodicals (3) [RC]	Güstrow	in existence 1803
School Masters' Reading Society	Borna	in existence 1804
Literary Museum	Gotha	in existence 1805
Journal Society [RC]	Hanover	in existence 1805

Details of dates not available:

Book Merchants' Reading Circle	Aachen
Reading circles (for newspapers) (several)	Ansbach
Reading Society [RL]	Hachenburg
Theological-Pedagogic Reading Society	Kaltennordheim and Ostheim
Reading Society	Olmütz
Reading Society	Troppau

MAPS

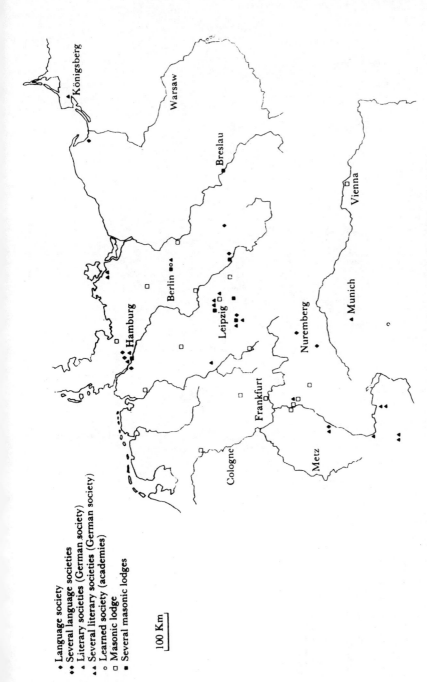

Map 1 Societies and foundings of societies from 1700 to 1745

Key:

- ♦ Language society
- ♦♦ Several language societies
- ▲ Literary societies (German society)
- ▲▲ Several literary societies (German society)
- ○ Learned society (academies)
- □ Masonic lodge
- ■ Several masonic lodges

100 Km

Königsberg
Warsaw
Breslau
Vienna
Hamburg
Berlin
Leipzig
Nuremberg
Munich
Frankfurt
Cologne
Metz

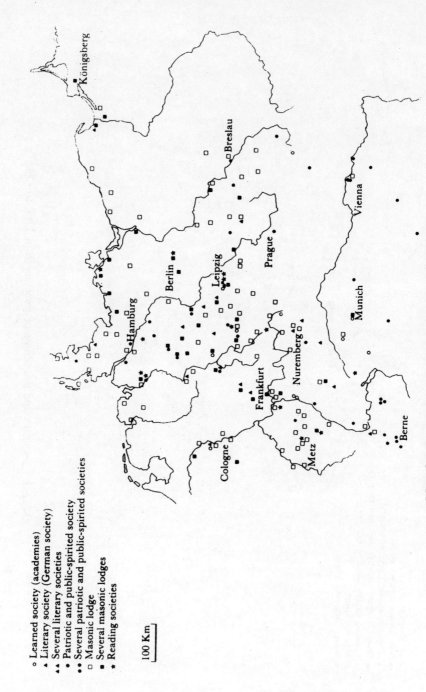

○ Learned society (academies)
▲ Literary society (German society)
▲▲ Several literary societies
● Patriotic and public-spirited society
●● Several patriotic and public-spirited societies
□ Masonic lodge
■ Several masonic lodges
★ Reading societies

100 Km

Map 2 Foundings of societies from 1746 to 1755

Königsberg

Breslau

Vienna

Berlin

Leipzig

Prague

Hamburg

Munich

Frankfurt

Nuremberg

Cologne

Metz

Berne

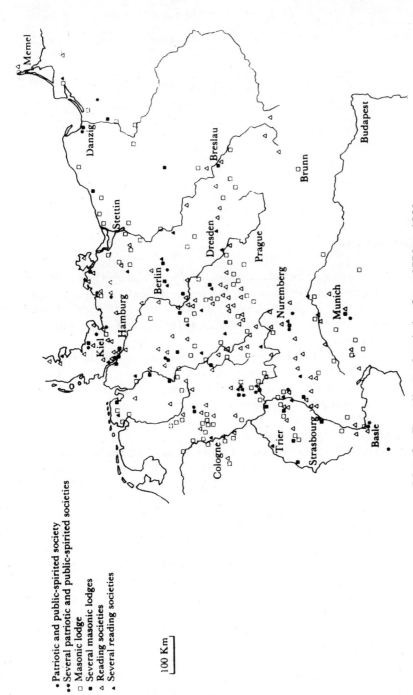

- • Patriotic and public-spirited society
- •• Several patriotic and public-spirited societies
- □ Masonic lodge
- ■ Several masonic lodges
- △ Reading societies
- ▲ Several reading societies

100 Km

Map 3 Foundings of societies from 1776 to 1880

Memel

Danzig

Stettin

Breslau

Brunn

Budapest

Dresden

Prague

Berlin

Hamburg

Kiel

Nuremberg

Munich

Cologne

Trier

Strasbourg

Basle

NOTES

INTRODUCTION

1 A. v. Harnack, *Geschichte der königlich Preussischen Akademie*, 1900; L. Hammermayer, *Geschichte der Bayerischen Akademie der Wissenschaften*, 1983; J. G. Findel, *Geschichte der Freimaurerei*, 1883; F. Runkel, *Geschichte der Freimaurerei in Deutschland*, 1931/2, and many others, see bibliography.

My sincere thanks are due to my assistants for their valuable support during the writing of this book, particularly Ludwig Linsmayer for his encouragement and criticism and Brigitte Gutjahr for her invaluable assistance in preparing the maps, analysing the membership lists and compiling the list of the societies of the Enlightenment.

2 E. Manheim, *Aufklärung und öffentliche Meinung. Studien zur Soziologie der Öffentlichkeit im 18. Jahrhundert*, edited by N. Schindler, Stuttgart, 1979; J. Habermas, *The Structural Transformation of the Public Sphere*, 1989.

3 T. Nipperdey, 'Verein als soziale Struktur im späten 18. und frühen 19. Jahrhundert', in Nipperdey, *Gesellschaft, Kultur, Theorie*, 1976.

4 O. Dann, 'Die Anfänge politischer Vereinsbildung in Deutschland', in *Festschrift Conze*, 1976. Other important studies include W. Dotzauer, 'Aufklärung und Sozietäten im 18. Jahrhundert', in *Geschichtliche Landeskunde* 21 (1980); U. Im Hof, *Das gesellige Jahrhundert*, 1982.

5 *Inter alia*, the essays by L. Hammermayer, O. Dann and W. Dotzauer. The literary reports of L. Hammermayer, 'Akademiebewegung und Wissenschaftsorganisation', in *Wissenschaftspolitik in Mittel- und Osteuropa*, 1976a, and 'Zur Geschichte der europäischen Freimaurerei und Geheimgesellschaften im Achtzehnten Jahrhundert', in *Eleusis*, 1976b, are important sources of further information.

6 *Inter alia*, R. Vierhaus (ed.), 'Deutsche patriotische und gemeinnützige Gesellschaften', in *Wolfenbütteler Forschungen*, vol. 8. 1980; P. C. Ludz (ed.), *Geheime Gesellschaften im 18. Jahrhundert*, 1979; H. Reinalter (ed.), *Freimaurer und Geheimbünde im 18. Jahrhundert in Mitteleuropa*, 1983; O. Dann (ed.), *Lesegesellschaften und bürgerliche Emanzipation*, 1981.

7 One of my early efforts, 'Die Aufklärungsgesellschaften in Deutschland im 18. Jahrhundert als Forschungsproblem', now in U. Herrmann (ed.), *Die Bildung des Bürgers. Die Formierung der bürgerlichen Gesellschaft und die Gebildeten im 18. Jahrhundert*, 1982, pp. 81–99.

8 A stimulating study is that by D. Roche, *Le siècle des lumières en province*, 1978, and also Roche, 'Die "Sociétés de pensée" und die aufgeklärte Elite des 18. Jahrhunderts in Frankreich', in H. U. Gumbrecht et al. (eds), *Sozialgeschichte der Aufklärung in Frankreich*, 1981, pp. 77–116. H. U. Gumbrecht, 'Literarische und geheime Gesellschaftsbildung im vorrevolutionären Frankreich: Akademien und Logen', in O. Dann (ed.), *Lesegesellschaften*, 1981, pp. 181–96.

CHAPTER I   ENLIGHTENMENT AND TRADITIONAL SOCIETY IN THE EIGHTEENTH CENTURY

1 For general socio-cultural studies on Germany, see B. Lutz (ed.), *Deutsches Bürgertum und literarische Intelligenz 1750–1800*, 1974; J. Schlumbohm, *Freiheit – Die Anfänge der bürgerlichen Emanzipationsbewegung in Deutschland im Spiegel ihres Leitwortes*, 1975; F. Kopitzsch, 'Die Sozialgeschichte der Aufklärung in Deutschland als Forschungsaufgabe', in Kopitzsch (ed.), *Aufklärung, Absolutismus und Bürgertum in Deutschland*, 1976a; H. H. Gerth, *Bürgerliche Intelligenz um 1800*, 1976; H. Kiesel and P. Münch, *Gesellschaft und Literatur im 18. Jahrhundert*, 1977; U. Herrmann (ed.), *'Die Bildung des Bürgers'. Die Formierung der bürgerlichen Gesellschaft und die Gebildeten im 18. Jahrhundert*, 1982; H. E. Bödeker, 'Strukturen der Aufklärungsgesellschaft in der Residenzstadt Kassel', in *Festschrift R. Vierhaus*, 1982 (an interesting effort); F. Kopitzsch, *Grundzüge einer Sozialgeschichte der Aufklärung in Hamburg und Altona*, 1982 (particularly the Introduction); Kopitzsch, 'Die deutsche Aufklärung. Leistungen, Grenzen, Wirkungen', in *Archiv für Sozialgeschichte* 23 (1983a); W. Ruppert, *Bürgerlicher Wandel*, 2nd edn, 1984.

CHAPTER 2   LEARNED AND LITERARY SOCIETIES IN THE SEVENTEENTH CENTURY

1 General: G. Hummel, *Die humanistischen Sodalitäten und ihr Einfluss auf die Entwicklung des Bildungswesens der Reformationszeit*, 1940; H.

Rupprich, *Humanismus und Renaissance in den deutschen Städten und an den Universitäten*, 1935.

2　F. von Bezold, 'Konrad Celtis, der deutsche Erzhumanist', in *Historische Zeitschrift* 49 (1883); C. Treml, 'Kommunikationsformen humanistischer Gelehrter um 1500', MA manuscript, 1982.

3　For some important accounts, see K. F. Otto, *Die Sprachgesellschaften des 17. Jahrhunderts*, 1972a; C. Stoll, *Sprachgesellschaften im Deutschland des 17. Jahrhunderts*, 1973; M. Bircher and F. v. Ingen (eds), *Sprachgesellschaften, Sozietäten, Dichtergruppen*, 1978.

4　K. Dissel, *Philip von Zesen und die Deutschgesinnte Genossenschaft*, 1890.

5　L. Neubaur, 'Zur Geschichte des Elbschwanenordens', in *Altpreussische Monatsschriften* 47 (1910).

6　Cf. Otto, *Sprachgesellschaften*, 1972a.

7　M. Bircher, *Joh. Wilhelm von Stubenberg (1619–1663) und sein Freundeskreis*, 1968.

8　F. Dix, 'Die tugendliche Gesellschaft', in *Mitteilungen der deutschen Gesellschaft* 6 (1877).

9　The following are still standard works of reference: F. W. Barthold, *Geschichte der Fruchtbringenden Gesellschaft*, 1848; F. Zöllner, *Einrichtung und Verfassung der Fruchtbringenden Gesellschaft vornehmlich unter dem Fürsten Ludwig zu Anhalt-Cöthen*, 1899.

10　G. Neumark, *Der Neu-Sprossende Teutsche Palmbaum*, Munich, 1970 (reprint), p. 25.

11　K. G. v. Hille, *Der Teutsche Palmbaum*, Munich, 1970 (reprint), p. 20.

12　J. Herdegen, *Historische Nachricht von dess löblichen Hirten-und Blumenordens an der Pegnitz Anfang und Fortgang; Festschrift zur 250jährigen Jubelfeier des Pegnesischen Blumenordens gegründet in Nürnberg*, 1894; B. L. Spahr, *The Archives of the Pegnesischer Blumenorden*, 1960; E. Mannack (ed.), *Die Pegnitz-Schäfer*, 1968.

13　Herdegen, *Historische Nachricht*, pp. 5–10.

14　Ibid., p. 3. See also R. van Dülmen, 'Sozietätsbildungen in Nürnberg im 17. Jahrhundert', in *Festschrift Bosl*, 1969, p. 177.

15　For general accounts, see J. Jansen, *Patriotismus und Nationalethos in den Flugschriften und Friedensspielen des Dreissigjährigen Krieges*, 1964; H. J. Berbig, *Das Nationalgefühl in Nürnberg nach dem Dreissigjährigen Krieg*, 1960.

16　Quoted from Otto, *Sprachgesellschaften*, 1972a, p. 46.

17　G. Schröttel, *Joh. Michael Dilherr und die vorpietistische Kirchenreform in Nürnberg*, 1962.

18　H.-J. Frank, *Catharina Regina von Greiffenberg. Leben und Welt*, 1967.

19　Herdegen, *Historische Nachricht*, p. 18.

20　G. E. Guhrauer, *Joachim Jungius und sein Zeitalter*, 1850; L. Keller, 'Comenius und die Akademien der Naturphilosophen des 17. Jahrhunderts', in *Monatshefte der Comenius-Gesellschaft*, 1895.

21 'Festschrift zur Gedenkfeier an die vor 300 Jahren in Schweinfurt erfolgte Gründung der Deutschen Akademie der Naturforscher', in *Veröffentlichungen des Historischen Vereins Schweinfurt*, 2, 1952; *Nunquam otiosus. Beiträge zur Geschichte der Präsidenten der Deutschen Akademie der Naturforscher Leopoldina*, 1970.

22 W. Artelt, Vom Akademiegedanken im 17. Jahrhundert, in *Nunquam otiosus*, 1970.

23 Quoted from J. Steudel, 'Leibniz und die Leopoldina', in *Nova Acta Leopoldina*, N. S. 16 (1953/4), p. 468.

CHAPTER 3   THE REPUBLIC OF SCHOLARS

1 For a general account of the problem of the Republic of Scholars, see G. Sauder, ' "Galante Ethica" und aufgeklärte Öffentlichkeit in der Gelehrtenrepublik', in Hansers *Sozialgeschichte der deutschen Literatur*, vol. 3, 1980. In addition, see L. Hammermayer, *Akademiebewegung und Wissenschaftsorganisationen: Stand der Forschung*, 1976a and J. Voss, 'Die Akademien als Organisationsträger der Wirtschaft im 18. Jahrhundert, in *Historische Zeitschrift* 231 (1980).

2 The most important accounts are L. Keller, *Gottfried Wilhelm Leibniz und die deutschen Sozietäten des 17. Jahrhunderts*, 1903; W. Totok, 'Leibniz als Wissenschaftsorganisator', in W. Totok and C. Haase (eds), *Leibniz*, 1966; W. Schneiders, 'Sozietätspläne und Sozialutopie bei Leibniz', in *Studia Leibniziana VII/1* (1975); W. Schneiders, 'Gottesreich und gelehrte Gesellschaft. Zwei politische Modelle bei G. W. Leibniz', in F. Hartmann and R. Vierhaus (eds), *Der Akademiegedanke im 17. und 18. Jahrhundert*, 1977.

3 A. v. Harnack, *Geschichte der königlich Preussischen Akademie der Wissenschaften zu Berlin*, 1900, pp. 71f.

4 Ibid. of 11 July 1700.

5 Denkschrift über den Zweck und Nutzen einer zu gründenden Sozietät der Wissenschaften zu Berlin (= G. W. Leibniz, *Politische Schriften*, vol. 2 (1967); p. 86).

6 Harnack, *Akademie der Wissenschaften*, vol. 2, p. 104.

7 Ibid.

8 Ibid.

9 Quoted from Totok, *Leibniz als Wissenschaftsorganisator*, p. 296.

10 *Festschrift zur Feier des 200jährigen Bestehens der Akademie der Wissenschaften in Göttingen*, 1951.

11 P. Fuchs, *Palatinatus Illustratus*, 1963; J. Voss, *Universität, Geschichtswissenschaft und Diplomatie im Zeitalter der Aufklärung*, 1979.

12 H.-H. Müller, *Akademie und Wirtschaft im 18. Jahrhundert*, 1975.

13 M. Spindler (ed.), *Electoralis Academiae Scientiarum Boicae Primordia. Briefe aus der Gründungszeit der Bayerischen Akademie der Wissenschaften*, 1959, pp. 82f.

14 L. Hammermayer, *Geschichte der Bayerischen Akademie der Wissenschaften*, 1983; A. Kraus, *Die historische Forschung an der churbayerischen Akademie der Wissenschaften 1759–1806*, 1959; A. Kraus, *Die naturwissenschaftliche Forschung an der Bayerischen Akademie der Wissenschaften im Zeitalter der Aufklärung*, 1978.

15 For a general account, see R. van Dülmen, 'Zum Strukturwandel der Aufklärung in Bayern', in *Festschrift Bosl*, 1973.

16 L. Hammermayer, 'Die Benediktiner und die Akademiebewegung im katholischen Deutschland 1720 bis 1770', in *Studien und Mitteilungen der Geschichte des Benediktinerordens* 70, 1960.

17 R. van Dülmen, 'Antijesuitismus und katholische Aufklärung in Deutschland', in *Historisches Jahrbuch* 89 (1969).

18 L. Hammermayer, *Geschichte der Bayerischen Akademie der Wissenschaften*, 1983, vol. 1, p. 354.

19 Ibid., p. 358.

20 Ibid., p. 355.

21 J. Gebele, *Peter von Osterwald*, 1891.

22 G. Lurz, *Die bayerische Mittelschule seit der Übernahme durch die Klöster bis zur Säkularisation*, 1905.

23 No standard reference work is available on this subject. For the only general study to date, see L. Keller, *Die Deutschen Gesellschaften des XVIII. Jahrhunderts und die moralischen Wochenschriften*, 1900.

24 C. Petersen, 'Die teutsch-übende Gesellschaft in Hamburg', in *Zeitschrift des Vereins für Hamburgische Geschichte*, vol. 2 (1847); also F. Kopitzsch, *Grundzüge einer Sozialgeschichte der Aufklärung in Hamburg und Altona*, 1982, pp. 265f.

25 H. Bodmer, 'Die Gesellschaft der Maler in Zürich und ihre Diskurse (1721–1723)', 1895; H. Brandes, *Die Gesellschaft der Maler und ihr literarischer Beitrag zur Aufklärung des 18. Jahrhunderts*, 1974.

26 Kopitzsch, *Grundzüge einer Sozialgeschichte der Aufklärung in Hamburg und Altona*, pp. 265ff.

27 Ibid.

28 Ibid.

29 Quoted in W. Martens, *Die Botschaft der Tugend*, 1971, p. 135.

30 Quoted from Kopitzsch, *Grundzüge einer Sozialgeschichte der Aufklärung in Hamburg und Altona*, p. 275.

31 Quoted from G. Sauder, 'Moralische Wochenschriften', in *Hansers Sozialgeschichte der deutschen Literatur*, vol. 3, p. 278.

32 For general accounts, see E. Wolff, *Gottscheds Stellung im deutschen Bildungsleben*, 1895; T. W. Danzel, *Gottsched und seine Zeit*, 1848; F. Neumann, 'Gottsched und die Leipziger Deutsche Gesellschaft', in *Archiv für Kulturgeschichte* 18 (1928).

33 E. Wolff, *Gottscheds Stellung im deutschen Bildungsleben*, part 1, 1895, pp. 3–14; G. Krause, *Gottsched und Flottwell*, 1893; P. Otto, *Die deutsche Gesellschaft in Göttingen*, 1898; F. Weber, 'Die bremische Deutsche Gesellschaft 1748–1793', 1910; E. Wolff, 'Die Deutschen Gesellschaften zu Erlangen und Altdorf im XVIII. Jahrhundert', in *Monatshefte der Comenius-Gesellschaft* 8 (1899).

34 Quoted from L. Hammermayer, *Geschichte der Bayerischen Akademie der Wissenschaften*, vol. 1, 1983, p. 30.

35 From W. Suchier, 'Die Mitglieder der Deutschen Gesellschaft in Göttingen', in *Zeitschrift des historischen Vereins für Niedersachsen*, 81 (1916).

36 Gottsched's message, in W. Killy (ed.), *18. Jahrhundert. Texte und Zeugnisse*, 1983, p. 858.

37 Taken from the Leipzig statutes, in ibid., p. 860.

38 Ibid., p. 862. G. Witkowski, *Geschichte des literarischen Lebens in Leipzig*, 1909.

39 Quoted from W. Rieck, *Joh. Christoph Gottsched*, 1972, pp. 46f.

40 The importance of attending a meeting of the German Society is revealed by the following comments of one of the members of the Berne Society:

> Thus were we taught, and we were all encouraged to continue reading selected material in the privacy of our own homes. Not least during these meetings, distinguished works of recent publication were read and discussed publicly, and thus, everyone benefited from the contributions of his fellows. In a nutshell, we were willing participants in this useful and necessary exercise for many years, and many of our number have enjoyed the intellectual and secular fruits of this activity throughout our lives. For my part, I pride myself on having learnt a great deal and on having gained innumerable hours of pleasure from these meetings; it was always with the greatest of pleasure that I sacrificed worthless and vulgar gambling evenings on the altar of this sensible and educational pastime. (Wolff, *Gottscheds*, vol. 2, p. 12.)

CHAPTER 4   ASSOCIATION OF 'CIVILIZED' MEN

1 There is no modern account available. Accounts still of importance are H. Boos, *Geschichte der Freimaurerei*, 2nd edn, Aarau, 1906; J. G. Findel, *Geschichte der Freimaurerei*, 1883; A. Kallweit, *Die Freimaurerei in Hessen-Kassel*, 1966; W. Keller, *Geschichte der Freimaurerei in Deutschland*, 1959; E. Lennhoff, *Die Freimaurer*, 1929; C. v. Nettelbladt, *Geschichte Freimaurerischer Systeme in England, Frankreich und Deutschland,*

1879; F. Runkel, *Geschichte der Freimaurerei in Deutschland*, 1931/2; A. Wolfstieg, *Werden und Wesen der Freimaurerei*, 1922/3, and particularly the following recent studies: W. Dotzauer, *Freimaurergesellschaften am Rhein*, 1977; R. Vierhaus, '*Aufklärung und Freimaurerei in Deutschland*', in H. Reinalter (ed.), Freimaurer und Geheimbünde; L. Hammermayer, 'Zur Geschichte der europäischen Freimaurerei und Geheimgesellschaften im 18. Jahrhundert', 1976b; a pioneering study is that of N. Schindler, 'Freimaurerkultur im 18. Jahrhundert', in Berdahl et al. (eds), *Klassen und Kultur*, 1982.

2 R. Koselleck, *Kritik und Krise*, 2nd edn, 1969, p. 64.
3 Cf. A. Wolfstieg, *Bibliographie der freimaurerischen Literatur*, 1913ff.
4 F. J. Schneider, *Die Freimaurerei und ihr Einfluss auf die geistige Kultur Deutschlands am Ende des 18. Jahrhunderts*, 1909.
5 R. Minder, *Glaube, Skepsis und Rationalismus*, 2nd edn, 1974, p. 171f. This contains the following reference to the lodge 'Zur Beständigkeit':

> Reiser joined the Order of Freemasons around this time. For many, this step is nothing more than another desire to follow the trend. For Reiser, however, this step heralded a complete transformation. The order and solemnity prevailing in the lodge of which Reiser became a member at that time fuelled his phantasy. The tender solidarity of the brothers was good for his soul, which for so long had had to forego the delights of friendship, and the great sympathy which everyone, especially the venerable Grand Master, displayed for his fate, overwhelmed him. The lodge atmosphere at that time was marked by effusiveness and piety: many a time, the openings and closings of meetings were accompanied by a prayer and tears, and some of the members had reached the stage where they yearned for association with the spirits whom they naively believed really did associate with the pure of heart. However, there was also fraternal harmony, and all vestiges of pride had been banished. The solemnity and ceremonies were designed to captivate the heart rather than the mind, but one was at pains to remove the peel and enjoy the fruits. Reiser was at peace in this circle. (K. F. Klischnig, *Erinnerungen aus den zehn letzten Lebensjahren meines Freundes Anton Reiser* [1794], pp. 47f.)

6 Cf. note 4 above.
7 H. C. Freiesleben, *Goethe als Freimaurer*, 1949. 'For some considerable time, I had hoped to have cause to become a Freemason. . . . The absence of this title was all that was preventing me from associating more closely with people whom I respected – and it is this sense of fraternity alone which causes me to seek admittance'

(B. v. Fritsch from 13 February 1780, in *Goethes Briefe* [1962], vol. 1, p. 294).

8   Quoted from Im Hof, *Das gesellige Jahrhundert*, p. 169.

9   G. E. Lessing, *Freimaurergespräche und anderes*, 1981.

10 J. G. Fichte, *Ausgewählte Politische Schriften*, 1970, (Vorlesungen über die Freimaurerei).

11 G. E. Lessing, *Freimaurergespräche*, p. 71.

12 F. Kopitzsch, *Grundzüge einer Sozialgeschichte der Aufklärung in Hamburg und Altona*, pp. 313ff. and 586ff.

13 W. Dotzauer, *Freimaurergesellschaften am Rhein*.

14 This is Schindler's estimate in *Freimaurerkultur im 18. Jahrhundert*, p. 208.

15 Ibid.

16 Ibid.

17 Cf. note 12 above.

18 H. Wagner (ed.), *Freimaurerei um Joseph II. Die Loge zur Wahren Eintracht*, 1980.

19 B. Beyer, *Freimauerei in München und Altbeiern*, pp. 113ff.

20 B. Beyer, *Geschichte der Grossloge 'Zur Sonne' in Bayreuth*, 1964, vol. 1, pp. 236ff.

21 'Alphabetische Liste der Mitglieder der Fr. M. Loge Minerva zu den Drey Palmen in Leipzig 1787' (I am indebted to Norbert Schindler for this reference).

22 W. Ebertz, *Geschichte des Orients Wetzlar*, 1893, pp. 57ff.

23 'Liste der gerecht und vollkommenen Loge Amalia in Weimar 5781' (I am indebted to Norbert Schindler for this reference).

24 A. Pauls, *Geschichte der Aachener Freimaurerei*, 1928, vol. 1, pp. 515ff.

25 E. Lennhoff and O. Posner, *Internationales Freimaurer-Lexikon*, 1932, p. 235.

26 Discussed in chapter 5.

27 H. Möller, 'Die Bruderschaft der Gold- und Rosenkreuzer. Struktur, Zielsetzung und Wirkung einer anti-aufklärerischen Geheimgesellschaft', in H. Reinalter (ed.), *Freimaurer und Geheimbünde*, pp. 199–239.

28 K. R. H. Frick, *Die Erleuchteten*, 1973, pp. 177ff.

29 Ibid., pp. 246ff.

30 L. Hammermayer, *Der Wilhelmsbader Freimaurerkonvent 1782*, 1980b.

31 W. Ebertz, *Geschichte des Orients Wetzlar*, p. 28; L. Keller, *Geschichte des eklektischen Freimaurerbundes*, 1857.

32 *Der sich selbst vertheidigende Freymäurer, Sammlung unterschiedlicher wohlverfassten Schriften*, Frankfurt/Leipzig, 1744, p. 117.

33 A. Pauls, *Geschichte der Aachener Freimaurerei*, vol. 1, p. 476.

34 Quoted from F. Runkel, *Geschichte der Freimaurerei in Deutschland*, vol. 1, pp. 154–8.

35 W. Ebertz, *Geschichte des Orients Wetzlar*, pp. 18ff.

36 Ibid., p. 22.
37 F. Runkel, *Geschichte der Freimaurerei in Deutschland*, vol. 1, p. 158. The following demands were made of the Freemason: 'He must free himself as far as possible from the shackles of prejudice, tread the straight path of Reason in his efforts to penetrate to the heart of Truth, eschew idleness, properly discharge the duties of his office and take pleasure in all kinds of useful activities' (Quoted from Pauls, *Geschichte der Aachener Freimaurerei*, vol. 1, p. 113).
38 *Patriotisches Archiv für Deutschland*, vol. 3, 1786.
39 General: H. Hubrig, *Die patriotischen Gesellschaften des 18. Jahrhunderts*, 1957; R. Vierhaus (ed.), 'Deutsche patriotische und gemeinnützige Gesellschaften', 1980.
40 Important: N. Schindler and W. Bonss, 'Praktische Aufklärung – ökonomische Sozietäten in Süddeutschland und Österreich im 18. Jahrhundert', in R. Vierhaus (ed.), *Deutsche patriotische und gemeinnützige Gesellschaften*, pp. 255–354.
41 H. Eichler, 'Die Leipziger Ökonomische Sozietät im 18. Jahrhundert', in *Jahrbuch für die Geschichte des Feudalismus* 2 (1978), p. 365; S. Graf, 'Aufklärung in der Provinz', manuscript, 1980, vol. 2, p. 69.
42 Cf. list contained in F. Euler, *Vom Gewerbefleiss zur Industrie*, 1967, pp. 127ff.
43 No detailed analysis of the extant lists has yet been conducted.
44 *Ausführliche Nachricht von der Hamburgischen Gesellschaft zur Beförderung der Künste und nützlichen Gewerbe*, 1792, p. 100. From the speech delivered by J. A. Reimarus on 15 April, 1790:

> Citizens from all feudal backgrounds congregate here together. By virtue of their different insights and experiences and their different occupations, both public and private, useful ideas which might otherwise have been smothered or lost are brought out into the open for general consideration and support. Friendly discussion and the constant awareness of the common purpose generate the agreement which is required in order that some among our number do not militate against the well-being of any persons, and hence, against the common good, during the unilateral execution of the area of responsibility with which they have been especially entrusted. . . . Their sole purpose should be to shed some light on useful proposals and to initiate detailed studies and investigations into their practicability with regard to local conditions and difficulties, and also a detailed examination of purpose and substance, thus, with a modest degree of candour, preparing the ground for deliberation lying outside the scope of the society's true sphere of influence. (Ibid., pp. 107ff.)

45 Cf. K. D. Sievers, 'Patriotische Gesellschaften in Schleswig-Holstein zwischen 1786 und 1829', in R. Vierhaus (ed.), *Deutsche patriotische und gemeinnützige Gesellschaften*, pp. 119–41.

46 G. Kowalewski, *Geschichte der Hamburgischen Gesellschaft zur Beförderung der Künste und nützlichen Gewerbe. Die Patriotische Gesellschaft zu Hamburg 1765–1965*, 1897; F. Kopitzsch, 'Die Hamburgische Gesellschaft zur Beförderung der Künste und nützlichen Gewerbe (Patriotische Gesellschaft von 1765) im Zeitalter der Aufklärung. Ein Überblick', in R. Vierhaus (ed.), *Deutsche patriotische und gemeinnützige Gesellschaften*, pp. 71–118.

47 Ibid., pp. 84f.

48 Ibid., p. 84.

49 Quoted from ibid., p. 95.

50 U. Im Hof, 'Die Helvetische Gesellschaft 1761–1798', in R. Vierhaus (ed.), *Deutsche patriotische und gemeinnützige Gesellschaften*, pp. 223–40.

51 Quoted from U. Im Hof, *Isaak Iselin und die Spätaufklärung*, 1967, p. 39.

52 U. Im Hof, 'Die Helvetische Gesellschaft', pp. 230f.

53 K. v. Reinhardstöttner, *Die sittlich-ökonomische Gesellschaft zu Burghausen*, 1895; N. Schindler and W. Bonss, 'Praktische Aufklärung', in R. Vierhaus (ed.) 1980, p. 283ff.; a standard work is S. Graf, 'Aufklärung in der Provinz', vol. 2, p. 20.

54 S. Graf, 'Gesellschaft der schönen Wissenschaften zu Oetting am Inn (1765–1769). Eine Studie zur Aufklärung in Bayern', in *Zeitschrift für bayerische Landesgeschichte* 46 (1983), pp. 81–137.

55 Graf, 'Aufklärung in der Provinz', vol. 2, p. 20.

56 J. Voss, 'Die Société Patriotique de Hesse-Hombourg (1775–1781). Der erste Versuch einer europäischen Koordinationsstelle für wissenschaftlichen Austausch', in R. Vierhaus (ed.), *Deutsche patriotische und gemeinnützige* Gesellschaften, pp. 195–222.

57 Hubrig, *Die patiotischen Gesellschaften*, pp. 65f.

58 Ibid., pp. 98f.

59 Cf. C. Grau, 'Herder, die Wissenschaft und die Akadamien seiner Zeit', in *Jahrbuch für Geschichte* 19 (1979).

CHAPTER 5   CLUBS OF THE ENLIGHTENMENT AND
POLITICAL ASSOCIATIONS

1 General: M. Prüsener, 'Lesegesellschaften im 18. Jahrhundert', 1972; O. Dann (ed.), *Lesegesellschaften und bürgerliche Emanzipation*, 1981; a standard work is O. Dann, 'Die Lesegesellschaften des 18. Jahrhunderts und der gesellschaftliche Aufbruch des deutschen

Bürgertums', in U. Herrmann (ed.), *Die Bildung des Bürgers*, 1982, pp. 100–19.

2   R. Engelsing, *Analphabetentum und Lektüre. Zur Sozialgeschichte des Lesens in Deutschland*, 1973a.

3   R. Engelsing, 'Die Perioden der Lesergeschichte in der Neuzeit', in R. Engelsing, *Sozialgeschichte deutscher Mittel- und Unterschichten*, 1973.

4   Quoted from M. Prüsener, *Lesegesellschaften*, pp. 379ff.

5   General: Martens, *Die Botschaft der Tugend*.

6   An example is Kopitzsch, *Grundzüge einer Sozialgeschichte der Aufklärung*, pp. 401ff.

7   As the Bonn Society was already known. For the purely social associations, cf. *inter alia* H. Freudenthal, *Vereine in Hamburg. Ein Beitrag zur Geschichte und Volkskunde der Geselligkeit*, 1968.

8   O. Dann, 'Die Lesegesellschaften des 18. Jahrhunderts', p. 103; Prüsener, *Lesegesellschaften*, pp. 518ff.

9   For details of actual numbers, cf. O. Dann, 'Die Lesegesellschaften', p. 5; Prüsener, *Lesegesellschaften*, pp. 531ff.

10   Cf. Prüsener, *Lesegesellschaften*, pp. 411ff.

11   Invitation to attend the founding of a reading society in Koblenz from 1783, in J. Hansen (ed.), *Quellen zur Geschichte des Rheinlandes im Zeitalter der Französischen Revolution*, 1935, vol. 1, p. 35.

> The means by which enlightenment and knowledge can be propagated and everyone afforded the same opportunity of enjoying their periods of occupational respite to the full are educational social intercourse and the constant reading of such material that reveals to the world the changes, variety, and peculiarites common to all countries and states, and the progress of human knowledge in all branches of science. The only possible way of achieving this objective is by means of an association of a number of people who pool their resources to procure the best political and learned newspapers, journals, periodicals and other generally useful writings, which are gradually enriching the world of literature, house them in one place where they are accessible for reading at any time of the day which is convenient and make the effort to extract benefit and pleasure from the concepts and knowledge gleamed from the reading matter by means of discussion and the reciprocal exchange of information.

12   Ibid., vol. 1, pp. 490ff.

13   From the statutes of the Karlsruhe Reading Society. Quoted from Prüsener, *Lesegesellschaften*, p. 253.

14   C. M. Kneisel, *Geschichtliche Nachrichten von der Lese- und Erholungs-*

gesellschaft in Bonn, 1837. Cf. also M. Braubach, 'Ein publizistischer Plan der Bonner Lesegesellschaft aus dem Jahre 1789', in M. Braubach, *Diplomatie und geistiges Leben*, 1969, pp. 764ff.

15 B. M. Milstein, *Eight Eighteenth Century Reading Societies*, 1972, pp. 12–14.

16 Ibid. Cf. also W. Dotzauer, 'Das aufgeklärte Trier', in *Geschichtliche Landeskunde* 9 (1973a).

17 B. M. Milstein, *Eight Eighteenth Century Reading Societies*.

18 K.-H. Pröve, *Von der ersten Lesegesellschaft zur Stadtbücherei*, 1967, p. 18; '...that members from a variety of feudal backgrounds associate with, and hence, meet and learn to respect, each other.' (p. 9).

19 O. Dann, *Lesegesellschaften*, p. 107.

20 Cf. the statutes of the Mainz Reading Society. Schünk, *Beiträge zur Mainzer Geschichte*, 1788, vol. 1, p. 20.

21 Cf. *inter alia* A. von Carnap, 'Zur Geschichte Wupperthals. Die geschlossene Gesellschaft in Elberfeld', in *Zeitschrift des Bergischen Geschichtsvereins* 1, (1863), p. 73.

22 Ibid.

23 *Johann Heinrich Jung-Stilling, Lebensgeschichte.* Edited by G. A. Benrath, Darmstadt, 1976, p. 341.

24 A. von Carnap, *Zur Geschichte Wupperthals. Die geschlossene Lesegesellschaft in Elberfeld*, pp. 58f.

25 M. Prüsener, *Lesegesellschaft*, pp. 425ff.

26 As can also be inferred from the names of the masonic lodges, this quest for harmony was common to all societies.

27 J. Hansen (ed.), *Quellen zur Geschichte des Rheinlandes*, vol. 4, pp. 140ff (exact year of publication not known).

28 Quoted from O. Dann, *Lesegesellschaften*, p. 111. From the statutes of the Stuttgart Reading Society, 1795:

> While not regarding a reading society as a necessity, any locality of any importance whose inhabitants are possessed of cultural aspirations nevertheless holds the conviction that such a society is an institution of public benefit. For the purpose of quenching a noble thirst for learning, of propagating knowledge of every kind and of improving taste and morals, and even the pleasures of societal life, these societies employ the most appropriate means to achieve the maximum benefit. (Quoted from M. Prüsener, *Lesegesellschaften*, p. 413.)

29 O. Dann, *Lesegesellschaften*, p. 113.

30 *Inter alia*, M. Braubach, *Ein publizistischer Plan*, p. 781.

31 Inter alia, Prüsener, *Lesegesellschaften*, p. 521. On the problem of

friendship, cf. F. Tenbruck, 'Freundschaft', in *Kölner Zeitschrift für Soziologie und Sozialpsychologie* 16 (1964); I. Kon, *Freundschaft. Geschichte und Sozialpsychologie der Freundschaft als soziale Institution und individuelle Beziehung*, 1979.

32 R. Bäsken, *Die Dichter des Göttinger Hains und die Bürgerlichkeit*, 1937; A. Kelletat (ed.), *Der Göttinger Hain*, 1972.

33 Letter from Voss to Brückner dated 20 September 1772:

> Oh, September 12th! You should have been there, my dearest friend! In the evening, the two Millers, Hahn, Hölty and I all went to a nearby village. The evening was unusually fine, and there was a full moon. We emersed ourselves completely in the beauty of nature. We partook of some roe in a peasant's hut before venturing forth into the fields where we discovered a small oak tree. At that moment, we all decided to swear a bond of frendship beneath the panoply of this sacred tree. We adorned our hats with oak leaves and laid them at the foot of the tree. Then, we all clasped hands around the tree and danced round in circles, calling upon the moon to bear witness to our bond and swearing eternal friendship. Finally, we pledged to judge each other with the utmost sincerity, to which end we would hold our regular meetings more frequently and in a more solemn atmosphere. (R. Bäsken, *Die Dichter des Göttinger Hains und die Bürgerlichkeit*, 1937, pp. 349f.).

34 R. Bäsken, *Die Dichter des Göttinger Hains und die Bürgerlichkeit*, 1937, pp. 390f.

35 G. Kaiser, *Klopstock. Religion und Dichtung*, 1963.

36 A. Kelletat, *Der Göttinger Hain*, p. 359.

37 M. Kirschstein, *Klopstocks Deutsche Gelehrtenrepublik*, 1928.

38 A. Kelletat, Der Göttinger Hain, p. 366.

39 Ibid., letters from Lichtenberg, pp. 366f.

40 F. Kopitzsch, *Grundzüge einer Sozialgeschichte der Aufklärung*, pp. 540f.

41 G. A. v. Halem, *Selbstbiographie*, 1840, pp. 86f.:

> At that time, Büsch's house was the meeting place for learned visitors from abroad where they were introduced to learned Hamburg societies. Pride of place among these societies was occupied by a so-called reading society, founded by Klopstock and to which I also gained admittance. Men and women were present in equal numbers and, if my memory serves me correctly, they met around six o'clock in the evening. Only the first hour was devoted to readings. The readers sat at a slightly raised table beneath the painting 'Theone, the ideal

reader' which the Kassel artist, Tischbein, had based on one of Klopstock's poems and presented to the society. On that occasion, Klopstock did not hold a reading. Among those who did was von Voght, who later became finance minister. He included my essay entitled 'A monument to trees' which I had submitted anonymously to the museum, among his contributions. After an hour, the reading circle formed into card groups. There were many who did not join such groups, however, including Klopstock, who was engaged in a lively conversation with the ladies, flirting and laughing with them. After the card games, dinner was served. This society existed for only a few short years; card playing and the presence of the ladies might have played a part in its premature dissolution.

42 H. Schieckel, 'Die Mitglieder der Oldenburgischen literarischen Gesellschaft von 1779', in *Oldenburger Jahrbuch* 78/9.

43 G. A. v. Halem, *Selbstbiographie*.

44 R. Engelsing, *Der Bürger als Leser*, 1974, pp. 259ff.

45 Ibid., p. 268.

46 Ibid.

47 L. Keller, 'Die Berliner Mittwochs-Gesellschaft. Ein Beitrag zur Geschichte der Geistesentwicklung am Ausgang des 18. Jahrhunderts', in *Monatshefte der Comenius-Gesellschaft* V (1896), pp. 67–94; H. Möller, *Aufklärung in Preussen*, 1974, pp. 229f; N. Hinske (ed.), *Was ist Aufklärung? Beiträge aus der Berlinischen Monatsschrift*, 3rd edn, 1981 (see Introduction); E. Hellmuth, 'Aufklärung und Pressefreiheit. Zur Debatte der Berliner Mittwochsgesellschaft während der Jahre 1783 und 1784', in *Zeitschrift für historische Forschung* 9 (1982), pp. 315–45.

48 Quoted from Möller, *Aufklärung in Preussen*, p. 232.

49 Ibid., p. 231.

50 Hinske (ed.), *Was ist Aufklärung?*, vol. 27.

51 W. H. Bruford, *Kultur und Gesellschaft im klassischen Weimar 1775–1806*, 1966, pp. 359ff. C. Schüddekopf, 'Die Freitagsgesellschaft', in *Goethe-Jahrbuch* 19 (1898), pp. 14–19.

52 From 'Tag-und Jahreshefte, 1796', in *Goethes Poetische Werke. Vollständige Ausgabe*, 1959, vol. 8 (Cotta), p. 1014.

53 From ibid., p. 1494; *Goethes Amtliche Schriften*, vol. 2, p. 200:

There is no doubt that anyone active in business who frequently engages in undertakings on other people's behalf is also obliged to socialize with people, to seek out like-minded companions whom he can exploit for his own purposes while at the same time serving their interests. . . . The champions of science are often alone and very isolated, although as a result of the widespread availability of books and the rapid circulation of all knowledge, they are unaware of their lack of social companionship. This is another area in which the spirit of solidarity should reign supreme, but all too often, the horizon is limited to the self, the school, overshadowing all else. Discord destroys the bond of companionship, and joint research often results in mutual estrangement. What good fortune that science, like everything else which has a truly solid foundation, can benefit as much from discord as from harmony, perhaps more so! It takes two to disagree, not one, and thus, even conflict steers us in the right direction.

54 Ibid., pp. 201f.
55 W. Flitner, *August Ludwig Hülsen und der Bund der Freien Männer*, 1913; P. Raabe (ed.), 'Das Protokollbuch der Gesellschaft der freien Männer in Jena 1794–1799', in *Festschrift Berend*, 1959.
56 Ibid., p. 337.
57 Ibid., p. 354.
58 Ibid., p. 348.
59 Ibid., p. 338. It would appear that the league was inspired by the 'Statutes of the Society of Free Men' which were published in the 'Neue Teutsche Merkur', G. St. in 1793 (pp. 129–32):

1 Our society is called the Society of Free Men. The candidness with which everyone is free to voice his opinion of the truth without fear of contradiction, and the meritorious fact that, unlike many other societies, we are subject not to the arbitrary commands of a fellow member but to a set of voluntarily adopted statutes, fully justify this description.

2 The primary purpose of this association is to enjoy the pleasure of company and to enhance our enjoyment of life within an intimate circle of noble friends. However, we also hope to be able to combine usefulness with pleasure, and together perhaps achieve something of merit which would have been beyond the capacity of the individual.

3 No person can be admitted as a member without universal approval, other than under the following exceptional circumstances: where, without giving a reason, a single member refuses to consent to the admittance of an applicant whom all the other members favour.

4 Everyone is obliged to observe the statutes as long as he wishes to remain a member of the society, though he is free to leave the society at any time of his choosing. However,

in this case, he is obliged to give his word of honour both verbally and in writing that he shall never abuse the confidences with which he has been entrusted to the detriment of any Free Man, and never betray any opinion voiced before the society to any third party as that of a member of this society. Everyone is obliged to give his word of honour immediately upon his admittance to the society that he shall faithfully observe this statute above all others.

5 Our meetings will be held twice weekly during the six winter months (from October to the end of March). There shall be one meeting, devoted solely to discussion, which is not subject to the statutes, and one meeting which is subject to the statutes. On the agreed dates, we shall congregate in the evenings after dinner at a particular location, the rent for which shall be met by everyone in equal measure, where everyone may bring his own wine, or whatever else he may prefer, or can order his requirements from the host.

60   A. v. Knigge, *Über den Umgang mit Menschen*, 1967, reprint, vol. 2, p. 166.

61   General: P. C. Ludz (ed.), *Geheime Gesellschaften im 18. Jahrhundert*; H. Reinalter (ed.), *Freimaurer und Geheimbünde im 18. Jahrhundert in Mitteleuropa*.

62   H. Möller, 'Die Bruderschaft der Gold- und Rosenkreuzer. Struktur, Zielsetzung und Wirkung einer anti-aufklärerischen Geheimgesellschaft', in H. Reinalter (ed.), *Freimaurer und Geheimbünde*, pp. 199–239. M. W. Fischer, *Die Aufklärung und ihr Gegenteil*, 1982.

63   J. Rogalla v. Bieberstein, *Die These von der Verschwörung 1776–1945. Philosophen, Freimaurer, Juden, Liberale und Sozialisten als Verschwörer gegen die Sozialordnung*, 1976. Also, K. Epstein, *Die Ursprünge des Konservativismus in Deutschland*, 1973, pp. 583ff.

64   General: R. le Forestier, *Les Illuminés de Bavière et la Franc-Maçonnerie*, 1915; R. van Dülmen, *Der Geheimbund der Illuminaten*, 2nd edn, 1977; N. Schindler, 'Der Geheimbund der Illuminaten: Aufklärung, Geheimnis und Politik', in H. Reinalter (ed.), *Freimaurer und Geheimbünde*, pp. 284–320; M. Agethen, *Geheimbund und Utopie. Illuminaten, Freimaurer und deutsche Spätaufklärung*, 1984.

65   R. Van Dülmen, *Der Geheimbund der Illuminaten*, pp. 31ff.

66   Ibid., p. 161.

67   Ibid., pp. 152f.

68   On von Knigge, cf. J. Popp, 'Weltanschauung und Hauptwerke des Frhr. Adolph v. Knigge', 1931; R. T. Grabe, *Das Geheimnis des Freiherrn v. Knigge*, 1936.

69   L. Hammermayer, *Der Wilhelmsbader Freimaurerkonvent 1782.*

70   M. Agethen, *Geheimbund und Utopie*; J. Hoffmann, *Jakob Mauvillon. Ein Offizier und Schriftsteller im Zeitalter der bürgerlichen Emanzipationsbewegung*, 1981.

71   E. Weis, *Montgelas 1759–1799. Zwischen Revolution und Reform*, 1971, pp. 33ff.

72   H. Reinalter, 'Die Freimaurerei zwischen Josephinismus und frühfranziszeiischer Reaktion. Zur gesellschaftlichen Rolle und indirekt politischen Macht der Geheimbünde im 18. Jahrhundert', in H. Reinalter (ed.), *Freimaurer und Geheimbünde*, pp. 35–84.

73   For a list-by-list analysis, cf. R. van Dülmen, *Der Geheimbund der Illuminaten*, pp. 439ff.

74   Cf. note 63 above.

75   R. van Dülmen, *Der Geheimbund der Illuminaten*, pp. 152f.

76   Ibid., pp. 212f.

77   Ibid., pp. 166ff. Also, R. Koselleck, 'Adam Weishaupt und die Anfänge der bürgerlichen Geschichtsphilosophie in Deutschland', in *Tijdschrift voor de Studie van de Verlichting* 4 (1976).

78   M. Agethen, *Geheimbund und Utopie*, pp. 164ff.

79   R. van Dülmen, *Der Geheimbund der Illuminaten*: In his speech of 1782, he prophesies:

> Princes and nations shall disappear from the face of the earth peacefully, mankind shall become one family and the world shall become a haven of reasonable people. Morality shall achieve this transformation, alone and imperceptibly. (p. 179)
>
> Thus, morality is the art of teaching people to achieve maturity, of jettisoning their nonage, venturing forth into adulthood and dispensing with the princes. (p. 184)
>
> They increase apathy towards the interests of the state, re-unite people from different nations and of different religions in a common bond, deprive the state of their labour and the Church of its most able minds and bring together people who had previously been strangers, indeed, might always have remained strangers. In consequence, they are undermining the state, though this might well have been their objective in the first place . . . (p. 192)

80   Ibid., pp. 207 and 211; N. Schindler, 'Der Geheimbund der Illuminaten: Aufklärung, Geheimnis und Politik', in H. Reinalter (ed.), *Freimaurer und Geheimbünde*.

81   R. van Dülmen, *Der Geheimbund der Illuminaten*, p. 222.

82   Ibid.

83 Ibid., pp. 53ff.

84 Ibid.

85 Ibid., pp. 329ff.

86 B. Beyer, *Geschichte der Münchener Freimaurerei des 18. Jahrhunderts*, 1973, pp. 104ff. An example:

> Extract from the minutes of the lodge of St Theodor vom guten Rath of 18 May 1781: (1) His Eminence opened the lodge of masters with due ceremony. (2) It was proposed to promote Brother Cassius to the grade of Master Mason. The proposal was carried forthwith due to his impending travels. (3) His Eminence bestowed the grade of Master Mason upon Brother Cassius with all due ceremony. (4) Brother Lullus delivered a speech on the subject of true Freemasonry. (5) Brother Theocritus's request for promotion to the grade of Master Mason was read out, and it was decided to grant his request at a future lodge meeting. (6) His Eminence performed the catechism and the meeting was closed in the usual manner. (p. 108)

87 R. van Dülmen, *Geheimbund der Illuminaten*, p. 390.

88 Except in Aachen. Cf. A. Pauls, *Geschichte der Aachener Freimaurerei*, 1928, vol. 1.

89 Cf. also M. Agethen, *Der Geheimbund und Utopie*, pp. 295ff.

90 R. van Dülmen, *Der Geheimbund der Illuminaten*, pp. 83ff.

91 J. Hansen (ed.), *Quellen*, vol. 1, p. 57.

92 *Memoiren des Karl Heinrich Ritters von Lang*, Brunswick, 1842, p. 96.

93 For general studies on German Jacobinism, cf. H. Reinalter, *Der Jakobinismus in Mitteleuropa*, 1981; W. Grab, *Ein Volk muss seine Freiheit selbst erobern. Zur Geschichte der deutschen Jakobiner*, 1984.

94 For an outstanding study, cf. A. Kuhn, *Jakobiner im Rheinland. Der Kölner konstitutionelle Zirkel von 1798*, 1976.

95 T. Blanning, *Reform und Revolution in Mainz 1743–1803*, 1974; F. Dumont, *Die Mainzer Republik von 1792/93. Studien zur Revolutionierung in Rheinhessen und der Pfalz*, 1982.

96 H. Scheel (ed.), *Die Mainzer Republik. Die Protokolle des Jakobinerklubs*, 1975, vol. 1, pp. 245f.

97 Ibid., p. 586.

98 Cf. also F. Dumont, *Die Mainzer Republik*.

99 In *Forsters Werke in zwei Bänden*, 1968, vol. 1, pp. 202f.

100 Reproduced in H. Scheel, *Die Mainzer Republik*, vol. 1.

101 Ibid., p. 107.

102 Ibid.

103 Ibid., (Introduction, p. 21).

104 For an analysis, cf. F. Dumont, *Die Mainzer Republik*.

105 H. Scheel, *Die Mainzer Republik*, vol. 1, p. 51.

106 For a study on Dorsch, cf. H. Mathy, 'Anton Joseph Dorsch (1758–1819). Leben und Werk eines rheinischen Jakobiners', in *Mainzer Zeitung* 62 (1967); for a study on Wedekind, cf. H. Mathy, 'Georg Wedekind. Die politische Gedankenwelt eines Mainzer Medizinalprofessors', in *Festschrift Petry* (1968), pp. 178–206; for studies on Forster, cf. K. Kersten, *Der Weltumsegler Jo. Gg. Adam Forster 1754–1794*, 1957 and R.-R. Wuthenow, *Vernunft und Republik. Studien zu Gg. Forsters Schriften*, 1970.

107 The statutes of the Cologne circle state: 'The objective and intention of this society is mutual instruction and enlightenment on the inalienable rights of man; the fraternal members shall endeavour to generate an atmosphere of solidarity and a true love of lawful freedom, and they shall do their utmost to further the interests of the common good in equal measure' (A. Kuhn, *Jakobiner im Rheinland*, p. 47).

SELECT BIBLIOGRAPHY

General

Agethen, Manfred, *Geheimbund und Utopie. Illuminaten, Freimaurer und deutsche Spätaufklärung*, Munich, 1984.

Aretin, Karl Otmar Frhr. von (ed.), *Der aufgeklärte Absolutismus*, Cologne, 1974.

Balázs, Eva. H. (ed.), *Beförderer der Aufklärung in Mittel- und Osteuropa. Freimaurer, Gesellschaften, Clubs*, Berlin, 1979.

Balet, Leo and Gerhard, E., *Die Verbürgerlichung der deutschen Kunst, Literatur und Musik im 18. Jahrhundert* (newly edited by G. Mattenklott), Frankfurt/Main, Berlin, Vienna, 1973.

Barnard, Frederick M., *Zwischen Aufklärung und politischer Romantik; eine Studie über Herders soziologisch-politisches Denken*, Berlin, 1964.

Barner, Wilfried et al., *Lessing. Epoche – Werk – Wirkung*, 2nd edn Munich, 1976.

Bartels, Adolf, *Freimaurerei und deutsche Literatur*, Munich, 1929.

Barton, Peter F., *Jesuiten, Jansenisten, Josephiner. Eine Fallstudie zur frühen Toleranzzeit, der Fall Innocentius Fessler*, part 1, Vienna, Cologne, Graz, 1968.

Barton, Peter F., *Ignatius Aurelius Fessler. Vom Barockkatholizismus zur Erweckungsbewegung*, Vienna, Cologne, Graz, 1969.

Barton, Peter F., *Erzieher, Erzähler, Evergeten. Ein Beitrag zur politischen Geschichte, Geistes- und Kirchengeschichte Schlesiens und Preussens 1786/88 bis 1796. Fessler in Schlesien*, Vienna, Cologne, Graz, 1980.

Berns, Jörg Jochen, '"Parteylichkeit" und Zeitungswesen zur Rekonstruktion einer medienpolitischen Diskussion an der Wende vom 17. zum 18. Jahrhundert', in W. F. Haug (ed.), *Massen – Medien – Politik* (= Argument-Sonderband 10) 1976, pp. 202–33.

Biedermann, Karl, *Deutschland im Achtzehnten Jahrhundert*, 4 vols., reprint, Aalen, 1969.

Bircher, Martin, *Joh. Wilhelm von Stubenberg (1619–1663) und sein Freundeskreis. Studien zur österreichischen Barockliteratur protestantischer Edelleute*, Berlin, 1968.

Bircher, Martin and Ingen, F. van (eds), *Sprachgesellschaften, Sozietäten, Dichtergruppen*, Hamburg, 1978.

Blackall, Eric A., *The Emergence of German as a Literary Language 1700–1775*, 2nd edn, Ithaca, 1978.

Blanning, Timothy C. W., *Reform and Revolution in Mainz, 1743–1803*, Cambridge, 1974.

Bleymehl, Helmut, 'Die Aufklärung in Nassau-Saarbrücken. Ein Beitrag zur Geschichte des aufgeklärten Absolutismus in den deutschen Kleinstaaten', Ph.D. dissertation, Bonn, 1962.

Bödeker, Hans Erich, 'Strukturen der Aufklärungsgesellschaft in der Residenzstadt Kassel', in *Festschrift R. Vierhaus* (1982), pp. 55–76.

Bogel, Else and Blühm, Elger, *Die deutschen Zeitungen des 17. Jahrhunderts*, 2 vols., Bremen, 1971.

Böhme, Gernot et al., *Experimentelle Philosophie. Ursprünge autonomer Wissenschaftsentwicklung*, Frankfurt/Main, 1977.

Braubach, Max, 'Die "Eudämonia" (1795–1798). Ein Beitrag zur deutschen Publizistik im Zeitalter der Aufklärung und der Revolution', in *Diplomatie und geistiges Leben im 17. und 18. Jahrhundert. Gesammelte Abhandlungen*, Bonn, 1969, pp. 834–61.

Braun, Hans-Joachim, *Technologische Beziehungen zwischen Deutschland und England von der Mitte des 17. Jahrhunderts bis zum Ausgang des 18. Jahrhunderts*, Düsseldorf, 1974.

Braun, Rudolf, *Industrialisierung und Volksleben. Veränderungen der Lebensformen unter Einwirkung der textilindustriellen Heimarbeit in einem ländlichen Industriegebiet vor 1800 (Zürcher Oberland)*, Erlenbach, Zurich, 1960.

Bruford, Walter H., *Kultur und Gesellschaft im klassischen Weimar 1774–1806*, Göttingen, 1966.

Bruford, Walter H., *Die gesellschaftlichen Grundlagen der Goethezeit*, Frankfurt/Main, Berlin, Vienna, 1975.

Brüggemann, Fritz, 'Der Kampf um die bürgerliche Welt- und Lebensanschauung in der deutschen Literatur des 18. Jahrhunderts', in *Deutsche Vierteljahresschrift für Literaturwissenschaft und Geistesgeschichte*, vol. 3 (1925), pp. 94–127.

Brunner, Horst, *Die poetische Insel. Inseln und Inselvorstellungen in der deutschen Literatur*, Stuttgart, 1967.

Brunner, Otto, *Adeliges Landleben und europäischer Geist*, Salzburg, 1949.

Brunschwig, Henri, *Gesellschaft und Romantik in Preussen im 18. Jahrhundert. Die Krise des preussischen Staates am Ende des 18. Jahrhunderts und die Entstehung der romantischen Mentalität*, Frankfurt/Main, Berlin, Vienna, 1976.

Bürger, Christa (ed.), *Aufklärung und literarische Öffentlichkeit*, Frankfurt/ Main, 1980.

Burggraf, Gudrun, *Christian Gotthilf Salzmann im Vorfeld der Französischen Revolution*, Germering, 1966.

Büsch, Otto, Grab, Walter, Schmädeke, J. and Wölk, Monika (eds), *Die demokratische Bewegung in Mitteleuropa im ausgehenden 18. und frühen 19. Jahrhundert. Ein Tagungsbericht*, Berlin, 1980.

Dann, Otto, 'Die Anfänge politischer Vereinsbildung in Deutschland', in *Soziale Bewegung und politische Verfassung (= Festschrift Conze)*, Stuttgart, 1976, pp. 197–232.

Dann, Otto, *Gleichheit und Gleichberechtigung. Das Gleichheitspostulat in der alteuropäischen Tradition und in Deutschland bis zum ausgehenden 19. Jahrhundert*, Berlin, 1980.

Danzel, T. W., *Gottsched und seine Zeit*, Leipzig, 1848.

Dickerhoff, Harald, 'Gelehrte Gesellschaften, Akademien, Ordensstudien und Universitäten. Zur sogen. "Akademiebewegung" vornehmlich im bayerischen Raum', in *Zeitschrift für bayerische Landesgeschichte* 45 (1985), pp. 37–66.

Dotzauer, Winfried, 'Aufklärung und Sozietäten im 18. Jahrhundert', in *Geschichtliche Landeskunde* 21 (1980), pp. 260–74.

Dreyfus, François, G., *Societés et mentalités à Mayence dans la seconde moitié du XVIIIe siècle*, Paris, 1968.

Dülmen, Richard van, 'Zum Strukturwandel der Aufklärung in Bayern', in *Festschrift Bosl – Zeitschrift für bayerische Landesgeschichte* 36 (1973), pp. 662–79.

Dülmen Richard van, *Die Utopie einer christlichen Gesellschaft. Joh. Valentin Andreae I*, Stuttgart, 1978a.

Dülmen, Richard van, 'Die Aufklärungsgesellschaften in Deutschland als Forschungsproblem', in *Francia* 5 (1978). Reprinted in U. Herrmann (ed.), 'Die Bildung des Bürgers' (1982), pp. 81–99.

Dumont, Franz, *Die Mainzer Republik von 1792/93. Studien zur Revolutionierung in Rheinhessen und der Pfalz*, Alzey, 1982.

Eichler, Arthur, *Die Landbewegung des 18. Jahrhunderts und ihre Pädagogik*, Langensalza, 1933.

Elias, Norbert, *The Civilizing Process*, Oxford, 1988.

Engel-Janosi, Friedrich (ed.), *Formen der europäischen Aufklärung. Untersuchungen zur Situation von Christentum, Bildung und Wissenschaft im 18. Jahrhundert*, Munich, 1976.

Engel-Janosi, Friedrich et al. (eds.), *Fürst, Bürger, Mensch. Untersuchungen zu politischen und soziokulturellen Wandlungen im vorrevolutionären Europa*, Munich, 1975.

Engelsing, Rolf, 'Die periodische Presse und ihr Publikum. Zeitungslektüre in Bremen von den Anfängen bis zur Franzosenzeit', in *Archiv für die Geschichte des Buchwesens* 4 (1962), particularly pp. 1481–1534.

Engelsing, Rolf, *Analphabetentum und Lektüre. Zur Sozialgeschichte des Lesens in Deutschland zwischen feudaler und industrieller Gesellschaft*, Stuttgart, 1973a.

Engelsing, Rolf, 'Die Perioden der Lesergeschichte in der Neuzeit', in R. Engelsing, *Zur Sozialgeschichte deutscher Mittel- und Unterschichten*, Göttingen, 1973b.

Engelsing, Rolf, *Der Bürger als Leser. Lesergeschichte in Deutschland 1500– 1800*, Stuttgart, 1974.

Epstein, Klaus, *Die Ursprünge des Konservativismus in Deutschland. Der Ausgangspunkt: Die Herausforderung durch die Französische Revolution 1770– 1806*, Frankfurt/Main, Berlin, Vienna, 1973.

Euler, Focko, *Vom Gewerbefleiss zur Industrie. Ein Beitrag zur Wirtschaftsgeschichte des 18. Jahrhunderts*, Berlin, 1967.

Fischer, Michael W., *Die Aufklärung und ihr Gegenteil. Die Rolle der Geheimbünde in Wissenschaft und Politik*, Berlin, 1982.

Frels, Onno, 'Die Entstehung einer bürgerlichen Unterhaltungskultur und das Problem der Vermittlung von Literatur und Öffentlichkeit in Deutschland um 1800', in Christa Bürger (ed.), *Aufklärung u. literar. Öffentlichkeit*. Frankfurt/Main, 1980.

Frick, Karl R. H., *Die Erleuchteten. Gnostisch-theosophische und alchemistisch-rosenkreuzerische Geheimgesellschaften bis zum Ende des 18. Jahrhunderts. Ein Beitrag zur Geistesgeschichte der Neuzeit*, Graz, 1973.

Frick, Karl R. H., *Licht und Finsternis. Gnostisch-theosophische und freimaurerisch-okkulte Geheimgesellschaften bis an die Wende zum 20. Jahrhundert* vol 2, Graz, 1975–8.

Gaus, Marianne, 'Das Idealbild der Familie in den Moralischen Wochenschriften und seine Auswirkungen in der deutschen Literatur des 18. Jahrhunderts', dissertation, Rostock, 1937.

Gay, Peter, *The Enlightenment: An Interpretation*, 2 vols., New York, 1967– 9.

Geiger, Max, *Aufklärung und Erweckung. Beiträge zur Erforschung Johann Heinrich Jung-Stillings und der Erweckungstheologie*, Zurich, 1963.

Gerth, Hans H., *Bürgerliche Intelligenz um 1800*, Göttingen, 1976.

Göpfert, Herbert G., *Vom Autor zum Leser. Beiträge zur Geschichte des Buchwesens*, Munich, Vienna, 1977.

Grab, Walter, *Demokratische Strömungen in Hamburg und Schleswig-Holstein zur Zeit der ersten französischen Republik*, Hamburg, 1966.

Grab, Walter, *Norddeutsche Jakobiner. Demokratische Bestrebungen zur Zeit der Französischen Revolution*, Frankfurt/Main, 1967.

Grab, Walter, *Ein Volk muss seine Freiheit selbst erobern. Zur Geschichte der deutschen Jakobiner*, Frankfurt/Main, 1984.

Grabe, Reinhold Thomas, *Das Geheimnis des Freiherrn v. Knigge*, Hamburg, 1936.

Graevenitz, Gerhard von, 'Innerlichkeit und Öffentlichkeit – Aspekte deutscher "bürgerlicher" Literatur im frühen 18. Jahrhundert', in *Deutsche Vierteljahresschrift für Literaturwissenschaft und Geistesgeschichte 49th year* (1975), Special edition, *18. Jahrhundert*, pp. 1–82.

Grassl, Hans, *Aufbruch zur Romantik. Bayerns Beitrag zur deutschen Geistesgeschichte 1765–1785*, Munich, 1968.

Grathoff, Erich, 'Deutsche Bauern- und Dorfzeitungen des 18. Jahrhunderts. Ein Beitrag zur Geschichte des Bauerntums, der öffentlichen Meinung und des Zeitungswesens', Ph.D. dissertation, Heidelberg, 1937.

Grimminger, Rolf, 'Aufklärung, Absolutismus und bürgerliche Individuen. Über den notwendigen Zusammenhang von Literatur, Gesellschaft und Staat in der Geschichte des 18. Jahrhunderts', in: R. Grimminger, (ed.), *Deutsche Aufklärung bis zur Französischen Revol. 1680–1789 (Hanser Sozialgeschichte der deutschen Literatur 3)*, Munich, 1980.

Guhrauer, Gottschalk Eduard, *Joachim Jungius und sein Zeitalter*, Stuttgart, Tübingen, 1850.

Gumbrecht, Hans U. et al. (eds), *Sozialgeschichte der Aufklärung in Frankreich*, Munich, Vienna, 1981.

Haacke, Wilmont, *Die politische Zeitschrift 1665–1965*, vol. 1, Stuttgart, 1968.

Haas, Norbert, *Spätaufklärung. Joh. Heinrich Merck zwischen Sturm und Drang und Französischer Revolution*, Kronberg/Taunus, 1975.

Haase, Carl, 'Obrigkeit und öffentliche Meinung in Kurhannover 1789–1803', in *Niedersächsisches Jahrbuch für Landesgeschichte*, vol. 39 (1967), pp. 191–294.

Habermas, Jürgen, *The Structural Transformation of the Public Sphere. An Inquiry into a Category of Bourgeois Society*, Cambridge, 1989.

Haferkorn, Hans J., 'Zur Entstehung der bürgerlich-literarischen Intelligenz und des Schriftstellers in Deutschland zwischen 1750 und 1800', in B. Lutz (ed.), *Deutsches Bürgertum und literarische Intelligenz 1750–1800*, Stuttgart, 1974.

Hansen, Josef (ed.), *Quellen zur Geschichte des Rheinlandes im Zeitalter der Französischen Revolution 1780–1801.* 4 vols., Bonn, 1931/8.

Hartmann, Klaus L. et al. (eds), *Schule und Staat im 18. und 19. Jahrhundert. Zur Sozialgeschichte der Schule in Deutschland*, Frankfurt/Main, 1974.

Hazard, Paul, *Die Krise des europäischen Geistes, 1680–1715*, Hamburg, 1939.

Hazard, Paul, *Die Herrschaft der Vernunft. Das europäische Denken im 18. Jahrhundert*, Hamburg, 1949.

Heimpel-Michel, Elisabeth, *Die Aufklärung. Eine historisch-systematische Untersuchung*, Langensalza, 1928.

Heinemann, Emma, 'Zur Geschichte der Staatsanschauungen während des 18. Jahrhunderts vor der Französischen Revolution', dissertation, Bonn, 1950.

Hermand, Jost (ed.), *Von deutscher Republik 1775–1795. Texte radikaler Demokraten*, Frankfurt/Main, 1975.

Herrmann, Ulrich (ed.), '*Die Bildung des Bürgers*'. *Die Formierung der bürgerlichen Gesellschaft und die Gebildeten im 18. Jahrhundert*, Weinheim, Basle, 1982.

Hertz, Frederick, *The Development of the German Public Mind. A Social History of German Political Sentiments, Aspirations and Ideas*, 2 vols., London, 1957–62.

Heydorn, Heinz-Joachim and Koneffke, Gernot, *Studien zur Sozialgeschichte und Philosophie der Bildung. I. Zur Pädagogik der Aufklärung*, Munich, 1973.

Hinrichs, Carl, *Preussentum und Pietismus. Der Pietismus in Brandenburg-Preussen als religiös-soziale Reformbewegung*, Göttingen, 1971.

Holborn, Hajo, 'Der deutsche Idealismus in sozialgeschichtlicher Beleuchtung', in H.-U. Wehler (ed.), *Moderne deutsche Sozialgeschichte*, 4th edn, Göttingen, 1973.

Hölscher, Lucian, *Öffentlichkeit und Geheimnis*, Stuttgart, 1979.

Horvath, Eva, 'Die Frau im gesellschaftlichen Leben Hamburgs. Meta Klopstock, Eva König, Elise Reimarus', in *Wolfenbütteler Studien zur Aufklärung* 3, (1976), pp. 175–94.

Im Hof, Ulrich, *Isaak Iselin und die Spätaufklärung*, Berne, Munich, 1967.

Im Hof, Ulrich, *Das gesellige Jahrhundert. Gesellschaft und Gesellschaften im Zeitalter der Aufklärung*, Munich, 1982.

Iven, Kurt, *Die Industrie-Pädagogik des 18. Jahrhunderts*, Berlin, Leipzig, 1929.

Jentsch, Irene, 'Zur Geschichte des Zeitungslesens in Deutschland am Ende des 18. Jahrhunderts. Mit besonderer Berücksichtigung der gesellschaftlichen Formen des Zeitungslesens', Ph.D. dissertation, Leipzig, 1929.

Kaiser, Gerhard, *Pietismus und Patriotismus im literarischen Deutschland. Ein Beitrag zum Problem der Säkularisation*, 2nd edn, Frankfurt/Main, 1973.

Keller, Ludwig, *Akademien, Logen und Kammern des XVII. und XVIII. Jahrhunderts*, Jena, 1912.

Kiesel, Helmuth and Münch, Paul, *Gesellschaft und Literatur im 18. Jahrhundert. Voraussetzungen und Entstehung des literarischen Markts in Deutschland*, Munich, 1977.

Kimpel, Dieter, *Der Roman der Aufklärung (Sammlung Metzler)*, Stuttgart, 1967.

Kirchner, Joachim, *Die Grundlagen des deutschen Zeitschriftenwesens. Mit einer Gesamtbibliographie der deutschen Zeitschriften bis zum Jahre 1790*, 2 parts, Leipzig, 1928–31.

Kirchner, Joachim, *Das deutsche Zeitschriftenwesen. Seine Geschichte und seine Probleme. Vol. I. Von den Anfängen bis zur Romantik*, 2nd edn, Wiesbaden, 1958.

Kofler, Leo, *Zur Geschichte der bürgerlichen Gesellschaft. Versuch einer verstehenden Deutung der Neuzeit*, Neuwied, East Berlin, 1966.

Kon, Igor S., *Freundschaft. Geschichte und Sozialpsychologie der Freundschaft als soziale Institution und individuelle Beziehung*, Reinbek, 1979.

König, Helmut, *Zur Geschichte der Nationalerziehung in Deutschland im letzten Drittel des 18. Jahrhunderts*, East Berlin, 1960.

Kopitzsch, Franklin (ed.), *Aufklärung, Absolutismus und Bürgertum in Deutschland. Zwölf Aufsätze*, Munich, 1976a.

Kopitzsch, Franklin, 'Aufgaben einer Sozialgeschichte der deutschen Intelligenz zwischen Aufklärung und Kaiserreich', in *Sozialwissenschaftliche Informationen für Unterricht und Studium* 5 (1976b), pp. 84–9.

Kopitzsch, Franklin, *Grundzüge einer Sozialgeschichte der Aufklärung in Hamburg und Altona*, 2 vols., Hamburg, 1982.

Kopitzsch, Franklin, 'Die Aufklärung in Deutschland. Zu ihren Leistungen, Grenzen und Wirkungen', in *Archiv für Sozialgeschichte* 23 (1983a), pp. 1–21.

Koselleck, Reinhardt, *Preussen zwischen Reform und Revolution. Allgemeines Landrecht, Verwaltung und Soziale Bewegung*, Stuttgart, 1967.

Koselleck, Reinhardt, *Kritik und Krise. Ein Beitrag zur Pathogenese der bürgerlichen Welt*, 2nd edn, Freiburg, Munich, 1969.

Kosyk, Kurt, *Vorläufer der Massenpresse. Ökonomie und Publizistik zwischen Reformation und Französischer Revolution*, Munich, 1972.

Krauss, Werner, 'Über die Konstellation der deutschen Aufklärung', in Krauss, Werner, *Studien zur deutschen und französischen Aufklärung*, East Berlin, 1963.

Krauss, Werner, *Perspektiven und Probleme. Zur französischen und deutschen Aufklärung und andere Aufsätze*, Neuwied, East Berlin, 1965.

Kreuzer, Helmut, *Gefährliche Lesesucht? Bemerkungen zur politischen Lektürekritik im ausgehenden 18. Jahrhundert*, Heidelberg, 1977.

Lampe, Joachim, *Aristokratie, Hofadel und Staatspatriziat in Kurhannover. Die Lebenskreise der höheren Beamten an den hannoverschen Zentral- und Hofbehörden 1714–1760*, 2 vols., Göttingen, 1963.

Langenbucher, Wolfgang, 'Die Demokratisierung des Lesens in der zweiten Leserevolution', in H. Göpfert (ed.), *Lesen und Leben*, Frankfurt/Main, 1975.

Lepenies, Wolf, *Melancholie und Gesellschaft*, Frankfurt/Main, 1972.

Liebel, Helen P., *Enlightened Bureaucracy versus Enlightened Despotism in Baden, 1760–1792*, Philadelphia, Pa. 1965.

Liebel, Helen P., 'Der aufgeklärte Absolutismus und die Gesellschaftskrise in Deutschland im 18. Jahrhundert', in W. Hubatsch (ed.), *Absolutismus*, Darmstadt, 1973.

Lindemann, Margot, *Deutsche Presse bis 1815*, Berlin, 1969.

Ludz, Peter Christian, 'Ideologie, Intelligenz und Organisation.

Bemerkungen über ihren Zusammenhang in der frühbürgerlichen Gesellschaft', in P. C. Ludz, *Ideologiebegriff und marxistische Theorie*, Opladen, 1976.

Ludz, Peter Christian (ed.), *Geheime Gesellschaften im 18. Jahrhundert*, Heidelberg, 1979.

Lutz, Bernd (ed.), *Deutsches Bürgertum und literarische Intelligenz 1750–1800*, Stuttgart, 1974.

Mälzer, Gottfried, 'Bücherzensur und Verlagswesen im 18. Jahrhundert', in *Archiv für die Geschichte des Buchwesens* 13/14 (1973), pp. 289–316.

Manheim, Ernest, 'The Communicator and his Audience: Liberals and Traditionalists in Eighteenth-Century Germany', in W. J. Cahnmann (ed.), *Sociology and History*, London, 1964.

Manheim, Ernest, Aufklärung und öffentliche Meinung. Studien zur Soziologie der Öffentlichkeit im 18. Jahrhundert. Edited by N. Schindler, Stuttgart, 1979.

Martens, Wolfgang, *Die Botschaft der Tugend. Die Aufklärung im Spiegel der deutschen Moralischen Wochenschriften*, Stuttgart, 1971.

Martens, Wolfgang, 'Die Geburt des Journalisten in der Aufklärung', in *Wolfenbütteler Studien zur Aufklärung*, vol. 1 (1974), pp. 84–98.

Mattenklott, Gerd and Scherpe, Klaus R. (eds), *Literatur der bürgerlichen Emanzipation im 18. Jahrhundert*, Kronberg/Taunus, 1973.

Mattenklott, Gerd and Scherpe, Klaus R. (eds), *Westberliner Projekt Grundkurs 18. Jahrhundert. Die Funktion der Literatur bei der Formierung der bürgerlichen Klasse Deutschlands im 18. Jahrhundert*, 2 vols., Kronberg/Taunus, 1974.

Mattenklott, Gerd and Scherpe, Klaus R. (eds), *Demokratisch-revolutionäre Literatur in Deutschland: Jakobinismus*, Kronberg/Taunus, 1975.

Milstein, Barney M., *Eight Eighteenth Century Reading Societies*, Berne, 1972.

Mog, Paul, *Ratio und Gefühlskultur. Studien zur Psychogenese und Literatur im 18. Jahrhundert*, Tübingen, 1976.

Möller, Helmut, *Die kleinbürgerliche Familie im 18. Jahrhundert. Verhalten und Gruppenkultur*, Berlin, 1969.

Möller, Horst, *Aufklärung in Preussen. Der Verleger, Publizist und Geschichts-schreiber Friedrich Nicolai*, Berlin, 1974.

Mühlpfordt, Günter, 'Karl Friedrich Bahrdt und die radikale Aufklärung', in *Jahrbuch des Instituts für Deutsche Geschichte* V (1976), pp. 49–100.

Musson, Albert (ed.), *Science, Technology and Economic Growth in the Eighteenth Century*, London, 1972.

Narr, Dieter, 'Fragen der Volksbildung in der späten Aufklärung', in *Württembergisches Jahrbuch für Volkskunde* (1959/60), pp. 38ff.

Nipperdey, Thomas, 'Verein als soziale Struktur im späten 18. und frühen 19. Jahrhundert', in T. Nipperdey, *Gesellschaft, Kultur, Theorie*, Göttingen, 1976.

Popp, Josef, 'Weltanschauung und Hauptwerke des Frhr. Adolph v. Knigge', dissertation, Munich, 1931.

Preussner, Eberhard, *Die bürgerliche Musikkultur. Ein Beitrag zur deutschen Musikgeschichte des 18. Jahrhunderts*, (1935) 2nd edn, Hamburg, 1954.

Raabe, Paul, 'Die Zeitschrift als Medium der Aufklärung', in *Wolfenbütteler Studien zur Aufklärung*, vol. 1 (1974), pp. 99–136.

Rasch, Wolfdietrich, *Freundschaftskultur und Freundschaftsdichtung im deutschen Schrifttum des 18. Jahrhunderts vom Ausgang des Barocks bis zu Klopstock*, Halle, 1936.

Reichert, Karl, 'Utopie und Staatsroman. Ein Forschungsbericht', in *Deutsche Vierteljahresschrift* 39 (1965), pp. 259–87.

Reinalter, Helmut, *Aufklärung, Absolutismus, Reaktion. Die Geschichte Tirols in der 2. Hälfte des 18. Jahrhunderts*, Vienna, 1974.

Reinalter, Helmut (ed.), *Jakobiner in Mitteleuropa*, Innsbruck, 1977.

Reinalter, Helmut, *Der Jakobinismus in Mitteleuropa. Eine Einführung*, Stuttgart, Berlin, Cologne, Mainz, 1981.

Reinalter, Helmut, *Aufklärung – Vormärz – Revolution. Mitteilung der internationalen Forschungsgruppe 'Demokratische Bewegungen in Mitteleuropa 1770–1850' an der Universität Innsbruck*, 2 vols., Innsbruck, 1982a.

Reinalter, Helmut, *Geheimbünde in Tirol. Von der Aufklärung bis zur Französischen Revolution*, Bozen, 1982b.

Reinalter, Helmut, 'Geheimgesellschaften und Freimaurerei im 18. Jahrhundert', in H. Reinalter, *Aufklärung – Vormärz – Revolution* 2 (1982c), pp. 27ff.

Reinalter, Helmut, 'Josephinismus, Geheimgesellschaften und Jakobinismus. Zur radikalen Spätaufklärung in der Habsburgermonarchie', in M. Drabek, R. Plaschke and A. Wandruszka (eds), *Ungarn und Österreich unter Maria Theresia und Joseph II.*, Vienna, 1982d.

Reinalter, Helmut (ed.), *Freimaurer und Geheimbünde im 18. Jahrhundert in Mitteleuropa*, Frankfurt/Main, 1983.

Rieck, Werner, *Joh. Christoph Gottsched. Eine kritische Würdigung seines Werkes*, Berlin, 1972.

Riedel, Manfred, 'Bürger, Staatsbürger, Bürgertum', in O. Brunner et al. (eds), *Geschichtliche Grundbegriffe, Historisches Lexikon zur politisch-sozialen Sprache in Deutschland*, vol. 1, Stuttgart, 1972, pp. 672–725.

Risse-Strumbies, Susanne D., *Erziehung und Bildung der Frau in der zweiten Hälfte des 18. Jahrhunderts*, Frankfurt/Main, 1980.

Ritter, Hermann. *Die pädagogischen Strömungen im letzten Drittel des 18. Jahrhunderts in den gleichzeitigen deutschen pädagogischen Romanen und romanhaften Darstellungen*, Halle, 1939.

Roche, Daniel, *Le siècle des lumières en province. Académies et académiciens provinciaux, 1680–1789*, 2 vols., Paris, 1978.

Roessler, Wilhelm, *Die Entstehung des modernen Erziehungswesens in Deutschland*, Stuttgart, 1961.

Rogalla v. Bieberstein, Johannes, *Die These von der Verschwörung 1776–*

1945. Philosophen, Freimaurer, Juden, Liberale und Sozialisten als Verschwörer gegen die Sozialordnung, (1976) 2nd edn, Berne, Frankfurt/Main, 1978.

Rossberg, Adolf, *Freimaurerei und Politik im Zeitalter der Französischen Revolution*, Berlin, 1942.

Ruppert, Wolfgang, *Bürgerlicher Wandel. Die Geburt der modernen deutschen Gesellschaft im 18. Jahrhundert*, (1981) 2nd edn, Frankfurt/Main, 1984.

Salomon, Albert, 'Der Freundschaftskult im 18. Jahrhundert in Deutschland. Versuch zur Soziologie einer Lebensform', in *Zeitschrift für Soziologie* 8 (1979), pp. 279–308.

Sauder, Gerhard, '"Verhältnismässige Aufklärung" – Zur bürgerlichen Ideologie am Ende des 18. Jahrhunderts', in *Jahrbuch der Jean-Paul-Gesellschaft* 9 (1974), pp. 102–26.

Scheel, Heinrich, *Süddeutsche Jakobiner, Klassenkämpfe und republikanische Bestrebungen im deutschen Süden Ende des 18. Jahrhunderts*, (1962) 2nd edn, East Berlin, 1971.

Scheel, Heinrich, 'Deutsche Jakobiner', in *Zeitschrift für Geschichtswissenschaft* 17, 7th year (1969), pp. 1131–40.

Scheel, Heinrich, *Die Begegnung deutscher Aufklärer mit der Revolution*, East Berlin, 1973.

Scheffers, Henning, *Höfische Konvention und die Aufklärung. Wandlungen des Honnête-homme-Ideals im 17. und 18. Jahrhundert*, Bonn, 1980.

Schenda, Rudolf, *Volk ohne Buch. Studien zur Sozialgeschichte der populären Lesestoffe 1770–1910*, Frankfurt/Main, 1970.

Schenda, Rudolf, *Der Lesestoff der kleinen Leute. Studien zur populären Literatur im 19. und 20. Jahrhundert*, Munich, 1976.

Schlumbohm, Jürgen, *Freiheit – Die Anfänge der bürgerlichen Emanzipationsbewegung in Deutschland im Spiegel ihres Leitwortes (c.1760–c.1800)*, Düsseldorf, 1975.

Schmidt, Peter and Hocke, Paul, *Literarische und politische Zeitschriften 1789–1805*, Stuttgart, 1975.

Schneider, Falko, *Aufklärung und Politik. Studien zur Politisierung der deutschen Spätaufklärung am Beispiel A. G. F. Rebmanns*, Wiesbaden, 1978.

Schneider, Franz, *Pressefreiheit und politische Öffentlichkeit. Studien zur politischen Geschichte Deutschlands bis 1848*, Neuwied, East Berlin, 1966.

Schneiders, Werner, *Die wahre Aufklärung. Zum Selbstverständnis der deutschen Aufklärung*, Freiburg, Munich, 1974.

Schober, Joyce, *Die deutsche Spätaufklärung (1770–1796)*, Frankfurt/Main, Berne, 1975.

Schöffler, Herbert, *Das literarische Zürich 1700–1750*, Leipzig, 1925.

Schultze, Johanna, *Die Auseinandersetzung von Adel und Bürgertum in den deutschen Zeitschriften der letzten drei Jahrzehnte des 18. Jahrhunderts 1773–1806*, reprint, Vaduz, 1965.

Schwieger, Klaus, 'Das Bürgertum in Preussen vor der Französischen Revolution', Ph.D. dissertation, (manuscript), Kiel, 1971.

Segeberg, Harro, 'Literarischer Jakobinismus in Deutschland. Theoretische und methodische Überlegungen zur Erforschung der radikalen Spätaufklärung', in B. Lutz (ed.), *Deutsches Bürgertum und literarische. Intelligenz 1750–1800*, Stuttgart, 1974.

Segebrecht, Wulf, 'Geselligkeit und Gesellschaft. Überlegungen zur Situation des Erzählens im geselligen Rahmen', in *Germanistisch-romanistiche Monatsschrift* 25 (1975), pp. 306–22.

Seiffert, Hans Werner, 'Zu Problemen der deutschen Aufklärung', in M. Kossok et al., *Aspekte der Aufklärungsbewegung*, East Berlin, 1974.

Sieveking, Heinrich, *Georg Heinrich Sieveking, Lebensbild eines Hamburgischen Kaufmanns aus dem Zeitalter der Französischen Revolution*, Berlin, 1913.

Sievers, Burkard, *Geheimnis und Geheimhaltung in sozialen Systemen*, Opladen, 1974.

Simmel, Georg, 'Das Geheimnis und die geheime Gesellschaft', in G. Simmel, *Soziologie. Untersuchungen über die Formen der Vergesellschaftung*, Munich, Leipzig, 1922.

Spengler, Karl, 'Die publizistische Tätigkeit des Freiherrn Adolf von Knigge während der Französischen Revolution', Ph.D. dissertation, Bonn, 1931.

Stadelmann, Rudolf and Fischer, Wolfram, *Die Bildungswelt des deutschen Handwerkers um 1800. Studien zur Soziologie des Kleinbürgers im Zeitalter Goethes*, Berlin, 1955.

Stecher, Martin, 'Die Erziehungsbestrebungen der deutschen moralischen Wochenschriften, ein Beitrag zur Geschichte der Pädagogik des 18. Jahrhunderts', dissertation, Leipzig, Langensalza, 1914.

Steiner, Gerhard, *Der Traum vom Menschenglück. Leben und literarische Wirksamkeit von Carl Wilhelm und Henriette Fröhlich*, Berlin, 1959.

Steiner, Gerhard, *Franz Heinrich Ziegenhagen und seine Verhältnislehre. Ein Beitrag zur Geschichte des utopischen Sozialismus in Deutschland*, Berlin, 1962.

Stephan, Inge, *Literarischer Jakobinismus in Deutschland (1789–1806)*, Stuttgart, 1976.

Stephan, Johann Gustav, *Die häusliche Erziehung in Deutschland während des XVIII. Jahrhunderts*, Wiesbaden, 1891.

Stratmann, Karl Wilhelm, *Die Krise der Berufserziehung im 18. Jahrhundert als Ursprungsfeld pädagogischen Denkens*, Ratingen, 1967.

Stuke, Horst, 'Aufklärung' in *Geschichtliche Grundbegriffe. Historisches Lexikon zur politisch-sozialen Sprache in Deutschland*, I, Stuttgart, 1972, pp. 243–342.

Tenbruck, Friedrich H., 'Freundschaft. Ein Beitrag zu einer Soziologie der persönlichen Beziehungen', in *Kölner Zeitschrift für Soziologie und Sozialpsychologie*, vol. 16 (1964), pp. 431–56.

Thalmann, Marianne, *Der Trivialroman des 18. Jahrhunderts und der romantische Roman. Ein Beitrag zur Entwicklungsgeschichte der*

Geheimbundmystik, Berlin, 1929.

Tönnies, Ferdinand, *Kritik der öffentlichen Meinung*, Berlin, 1922.

Tönnies, Ferdinand, *Gemeinschaft und Gesellschaft. Grundbegriffe der reinen Soziologie*, 2nd edn, Berlin, 1926.

Ulbricht, Günter, 'Der Philanthropismus – eine fortschrittliche pädagogische Reformbewegung der deutschen Aufklärung', in *Pädagogik* 10 (1955), pp. 750–64.

Valjavec, Fritz, *Die Entstehung der politischen Strömungen in Deutschland. 1770–1815*, Munich, 1951.

Viatte, Auguste, *Les sources occultes du Romantisme, Illuminisme, Théosophie 1770–1820*, 2 vols., Paris, 1965.

Vierhaus, Rudolf, 'Politisches Bewusstsein in Deutschland vor 1789', in *Der Staat* 6 (1967), pp. 175–98.

Vierhaus, Rudolf, 'Deutschland im 18. Jahrhundert: soziales Gefüge, politische Verfassung, geistige Bewegung', in *Lessing und die Zeit der Aufklärung*, Göttingen, 1968.

Vierhaus, Rudolf (ed.), *Der Adel vor der Revolution. Zur sozialen und politischen Funktion des Adels im vorrevolutionären Europa*, Göttingen, 1971.

Vierhaus, Rudolf, 'Bildung', in *Geschichtliche Grundbegriffe. Historisches Lexikon zur politisch-sozialen Sprache in Deutschland*, I, Stuttgart, 1972, pp. 508–51.

Vierhaus, Rudolf, 'Aufklärung und Freimaurerei in Deutschland', in *Das Vergangene und die Geschichte, Festschrift Wittram*, Göttingen, 1973.

Vierhaus, Rudolf, *Germany in the Age of Absolutism*, Cambridge, 1988.

Vierhaus, Rudolf (ed.), 'Deutsche patriotische und gemeinnützige Gesellschaften', in *Wolfenbütteler Forschungen*, vol. 8, Munich, 1980.

Vierhaus, Rudolf (ed.), *Bürger und Bürgerlichkeit im Zeitalter der Aufklärung*, Heidelberg, 1981.

Vogt, Erika, *Die gegenhöfische Strömung in der deutschen Barockliteratur*, Leipzig, 1932.

Wangermann, Erich, *Von Joseph II. zu den Jakobinerprozessen*, Vienna, Frankfurt/Main, Zurich, 1966.

Weil, Hans, *Die Entstehung des deutschen Bildungsprinzips*, (1930) 2nd edn, Bonn, 1967.

Wenck, Woldemar, *Deutschland vor 100 Jahren*, 2 vol., Leipzig 1887/1890.

Winckler, Lutz, *Kulturwarenproduktion. Aufsätze zur Literatur-und Sprachsoziologie*, Frankfurt/Main, 1973.

Witkowski, Georg, *Geschichte des literarischen Lebens in Leipzig*, Leipzig, Berlin, 1909.

Wittmann, Reinhard, 'Der lesende Landmann. Zur Rezeption aufklärerischer Bemühungen durch die bäuerliche Bevölkerung im 18. Jahrhundert', in *Studien zur Geschichte der Kulturbeziehungen in Mittel- und Osteuropa*, vol. 2 (1973), pp. 142–96.

Wittmann, Walter, 'Beruf und Buch im 18. Jahrhundert. Ein Beitrag zur

Erfassung und Gliederung der Leserschaft im 18. Jahrhundert, insbes. unter Berücksichtigung des Einflusses auf die Buchproduktion', dissertation, Frankfurt/Main, 1934.

Wolff, Eugen, *Gottscheds Stellung im deutschen Bildungsleben*, 2 vols., Kiel, Leipzig, 1895.

Wolff, Hans Martin, *Die Weltanschauung der deutschen Aufklärung in geschichtlicher Entwicklung*, 2nd edn, Berne, Munich, 1963.

Wuthenow, Ralph-Rainer (ed.), *Zwischen Absolutismus und Aufklärung: Rationalismus, Empfindsamkeit, Sturm und Drang 1740–1786*, vol. 4: *Deutsche Literatur. Eine Sozialgeschichte*, edited by H. A. Glaser, Hamburg, 1980.

Wuttke, Heinrich, *Die deutschen Zeitschriften und die Entstehung der öffentlichen Meinung. Ein Beitrag zur Geschichte des* Zeitungswesens, 2nd edn, Leipzig, 1875.

Yates, Frances A., *The Rosicrucian Enlightenment*, London, 1986.

Zimmermann, Rolf Christian, *Das Weltbild des jungen Goethe. Studien zur hermetischen Tradition des deutschen 18. Jahrhunderts I. Elemente und Fundamente*, Munich, 1969.

Specialist

Aigner-Abafi, Ludwig, *Geschichte der Freimaurerei in Österreich-Ungarn*. 5 vols., Budapest, 1890–3.

Artelt, Walter, 'Vom Akademiegedanken im 17. Jahrhundert', in *Nunquam otiosus. Beiträge zur Geschichte der Präsidenten der Deutschen Akademie der Naturforscher Leopoldina*, Halle, 1970.

Aus vergangenen Tagen. Geschichtliche Bilder aus der St Johannisloge zur Verschwiegenheit 1775/1925, Berlin, year not cited (1925).

Bäschlin, Conrad, *Die Blütezeit der ökonomischen Gesellschaften in Bern 1759 bis 1766*, Campen, 1917.

Bäsken, Rothraud, *Die Dichter des Göttinger Hains und die Bürgerlichkeit. Eine literatursoziologische Studie*, Königsberg, 1937.

Die Basler Christentumsgesellschaft = Pietismus und Neuzeit. Ein Jahrbuch zur Geschichte des neueren Protestantismus, vol. 7 (1981).

Begemann, Wilhelm, *Die Fruchtbringende Gesellschaft und Johann Valentin Andreä*, Berlin, 1911.

Beneke, Otto, *Die literarische Gesellschaft von 1790*, Hamburg, 1866.

Beyer, Bernhard, *Geschichte der Grossloge 'Zur Sonne' in Bayreuth*. 3 vols., Frankfurt/Main, 1954.

Beyer, Bernhard, *Geschichte der Münchner Freimaurerei des 18. Jahrhunderts. Ein Beitrag zur Geschichte Altbaierns*, Hamburg, 1973.

Biereye, Johannes, *Geschichte der Akademie gemeinnütziger Wissenschaften zu Erfurt 1754–1929*, Erfurt, 1930.

Birkner, Gottlieb, *Geschichte der Loge 'Zu den drei Pfeilen' i. Or. Nürnberg während des ersten Jahrhunderts ihres Bestehens 1789–1889*, Nuremberg, 1889.

Bischoff, Theodor and Schmid, August (eds), *Festschrift zur 250jährigen Jubelfeier des Pegnesischen Blumenordens*, Nuremberg, 1894.

Bodmer, Hans, 'Die Gesellschaft der Maler in Zürich und ihre Diskurse (1721–1723)', dissertation, Zurich, Frauenfeld, 1895.

Bokov, Charles von, *Winkelmass und Zirkel. Die Geschichte der Freimaurer*, Vienna, 1980.

Boos, Heinrich, *Geschichte der Freimaurerei. Ein Beitrag zur Kultur- und Literaturgeschichte des 18. Jahrhunderts*, 2nd edn, Aarau, 1906 (reprint, Wiesbaden, 1969).

Bradish, Joseph A. von, 'Der "Erzhumanist" Celtis und das Wiener "Dichterkollegium". Ein Beitrag zur deutschen Kulturkunde', in *Monatshefte für Deutschen Unterricht* 28 (1936), pp. 157–64.

Brandes, Helga, *Die Gesellschaft der Maler und ihr literarischer Beitrag zur Aufklärung des 18. Jahrhunderts*, Bremen, 1974.

Brandt, Ahasver von, 'Das Lübecker Bürgertum zur Zeit der Gründung der "Gemeinnützigen" – Menschen, Ideen und soziale Verhältnisse', in *Der Wagen. Ein Lübeckisches Jahrbuch* (1966), pp. 18–33.

Braubach, Max, 'Ein publizistischer Plan der Bonner Lesegesellschaft aus dem Jahre 1789. Ein Beitrag zu den Anfängen politischer Meinungsbildung', in M. Braubach, *Diplomatie und geistiges Leben im 17. und 18. Jahrhundert. Gesammelte Abhandlungen*, Bonn, 1969.

Brockdorff, Cay von, 'Gelehrte Gesellschaften im 17. Jahrhundert', dissertation, Kiel, 1940.

Bröcker, Carl, *Die Freimaurerlogen Deutschlands von 1737 bis 1893*, Berlin, 1894.

Brunner, Otto, 'Die Patriotische Gesellschaft in Hamburg im Wandel von Staat und Gesellschaft', in O. Brunner, *Neue Wege der Verfassungs- und Sozialgeschichte*, 2nd edn, Göttingen, 1968.

Bulling, Klaus, *Bibliographie zur Fruchtbringenden Gesellschaft (Marginale Blätter der Pirckheimer Gesellschaft 18)*, 1965.

Carnap, A. von, 'Zur Geschichte Wupperthals. Die geschlossene Lesegesellschaft in Elberfeld', in *Zeitschrift des Bergischen Geschichtsvereins* 1 (1863), pp. 54–104.

Contiades, Ion (ed.), *Gotthold Ephraim Lessings 'Ernst und Falk'. Mit den Fortsetzungen Joh. Gottfr. Herders und Fr. Schlegels*, Frankfurt/Main, 1968.

Dahl, Wilhelm, *Abriss der Geschichte der Loge Carl zur gekrönten Säule von 1744 bis 1894*, Brunswick, 1894.

Dann, Otto, 'Die Lesegesellschaften des 18. Jahrhunderts und der gesellschaftliche Aufbruch des deutschen Bürgertums', in H. Göpfert (ed.), *Buch und Leser*, Hamburg, 1977, now in U. Hermann (ed.), *Die Bildung des Bürgers* (1982).

Dann, Otto, 'Zur Gründung der Bonner Lesegesellschaft im

ausgehenden 18. Jahrhundert', in *Bonner Geschichtsblätter* 30 (1978), pp. 66–81.

Dann, Otto (ed.), *Lesegesellschaften und bürgerliche Emanzipation. Ein europäischer Vergleich*, Munich, 1981.

d'Elvert, Christian, *Die gelehrten Gesellschaften in Mähren und österreichisch Schlesien*, Brünn, 1853.

Demeter, Karl, *Die Frankfurter Loge zur Einigkeit 1742–1966*, Frankfurt/Main, 1967.

Denk, Viktor Martin Otto, *Fürst Ludwig zu Anhalt-Cöthen und der erste deutsche Sprachverein. Zum 300jährigen Gedächtnis an die Fruchtbringende Gesellschaft*, Marburg, 1917.

Deutsche Jakobiner, Mainzer Republik und Cisrhenanen. Exhibition organized by the National Archive and the city of Mainz, catalogue edited by Fritz Schütz: vol. 1 *Handbuch Beitrag zur demokratischen Tradition in Deutschland*; vol. 2, *Bibliographie zur deutschen linksrheinischen Revolutionsbewegung in den Jahren 1792–93. Ein Nachweis zu zeitgenössischen Schriften mit den heutigen Standorten*; vol. 3, *Katalog*, Mainz, 1981.

Dierauer, Johann, *Die Toggenburger Moralische Gesellschaft. Ein Kulturbild aus der zweiten Hälfte des 18. Jahrhunderts*, St Gallen, 1913.

Dissel, Karl, *Philipp von Zesen und die Deutschgesinnte Genossenschaft*, Hamburg, 1890.

Dix, Franz, 'Die tugendliche Gesellschaft', in *Mitteilungen der Deutschen Gesellschaft* 6 (1899), pp. 45–129.

Dotzauer, Winfried, 'Bonner aufgeklärte Gesellschaften und geheime Sozietäten bis zum Jahr 1815, unter bes. Berücksichtigung des Mitgliederbestandes der Freimaurerloge "Frères courageux" in der napoleonischen Zeit', in *Bonner Geschichtsblätter* 24 (1971), pp. 78ff.

Dotzauer, Winfried, 'Mainzer Illuminaten und Freimaurer vom Ende der kurfürstlichen Zeit bis zu den Freiheitskriegen', in *Nassauische Annalen* 83 (1972a), pp. 120ff.

Dotzauer, Winfried, 'Die Städte Landau, Zweibrücken und Speyer und ihre aufgeklärten Gesellschaften vom Ende des Ancien Régime bis zum Ende des napoleonischen Zeitalters, unter bes. Berücksichtigung der Freimaurerlogen', in *Zeitschrift für die Geschichte des Oberrheins* 120 (1972b), pp. 303ff.

Dotzauer, Winfried, 'Das aufgeklärte Trier. Freimaurergesellschaften und Lesegesellschaften bis zum Ende der napoleonischen Zeit', in *Geschichtliche Landeskunde* 9 (1973a), pp. 214ff.

Dotzauer, Winfried, 'Die Mitglieder der Kölner Freimaurerlogen, inbes. der Loge 'Le Secret des Trois Rois' vom Ende des alten Reiches bis zu den Freiheitskriegen', in *Jahrbuch des Kölner Geschichtsvereins* 34 (1973b), pp. 214ff.

Dotzauer, Winfried, 'Lesegesellschaft und Loge "Trois flammes vicifiantes" in Neustand', in *Blätter Pfälzer Kulturgeschichte* 42 (1975), pp. 59–70.

Dotzauer, Winfried, *Freimaurergesellschaften am Rhein. Aufgeklärte Sozietäten auf dem linken Rheinufer vom Ausgang des Ancien Régime bis zum Ende der Napoleonischen Herrschaft*, Wiesbaden, 1977.

Douglas, Knoop and Jonas, G. T., *Genesis of Freemasonry*, Manchester, 1947.

Dülmen, Richard van, 'Sozietätsbildung in Nürnberg im 17. Jahrhundert', in *Festschrift Bosl*, 1969.

Dülmen, Richard van, *Der Geheimbund der Illuminaten*, 2nd edn, Stuttgart, 1977.

Dülmen, Richard van, 'Prophetie und Politik. Johann Permeier und die "Societas regalis Jesu Christi" (1631–1643)', in *Zeitschrift für bayerische Landesgeschichte* 41 (1978b), pp. 417–73.

Dülmen, Richard van, 'Reformationsutopie und Sozietätsprojekte bei Joh. Valentin Andreae', in *Francia* 6 (1979), pp. 299–318.

Dünnhaupt, Gerhard, 'Dietrich v. d. Werde and the "Fruchtbringende Gesellschaft"', in *MLR* 69 (1974), pp. 796–804.

Dzwonek, Ulrich et al., '"Bürgerliche Oppositionsliteratur zwischen Revolution und Reformismus". F. G. Klopstocks Deutsche Gelehrtenrepublik und Bardendichtung als Dokumente der bürgerlichen Emanzipationsbewegung in der zweiten Hälfte des 18. Jahrhunderts', in B. Lutz (ed.), *Deutsches Bürgertum und literarische Intelligenz 1750–1800*, Stuttgart, 1974.

Eckhardt, Hellmuth, 'Aufklärung und Pressefreiheit. Zur Debatte der Berliner Mittwochsgesellschaft während der Jahre 1783 und 1784', in *ZHG* 9 (1982), pp. 315–45.

Eich, Ludwig, *Die gelehrten Gesellschaften der Pfalz*, Speyer, 1926.

Eichler, Helga, 'Die Leipziger Ökonomische Sozietät im 18. Jahrhundert', in *Jahrbuch für die Geschichte des Feudalismus* 2 (1978), pp. 357–86.

Engel, Leopold, *Geschichte des Illuminatenordens. Ein Beitrag zur Geschichte Bayerns*, Berlin, 1906.

Erlenmeier, Albrecht, *Die Namen der Freimaurerlogen, eine geschichtliche Untersuchung*, Leipzig, 1917.

Falsi, Robert, 'Die Dienstags-Companie, eine unbekannte literarische Gesellschaft aus Bodmers Kreis', in *Zürcher Taschenbuch* (1918), pp. 135–61.

Fay, Bernard, 'Learned Societies in Europe and America in the Eighteenth Century', in *American Historical Review* 37 (1932), pp. 255–66.

'Festschrift zur Gedenkfeier an die vor 300 Jahren in Schweinfurt erfolgte Gründung der Deutschen Akademie der Naturforscher (Kaiserlich Leopoldinisch-Carolinisch Deutsche Akademie der Naturforscher)', in *Veröffentlichungen des Historischen Vereins Schweinfurt* 2, Schweinfurt, 1952.

Findel, Josef Gottfried, *Geschichte der Freimaurerei von der Zeit ihres Entstehens bis auf die Gegenwart.* 2 vols., 5th edn, Leipzig, 1883.

Flitner, Wilhelm, *August Ludwig Hülsen und der Bund der freien Männer*, Jena, 1913.

Flohr, August, *Geschichte der Grossen Loge von Preussen, gen. Royal York zur Freundschaft im Orient in Berlin*, Berlin, 1898.

le Forestier, Réne, *Les Illuminés de Bavière et la Franc-Maçonnerie Allemande*, Paris, 1915.

le Forestier, Réne, *La Franc-Maçonnerie Templière et Occultiste aux XVIIIe et XIXe siècles*, Paris, Louvain, 1970.

Fretz, Diethelm, 'Die Entstehung der Lesegesellschaft von Wädenswil', in *XI. Neujahrsblatt der Lesegesellschaft Wädenswil für 1940*, p. 113.

Freude, Felix, 'Die Kaiserlich Französische Akademie der freien Künste und Wissenschaften', in *Zeitschrift des Historischen Vereins für Schwaben und Neuburg* 34 (1908), pp. 1–132.

Fuchs, Peter, *Palatinatus Illustratus. Die historische Forschung an der Kurpfälzischen Akademie der Wissenschaften*, Mannheim, 1963.

Full, Viktoria, 'Die Agrikultursozietäen und ihr Einfluss auf die Landwirtschaft der österreichisch-ungarischen Monarchie im 18. Jahrhundert', Ph.D. dissertation, (manuscript), Vienna, 1937.

Geist, Lorenz, *Kurzgefasste Geschichte der Freimaurerlogen 'Joseph zur Einigkeit' i. Or. Nürnberg 1761–1861*, Nuremberg, 1861.

Geppert, Ernst G., *Die Freimaurer-Logen Deutschlands 1737 bis 1972*, Hamburg, 1974.

Geppert, Ernst G., *Die Herkunft, die Gründer, die Namen der Freimaurerlogen in Deutschland seit 1937*, Hamburg, 1976.

Gerber, Georg, 'Die Neu-Atlantis des Francis Bacon und die Entstehung der Academia Naturae Curiosorum (Leopoldina) und der Societät der Wissenschaften zu Berlin', in *Wissenschaftliche Annalen* 4 (1955), pp. 552–60.

Gerteis, Klaus, 'Bildung und Revolution. Die deutschen Lesegesellschaften am Ende des 18. Jahrhunderts', in *Archiv für Kulturgeschichte* 23 (1971). pp. 127–39.

Glaser-Gerhard, Ernst (ed.), *Zur Geschichte der Grossen Landesloge der Freimaurer von Deutschland*, Berlin, 1970.

Goldschmidt, Léon, *Die litterarische Gesellschaft zu Hamburg. Ein Rückblick auf die ersten zehn Jahre ihres Bestehens*, Hamburg, 1901.

Graf, Sieglinde, 'Aufklärung in der Provinz. Die kurbayerische "Gesellschaft sittlich- und landwirtschaftlicher Wissenschaften" in Altötting und Burghausen 1765–1802', dissertation, (manuscript), Munich, 1982.

Graf, Sieglinde, 'Gesellschaft der schönen Wissenschaften zu Oetting am Inn (1765–1769). Eine Studie zur Aufklärung in Bayern', in *Zeitschrift für bayerische Landesgeschichte* 46 (1983), pp. 81–137.

Grantzow, Hans, *Geschichte des Göttinger und des Vossischen Musenalmanachs*, Berlin, 1909.

Grau, Conrad, 'Herder, die Wissenschaft und die Akademien seiner Zeit', in *Jahrbuch für Geschichte* 19 (1979), pp. 89–114.

Guggisberg, Kurt and Vahlen, Hermann, *Kundige Aussaat, köstliche Frucht. Die ökonomische Sozietät von Bern*, Berne, 1958.

Haase, Carl, *Der Bildungshorizont der norddeutschen Kleinstadt am Ende des 18. Jahrhunderts. Zwei Bücherverzeichnisse der Lesegesellschaften in Wunstorf aus dem Jahre 1794, Festschrift Aubin*, vol. 2, Wiesbaden, 1965.

Haase, Carl, 'Leihbüchereien und Lesegesellschaften im Elbe-Weser-Winkel zu Ausgang des 18. Jahrhunderts', in *Stader Jahrbuch* 1977, pp. 7–30.

Hammermayer, Ludwig, 'Die Benediktiner und die Akademiebewegung im katholischen Deutschland 1720 bis 1770', in *Studien und Mitteilungen der Geschichte des Benediktinerordens* 70 (1960), pp. 45–146.

Hammermayer, Ludwig, 'Marianus Brockie und Oliver Legipont. Zur benediktinischen Wissenschafts- und Akademiegeschichte des 18. Jahrhunderts', in *Studien und Mitteilungen der Geschichte des Benediktinerordens* 71 (1961), pp. 69–121.

Hammermayer, Ludwig, 'Der Geheimbund der Illuminaten und Regensburg', in *Verhandlungen des historischen Vereins für Oberpfalz und Regensburg* 110 (1970), pp. 69ff.

Hammermayer, Ludwig, 'Akademiebewegung und Wissenschaftsorganisation. Formen, Tendenzen und Wandel in Europa während der zweiten Hälfte des 18. Jahrhunderts', in *Wissenschaftspolitik in Mittel- und Osteuropa* (1976a), pp. 1–84.

Hammermayer, Ludwig, 'Zur Geschichte der europäischen Freimaurerei und Geheimgesellschaften im Achtzehnten Jahrhundert. Genese, Historiographie, Forschungsprobleme', in *Eleusis. Organ des Deutschen Obersten Rates der Freimaurer des Alten und Angenommenen Schottischen Ritus*, 31st year, no. 6 (Nov./Dec. 1976b), pp. 367–88.

Hammermayer, Ludwig, 'Illuminaten in Bayern. Zu Geschichte, Fortwirken und Legende des Geheimbundes', in H. Glaser (ed.), *Krone und Verfassung. König Max I. Joseph und der neue Staat. Beiträge zur Bayerischen Geschichte und Kunst 1799–1825*, Munich, Zurich, 1980a.

Hammermayer, Ludwig, *Der Wilhelmsbader Freimaurerkonvent 1782. Ein Höhe- und Wendepunkt in der Geschichte der deutschen und europäischen Geheimgesellschaften*, Heidelberg, 1980b.

Hammermayer, Ludwig, 'Zur Geschichte und Historiographie der deutschen Freimaurerei vom 18. bis 20. Jahrhundert', in *Kulturbeziehungen in Mittel- und Osteuropa im 18. und 19. Jahrhundert, Festschrift Ischreyt*, Berlin, 1982.

Hammermayer, Ludwig, *Geschichte der Bayerischen Akademie der Wissenschaften 1759–1807*, vol. 1, *Gründungs- und Frühgeschichte 1759–1769*, vol. 2 *Zwischen Stagnation, Aufschwung und Illuminatenkrise 1769–1786*, Munich, 1983.

Harnack, Adolff von, *Geschichte der königlich Preussischen Akademie der Wissenschaften zu Berlin*, 3 vols., Berlin, 1900.

Hartmann, Fritz and Vierhaus, Rudolf (eds), *Der Akademiegedanke im 17.*

und 18. Jahrhundert, Bremen, Wolfenbüttel, 1977.

Hennings, Johannes, *Geschichte der Johannis-Loge 'Zum Füllhorn' zu Lübeck 1772–1922*, Lübeck, 1922.

Hensing, Ulrich, 'Acta Eruditorum (1682–1782)', in H.-D. Fischer (ed.), *Deutsche Zeitschriften des 17. und 20. Jahrhunderts*, Pullach, 1973.

Herrmann, Ulrich, 'Lesegesellschaften an der Wende des 18. Jahrhunderts', in *Archiv für Kulturgeschichte* 57 (1975), pp. 475–84.

Hieber, Otto, *Geschichte der Vereinigten Johannis-Loge zum Todtenkopf und Phönix zu Königsberg i. P.*, Königsberg, 1897.

Hoffmann, Jochen, 'Bedeutung und Funktion des Illuminatenordens in Norddeutschland', in *Zeitschrift für bayerische Landesgeschichte* 45 (1982), pp. 363–92.

Hofmann, Franz, '"Panorthosia". J. A. Kommenskys Plan der Universalreform', in *Pädagogik* II (1956), pp. 756–67.

Hubbertz, Erich, *Zwei Jahrhunderte Freimaurerei am Niederrhein. Geschichte der Freimaurerloge Pax Inimica Malis in Emmerich. Mit einer Matrikel von 1793–1935*, Kleve, 1979.

Hubrig, Hans, *Die patriotischen Gesellschaften des 18. Jahrhunderts*, Weinheim, 1957.

Hummel, Gerhard, *Die humanistischen Sodalitäten und ihr Einfluss auf die Entwicklung des Bildungswesens der Reformationszeit*, Leipzig, 1940.

Im Hof, Ulrich, 'Die Helvetische Gesellschaft als Jugendbewegung', in *Der Schweizerische Zofingerverein 1819–1969*, Berne, 1969.

Ingen, Ferdinand van, 'Die Sprachgesellschaften des 17. Jahrhunderts. Versuch einer Korrektur', in *Daphnis* I (1972), pp. 14–28.

Ischer, Rudolf, *Johann Georg Altmann (1695–1758). Die deutsche Gesellschaft und die moralischen Wochenschriften in Bern*, Berne, 1902.

Joachim, Johannes, *Die Anfänge der königlichen Sozietät der Wissenschaften zu Göttingen*, Berlin, 1936.

Julku, Kyösti, *Die revolutionäre Bewegung im Rheinland am Ende des 18. Jahrhunderts*, 2 vols., Helsinki, 1965 and 1969.

Kallweit, Adolf, *Die Freimaurerei in Hessen-Kassel. Königliche Kunst durch zwei Jahrhunderte*, Baden-Baden, 1966.

Keller, Helmut, 'Dr Johann Laurentius Bausch (1605–1665). Gründer der Academia Naturae-Curiosorum', dissertation, Würzburg, 1955.

Keller, Ludwig, 'Comenius und die Akademien der Naturphilosophen des 17. Jahrhunderts', in *Monatshefte der Comenius-Gesellschaft* 1895.

Keller, Ludwig, *Die Deutschen Gesellschaften des XVIII. Jahrhunderts und die moralischen Wochenschriften, ein Beitrag zur Geschichte des deutschen Bildungswesens*, Berlin, 1900.

Keller, Ludwig, *Gottfried Wilhelm Leibniz und die deutschen Sozietäten des 17. Jahrhunderts*, Berlin, 1903.

Keller, Ludwig, 'Die Grossloge zum Palmbaum und die sogenannten Sprachgesellschaften des XVII. Jahrhunderts', in *Monatshefte der Comenius-Gesellschaft* 16 (1907), pp. 189–236.

Keller, Ludwig, *Die Akademien der Renaissance und ihre Nachfolger: Monatshefte der Comenius-Gesellschaft*, n. v., no. 3 (1911), pp. 97–115.

Keller, Wilhelm, *Geschichte des eklektischen Freimaurerbundes*, Giessen, 1957.

Keller, Wilhelm, *Geschichte der Freimaurerei in Deutschland*, Giessen, 1959.

Kirschstein, Max, *Klopstocks Deutsche Gelehrtenrepublik*, Berlin, Leipzig, 1928.

Kneisel, C. M., *Geschichtliche Nachrichten von der Lese- und Erholungsgesellschaft in Bonn*, Bonn, 1837.

Kobuch, A., 'Die Deutsche Union. Radikale Spätaufklärung, Freimaurerei und Illuminatismus am Vorabend der Französischen Revolution', in *Beiträge zur Archivwissenschaft und Geschichtsforschung* 10 (1977), pp. 278ff.

Kopitzsch, Franklin, 'Der Aufklärung verpflichtet. Zu den Anfängen der Hamburger "Gesellschaft der Freunde des Vaterländischen Schul- und Erziehungswesens"', in *175 Jahre Gesellschaft der Freunde des vaterländischen Schul- und Erziehungswesens*. Gewerkschaft Erziehung und Wissenschaft Landesverband, Hamburg, Hamburg, year not cited (1981), pp. 16–33.

Kopitzsch, Franklin, 'Lesegesellschaften und Aufklärung in Schleswig-Holstein', in *Zeitschrift für Schleswig-Holsteinische Geschichte* 108 (1983b), pp. 141–70.

Koselleck, Reinhardt, 'Adam Weishaupt und die Anfänge der bürgerlichen Geschichtsphilosophie in Deutschland', in *Tijdschrift voor de Studie van de Verlichting* 4 (1976), pp. 317–28.

Kovács, Elisabeth, 'Zur Geschichte der Freimaurer in Österreich', in *Religion, Wissenschaft, Kultur. Jahrbuch der Wiener katholischen Akademie* 25/2 (1976/7), pp. 111f.

Kowalewski, Gustav, *Geschichte der Hamburgischen Gesellschaft zur Beförderung der Künste und nützlichen Gewerbe* (Patriotische Gesellschaft). Gestiftet im Jahre 1765, 3 vols., Hamburg, 1897.

Kowalewski, Gustav, *Marksteine aus dem Leben der Patriotischen Gesellschaft. Jahrbuch der Hamburgischen Gesellschaft zur Beförderung der Künste und nützlichen Gewerbe*, Hamburg, 1904.

Kraus, Andreas, *Die historische Forschung an der churbayerischen Akademie der Wissenschaften 1759–1806*, Munich, 1959.

Kraus, Andreas, *Die naturwissenschaftliche Forschung an der Bayerischen Akademie der Wissenschaften im Zeitalter der Aufklärung*, Munich, 1978.

Krause, Gottlieb, *Urkundlicher Beitrag der deutschen Sprachgesellschaften im 17. Jahrhundert* (also under the title, *Der Fruchtbringenden Gesellschaft ältester Ertzschrein*), Leipzig, 1855.

Krause, Gottlieb, *Gottsched und Flottwell, die Begründer der Deutschen Gesellschaft in Königsberg*, Leipzig, 1893.

Krauss, Werner, 'Entwicklungstendenzen der Akademien im Zeitalter der Aufklärung', in W. Krauss, *Studien zur deutschen und französischen Aufklärung*, East Berlin, 1963.

Krivanec, Ernest, 'Die Freimaurerei in der Theresianischen Epoche', in W. Koschatzky (ed.), *Maria Theresa und ihre Zeit* Salzburg, Vienna, 1980.

Krocker, Ernst, '200 Jahre Deutsche Gesellschaft. Beiträge zur deutschen Bildungsgeschichte. Festschrift zur 200-Jahr-Feier der Deutschen Gesellschaft in Leipzig 1727–1927', in *Mitteilungen der Deutschen Gesellschaft zur Erforschung vaterländischer Sprache und Alterthümer in Leipzig* 12 (1927), pp. 7–27.

Kroker, Werner, *Wege zur Verbreitung technischer Kenntnisse zwischen England und Deutschland in der zweiten Hälfte des 18. Jahrhunderts*, Berlin, 1971.

Kuhn, Axel, *Jakobiner im Rheinland. Der Kölner konstitutionelle Zirkel von 1798*, Stuttgart, 1976.

Kuhn, Axel, *Linksrheinische deutsche Jakobiner. Aufrufe, Reden, Protokolle, Briefe und Schriften 1794–1801*, Stuttgart, 1978.

Lachmann, Heinrich, *Geschichte und Gebräuche der maurerischen Hochgrade und Hochgradsysteme*, Brunswick, 1866.

Lang, Gustav, *Aus dem Ordensleben des 18. Jahrhunderts. Typische Vertreter der Strikten Observanz*, Heilbronn, 1929.

Lefftz, Joseph, *Die gelehrten und literarischen Gesellschaften im Elsass vor 1870*, Colmar, 1931.

Leicht, Walter H., 'Die Gründung der Deutschen Akademie der Naturforscher', in *Festschrift zur Gedenkfeier an die vor 300 Jahren in Schweinfurt erfolgte Gründung der Deutschen Akademie der Naturforscher*, 1953.

Lennhoff, Eugen, *Die Freimaurer*, Zurich, Leipzig, Vienna, 1929.

Lennhoff, Eugen, and Posner, Oskar, *Internationales Freimaurer-Lexikon* (1932), 2nd edn, Zurich, Vienna, 1965.

Lennhoff, Eugen, and Gebühr, Werner, *Politische Geheimbünde*, 3nd edn, Munich, Vienna, 1968.

Lenning (= Hesse), C., *Enzyklopädie der Freimaurerei*, 3 vols., Leipzig, (edited by Friedrich Mossdorf), 1822–8.

Liebermann, Karl, *Im Wandel der Zeiten. 125 Jahre Loge Karl zum Rautenkranz in Hildburghausen 1787–1912*, Hildburghausen, 1912.

Lincke, Philip, *Geschichte der Loge Ferdinand zur Glückseligkeit i. Or. zu Magdeburg und chronologisch-geordnetes General-Verzeichnis aller Mitglieder derselben*, place of publication not cited, (Magdeburg), 1824.

Lindner, E. J., *Freimaurerisches Brauchtum in Bildern 1730–1840*, Bayreuth, 1969.

Mannack, Eberhard (ed.), *Die Pegnitz-Schäfer. Nürnberger Barockdichtung*, Stuttgart, 1968.

Kartin, Moritz, *Konrad Celtis und die rheinische Gelehrtengesellschaft. Ein Beitrag zur Geschichte des Humanismus in Deutschland*, Ludwigshafen, 1903.

Marwinski, Felicitas, 'Die literarische Gesellschaft zu Altenburg – ein Seitenstück zur Geschichte des Altenburger Bibliothekswesens', in

Zentralblatt für Bibliothekswesen 94 (1980), pp. 209–19.

Marwinski, Felicitas, 'Die Frankenhäuser Lesegesellschaft von 1795', in *Marginalien* 82 (1981), pp. 63–83.

Marx, Arnold, *Die Gold- und Rosenkreuzer. Ein Mysterienbund des ausgehenden 18. Jahrhunderts in Deutschland*, Zeulenroda, Leipzig, 1929.

Mathy, Helmut, 'Gelehrte, literarische, okkulte und studentische Vereinigungen und Gesellschaften in Mainz am Ende des 18. Jahrhunderts', in *Jahrbuch der Vereinigung 'Freunde der Universität Mainz'* 18 (1969), pp. 70–95.

Matthaei, Henning, *Untersuchungen zur Frühgeschichte der deutschen Berufsschule, dargestellt am Wirken der Patriotischen Gesellschaft zu Hamburg im 18. Jahrhundert*, Hamburg, 1967.

Menge, Georg Friedrich, *Geschichte der Freimaurerloge Pforte zum Tempel des Lichts in Hildesheim und der vor ihr daselbst bestandenen Logen*, Hildesheim, 1863.

Mensing, W., *Der Freimaurer-Konvent von Wilhelmsbad*, Bayreuth, 1974.

Möller, Dieter (ed.), *Fünf frühe Freimaurerreden, 1726/37*, Bayreuth, 1966.

Mühlpfordt, Günther, 'Lesegesellschaften und bürgerliche Umgestaltung. Ein Organisationsversuch des deutschen Aufklärers Bahrdt vor der Französischen Revolution', in *Zeitschrift für Geschichtswissenschaften* 28 (1980), pp. 730–51.

Mühlpfordt, Günther, 'Ein radikaler Geheimbund vor der Französischen Revolution. Die "Union" K. F. Bahrdts', in *Jahrbuch für die Geschichte des Feudalismus* 5 (1981), pp. 379–413.

Müller, Hans-Heinrich, *Akademie und Wirtschaft im 18. Jahrhundert. Agrarökonomische Preisaufgaben und Preisschriften der Preussischen Akademie der Wissenschaften (Versuch, Tendenzen und Überblick)*, Berlin, 1975.

Müller, Johannes, *Die Wissenschaftlichen Vereine und Gesellschaften Deutschlands im 19. Jahrhundert*, 3 vols., Berlin, 1883–1917.

Müller, Kurt, 'Zur Enstehung und Wirkung der wissenschaftlichen Akademien und gelehrten Gesellschaften des 17. Jahrhunderts', in H. Rössler and G. Franz (eds), *Universitäten und Gelehrtenstand 1400–1800* (1970), pp. 127–44.

Müller, Paul, *Untersuchungen zum Problem der Freimaurerei bei Lessing, Herder und Fichte*, Berne, 1965.

Müssel, Karl, 'Die Akademie der freien Künste und Wissenschaften in Bayreuth (1756–1763)', in *Archiv für Geschichte in Oberfranken* 61 (1981), pp. 33–57.

Nabholz, Hans, *Die Helvetische Gesellschaft 1761–1848*, Zurich, 1961.

Naudon, Paul, *Geschichte der Freimaurerei*, Frankfurt/Main, 1982.

Nettelbladt, Christian Frh. von, *Geschichte Freimaurerischer Systeme in England, Frankreich und Deutschland*, Berlin, 1879.

Neubaur, L., 'Zur Geschichte des Elbschwanenordens', in *Altpreussische Monatsschriften* 47 (1910), pp. 113–83.

Neumann, Friedrich, 'Gottsched und die Leipziger Deutsche Gesellschaft', in *Archiv für Kulturgeschichte* 18 (1928), pp. 194–212.

Olbrich, Karl, *Die Freimaurer im deutschen Volksglauben. Die im Volke umlaufenden Vorstellungen und Erzählungen von den Freimaurern*, Breslau, 1930.

Otto, Karl F., *Die Sprachgesellschaften des 17. Jahrhunderts*, Stuttgart, 1972a.

Otto, Karl F., 'Zu Zesens Zünften', in F. van Ingen (ed.), *Philipp von Zesen*, 1972b.

Otto, Karl F., 'Die Frauen der Sprachgesellschaften', in A. Buck et al. (eds), *Europäische Hofkultur im 16. und 17. Jahrhundert III*, Hamburg, 1981.

Otto, Paul, *Die Deutsche Gesellschaft in Göttingen*, Munich, 1898.

Die Patriotische Gesellschaft zu Hamburg 1765–1965. Festschrift der Hamburgischen Gesellschaft zur Beförderung der Künste und nützlichen Gewerbe, Hamburg, 1965.

Pauls, August, *Geschichte der Aachener Freimaurerei*, vol. 1 *Die Aachener Freimaurerei in der reichsstädtischen Zeit* (up to the end of Sept. 1794), Clausthal-Zellerfeld, 1928.

Pauls, August, *Düsseldorfer Freimaurerei im 18. Jahrhundert*, Clausthal-Zellerfeld, 1929.

Petersen, Christian, 'Die teutsch-übende Gesellschaft in Hamburg', in *Zeitschrift des Vereins für Hamburgische Geschichte*, vol. 2 (1847), pp. 533–64.

Peuckert, Will-Erich, *Das Rosenkreuz*, with an Introduction edited by R. C. Zimmermann ('Pansophie', part 3), 2nd edn, Berlin, 1973.

Posner, Oskar, *Bilder zur Geschichte der Freimaurerei*, Reichenberg, 1927.

Pröve, Karl-Heinz, *Von der ersten Lesegesellschaft zur Stadtbücherei. Ein Kapitel Würzburger Kulturgeschichte*, Würzburg, 1967.

Prüsener, Marlies, 'Lesegesellschaften im 18. Jahrhundert. Ein Beitrag zur Lesegeschichte', in *Börsenblätter für die deutsche Buchhandlung* 28/10, Frankfurt/Main, 1972.

Prüsener, Marlies and Göpfert, Herbert G., 'Lesegesellschaften', in *Buchkunst und Literatur in Deutschland 1750–1850*, Hamburg, 1977.

Raabe, Paul (ed.), 'Das Protokollbuch der Gesellschaft der freien Männer in Jena 1779–1794', in *Festschrift Berend*, Weimar, 1959.

Reber, Joseph, *Johann Amos Comenius und seine Beziehungen zu den Sprachengesellschaften. Denkschrift zur Feier des vierteltausendjährigen Bestehens des Pegnesischen Blumenordens zu Nürnberg*, Leipzig, 1895.

Reinhardstöttner, Karl von, *Die sittlich-ökonomische Gesellschaft zu Burghausen*, Ansbach, 1895.

Richter, Walter, 'Concordienlogen im Orden der Unzertrennlichen. Ein Beitrag zur Geschichte der Aufklärung', in *Göttinger Jahrbuch* (1974), pp. 107–31.

Rosenstrauch-Königsberg, Edith, *Freimaurerei im josephinischen Wien. Aloys*

Blumenaus Weg vom Jesuiten zum Jakobiner, Vienna, Stuttgart, 1975.

Rosenstrauch-Königsberg, Edith, 'Ausstrahlungen des "Journals für Freimaurer"', in E. H. Balázs (ed.), *Beförderer der Aufklärung in Mittel- und Osteuropa*, Berlin, 1979.

Rosenstrauch-Königsberg, Edith, 'Radikalaufklärerische Geheimbünde in der Habsburgermonarchie zur Zeit der Französischen Revolution (1785–1795)', in O. Büsch and W. Grab (eds), *Die demokratische Bewegung in Mitteleuropa im ausgehenden 18. und frühen 19. Jahrhundert*, Berlin, 1980.

Rosenthal, Otto, *Beiträge zur Geschichte der Loge zum Pilgrim zu Berlin 1776 bis 1901*, place of publication not cited (Berlin), 1901.

Rübberdt, Rudolf, 'Die ökonomischen Sozietäten. Ein Beitrag zur Wirtschaftsgeschichte des XVIII. Jahrhunderts', dissertation, Würzburg, 1934.

Ruckstuhl, Karl, 'Geschichte der Lese- und Erholungsgesellschaft in Bonn', in *Bonner Geschichtsblätter* 15 (1961), pp. 26–75.

Runkel, Ferdinand, *Die Johannes-Loge zur Beständigkeit von 1775 bis 1925. Zum 150jährigen Stiftungsfest*, Berlin, 1925a.

Runkel, Ferdinand, *Die Loge zur Beständigkeit i. Or. Berlin von 1775–1925*, Berlin, 1925b.

Runkel, Ferdinand, *Geschichte der Freimaurerei in Deutschland*, 3 vols., Berlin, 1931/2.

Saarbrücker Casino-Chronik 1796–1896, Saarbrücken, 1896.

Saliger, Wilhelm, *Die gelehrte Donaugesellschaft und die Anfänge des Humanismus in Österreich*, Olmütz, 1876.

Schalk, Fritz, 'Die Akademien und die Entstehung neuer Wissenschaften im Zeitalter der Aufklärung', in *Berichte zur Wissenschaftsgeschichte* 1 (1978), pp. 37–42.

Scheel, Heinrich (ed.), *Die Mainzer Republik I. Protokolle des Jakobinerklubs*, Berlin, 1975.

Scheibe, Jorg, *Der 'Patriot' (1724–1726) und sein Publikum. Untersuchungen über die Verfassergesellschaft und die Leserschaft einer Zeitschrift der frühen Aufklärung*, Göppingen, 1973.

Schick, Hans, *Das ältere Rosenkreuzertum. Ein Beitrag zur Enstehungsgeschichte der Freimaurerei*, Berlin, 1942.

Schieckel, Harald, 'Die Mitglieder der "Oldenburgischen Literarischen Gesellschaft von 1779" seit ihrer Gründung. Soziale Herkunft – Gesellschaftliche Stellung – Lebensdaten', in *Oldenburger Jahrbuch* 78/9, pp. 1–7.

Schiffmann, Gustav Adolf, *Die Entstehung der Rittergrade in der Freimaurerei um die Mitte des XVIII. Jahrhunderts*, Leipzig, 1882.

Schindler, Norbert, 'Freimaurerkultur im 18. Jahrhundert. Zur sozialen Funktion des Geheimwissens in der entstehenden bürgerlichen Gesellschaft', in R. M. Berdahl et al. (eds), *Klassen und Kultur*, Frankfurt/Main, 1982, pp. 205–62.

Schmidt, Heinz, *Das Vereinsleben der Stadt Weinheim an der Bergstrasse. Volkskundliche Untersuchung zum kulturellen Leben einer Mittelstadt*, Weinheim, 1963.

Schneider, Ferdinand Josef, *Die Freimaurerei und ihr Einfluss auf die geistige Kultur Deutschlands am Ende des 18. Jahrhunderts*, Prague, 1909.

Schneider, G., *Festschrift der Loge zu den drei Seraphim im Orient Berlin*, Berlin, 1924.

Schneider, Herbert, *Deutsche Freimaurerbibliothek. Verzeichnis der Bibliothek des Deutschen Freimaurer-Museums Bayreuth*, Hamburg, 1977.

Schneiders, Werner, 'Sozietätspläne und Sozialutopie bei Leibniz', in *Studia Leibniziana VII/1* (1975), pp. 58–80.

Schnetze, Johann, *Quellen zur Geschichte der Rosenkreuzer des 18. Jahrhunderts*, Leipzig, 1929.

Schöne, Albrecht, *Kürbishütte und Königsberg. Modellversuch einer sozialgeschichtlichen Entzifferung poetischer Texte. – Am Beispiel Simon Dachs*, Munich, 1975.

Schreiber, O., *Die St Johannisloge Memphis i. Or. Memel (1776–1926)*, place of publication not cited (Memel), 1926.

Schumann, E., *Geschichte der naturforschenden Gesellschaft zu Danzig*, Danzig, 1895.

Schuster, Georg, *Die geheimen Gesellschaften, Verbindungen und Orden*, 2 vols., Leipzig, 1906.

Seeger, L., *Geschichte der Freimaurerei in Celle*, Celle, 1911.

Siefert, Helmut, 'Das naturwissenschaftliche und medizinische Vereinswesen im deutschen Sprachgebiet (1750–1850). Idee und Gestalt', dissertation, Marburg, 1967.

Siegfried, Paul, 'Die Basler Gesellschaft', in *Festschrift zur 150. Stiftungsfeier der Gemeinnützigen Gesellschaft 1777–1927*, Basle, 1927.

Silagi, Denis, *Jakobiner in der Habsburger-Monarchie*, Vienna, Munich, 1962.

Spahr, B. Lee, *The Archives of the Pegnesischer Blumenorden. A Survey and Reference Guide*, 1960.

Speich, Daniel, *Une société de lecture à la fin du 18e et au début du 19e siècle. La 'Allgemeine Lesegesellschaft' de Bâles 1787/1831*, Basle, 1975.

Staehelin, Ernst, *Die Christentumsgesellschaft in der Zeit der Aufklärung und der beginnenden Erweckung*, Basle, 1970.

Steffens, Manfred, *Freimaurer in Deutschland. Bilanz eines Vierteljahrtausends*, Flensburg, (1965), 2nd edn, Frankfurt/Main 1966.

Stephan, Inge, 'Theorie und Praxis des Literarischen Jakobinismus in Deutschland', in *Studien zur Literatur. Festschrift Beck*, Heidelberg, 1979.

Stern, Leo, *Zur Geschichte und wissenschaftlichen Leistung der deutschen Akademie der Naturforscher 'Leopoldina'*, Berlin, 1952.

Steudel, Johannes, 'Leibniz und die Leopoldina', in *Nova Acta Leopoldina*, n. s. 16 (1953/4), pp. 465–74.

Stoll, Christoph, *Sprachgesellschaften im Deutschland des 17. Jahrhunderts*,

Munich, 1973.

Strahm, G., *Die Ökonomische Gesellschaft von Bern*, Berne, 1947.

Stübel, Bruno, 'Die Deutsche Gesellschaft in Leipzig von ihrem Entstehen bis zur Gegenwart', in *Mitteilungen der Deutschen Gesellschaft zur Erforschung vaterländischer Sprache und Alterthümer in Leipzig* 6 (1877), pp. 1–41.

Suchier, Wolfram, 'Die Mitglieder der Deutschen Gesellschaft in Göttingen von 1738 bis Anfang 1755', in *Zeitschrift des historischen Vereins für Niedersachsen* 81 (1916), pp. 44–124.

Taute, Reinhold, *Der Wilhelmsbader Konvent und der Zusammenbruch der Strikten Observanz*, Berlin, 1909.

Teufel, Walther, *Geschichte der Freimaurerei in den Gebieten des heutigen Saarlandes und in den angrenzenden Ländern*, Baden-Baden, 1964.

Teufel, Walther, *Der Alte und Angenommene Schottische Ritus und seine Vorläufer*, Hamburg, 1966.

Theilig, Wolfgang, 'Die Stadtlesegesellschaft von Zeulenroda. Ein Beitrag zur Lektüre-Forschung des 19. Jahrhunderts', in *Marginalien. Zeitschrift für Buchkunst und Bibliophilie* 63 (1976), pp. 14–22.

Thiele, Rudolf, *Die Gründung der Akademie nützlicher Wissenschaften zu Erfurt*, Erfurt, 1904.

Totok, Wilhelm, 'Leibniz als Wissenschaftsorganisator', in W. Totok and C. Haase (eds), *Leibniz*, Hanover, 1966.

Träger, Claus (ed.), *Mainz zwischen Rot und Schwarz. Die Mainzer Revolution 1792–1793*, Berlin, 1963.

Treml, Christine, 'Kommunikationsformen humanistischer Gelehrter um 1500. Konrad Celtis und der Kreis seiner Freunde und Sodalen', MA, (manuscript), Munich, 1982.

Trommsdorf, H., *Die Freimaurerei in Pyrmont. Beiträge zur Kulturgeschichte Niedersachsens im 18. Jahrhundert*, Göttingen, 1928.

Viola, Siegfried, *Aus den Anfängen der schweizerischen Gemeinnützigkeitsbewegung mit bes. Berücksichtigung des Kantons Zürich*, Zurich, 1941.

Voegt, Hedwig, Die deutsche jakobinische Literatur und Publizistik 1789–1800, East Berlin, 1955.

Voigt, Günther, *Die Dichter der aufrichtigen Tannengesellschaft zu Strassburg*, Berlin, 1899.

Voss, Jürgen, *Universität, Geschichtswissenschaft und Diplomatie im Zeitalter der Aufklärung. Johann David Schöpflin 1694–1771*, Munich, 1979.

Voss, Jürgen, 'Die Akademien als Organisationsträger der Wissenschaften im 18. Jahrhundert', in *Historische Zeitschrift* 231 (1980), pp. 34–74.

Wagner, H., 'Die Loge "Zur wahren Eintracht" 1781–1785. Das Ende der österreichischen Freimaurerei im 18. Jahrhundert', in Festschrift 'Fünf Jahre Libertas', Vienna, 1965.

Wagner, H., 'Die politische und kulturelle Bedeutung der Freimaurerei im 18. Jahrhundert', in E. H. Balázs, L. Hammermayer, H. Wagner and J. Wojtowicz (eds), *Beförderer der Aufklärung in Mittel- und Osteuropa. Freimaurerei, Gesellschaften, Clubs*, Berlin, 1979.

Weber, Franz, 'Die bremische Deutsche Gesellschaft 1748–1793', dissertation, Königsberg, 1910.

Wehrhan, Karl, *Die Freimaurerei im Volksglauben. Geschichte, Sagen und Erzählungen des Volkes über die Geheimnisse der Freimaurerei und ihre Kunst*, Berlin-Lankwitz, 1919.

Witkowski, Georg, 'Die Deutsche Gesellschaft in Leipzig', in *Minerva-Zeitschrift* (August, 1927), pp. 165ff.

Wolff, Eugen, 'Die Deutschen Gesellschaften zu Erlangen und Altdorf im XVIII. Jahrhundert', in *Monatshefte der Comenius-Gesellschaft* 8 (1899), pp. 209–20.

Wolfstieg, August, *Bibliographie der freimaurerischen Literatur*, 3 vols., and supplementary vol., Burg, near Munich, 1913ff.

Wolfstieg, August, *Ursprung und Entwicklung der Freimaurerei. Ihre geschichtlichen, sozialen und geistigen Wurzeln*, vols. 1–3, Berlin, 1920.

Wolfstieg, August, *Werden und Wesen der Freimaurerei*, 5 vols., Berlin, 1922/3.

Wülker, L., *Geschichte der Loge 'Zur Ceder' 1777 bis 1927*, Hanover, 1927.

Zeitz, Karl-Hermann, *Loge 'Absalom zu den drei Nesseln' zu Hamburg, gestiftet 1737. 220 Jahre Freimaurerei in Deutschland*, Hamburg, 1957.

Ziegler, Hans, 'Die Landauer Gesellschaft der Konstitutionsfreunde (Jakobinerklub: 1791–1795)', in *Mitteilungen des Historischen Vereins der Pfalz 73* (1976), pp. 221–94.

Zöllner, Friedrich, *Einrichtungen und Verfassung der Fruchtbringenden Gesellschaft vornehmlich unter dem Fürsten Ludwig zu Anhalt-Cöthen*, Berlin, 1899.

INDEX